IMAGES
of America

AROUND RAQUETTE LAKE

On the cover: The Raquette Lake House, located in the village, was later enlarged with new services added. The great fire of February 20, 1927, claimed the building, a store, and a steamship. (Author's collection.)

IMAGES
of America

AROUND RAQUETTE LAKE

James M. Kammer

ARCADIA
PUBLISHING

ISBN 978-0-7385-4984-2

Published by Arcadia Publishing
Charleston, South Carolina

Printed in the United States of America

Library of Congress Catalog Card Number: 2006938007

For all general information contact Arcadia Publishing at:
Telephone 843-853-2070
Fax 843-853-0044
E-mail sales@arcadiapublishing.com
For customer service and orders:
Toll-Free 1-888-313-2665

Visit us on the Internet at www.arcadiapublishing.com

Dedicated to the people of Raquette Lake,
both past and present, who created the places and events
that have made this area what it is today

Contents

ACKNOWLEDGMENTS

The following folks, with their hands-on experience, knowledge, and interest, were invaluable in helping to make this book a reality: Bob and Darlene Berdeen, the late Marion and Jim Bird, Jim Dillion, Bob Egonhofer, George Fuge, Steve Gautier, Bonnie Halstead, the late Francis "Skipper" Havinga, Rhonda Jacobs, Don Langham, Doris Lamphear, Gail Murray, Mary Simons, and Maurice Waldron.

All images are from the author's collection.

INTRODUCTION

Since the 1800s, Raquette Lake has had a strong magnetism, drawing people back for return visits and, in some cases, for permanent stays. It has a very irregular shoreline of almost 100 miles, with numerous bays, islands, rivers, and other points of interest. Along with tourism, the area has plentiful lumber, winter ice, venison, and fish to bolster the local economy.

In the beginning, however, Raquette was not easy to access. No formal roads existed, and anyone interested in reaching the lake had to rely on a local guide. Once here, the weary travelers were rewarded by a pristine and secluded place where they could camp, hunt, and fish.

Architect and builder William West Durant is credited with tapping Raquette's potential by establishing the first of many great camps. These buildings were really the furthest idea from camps, as they offered every possible convenience and pastime. To this day, the great camp remains a preferred style for a summer home or year-round establishment, not only in New York State but far beyond.

As word got around, more and more people wanted to sample the Adirondack experience, and before long, hotels and inns appeared around the lake. Travelers found quality accommodations at places like Under the Hemlocks, Camp Fairview, Brightside Camp, Hunters Rest, and the Antlers. People of note, however, were not satisfied with just visiting; they bought or built their own homes. Soon the list of names at Raquette rivaled many top 10 lists: Vanderbilt, Morgan, Carnegie, and Collier. These families invited their friends, who included Benjamin Harrison, Ulysses S. Grant, Alexander Graham Bell, Henry Ford, Thomas Edison, and Harvey Firestone.

Although the Great Depression, rising costs, and mere convenience eventually led to the departure of these golden era people, their legacy remains as a part of Raquette Lake.

One

THE MARION RIVER AND CENTRAL PORTION OF THE LAKE

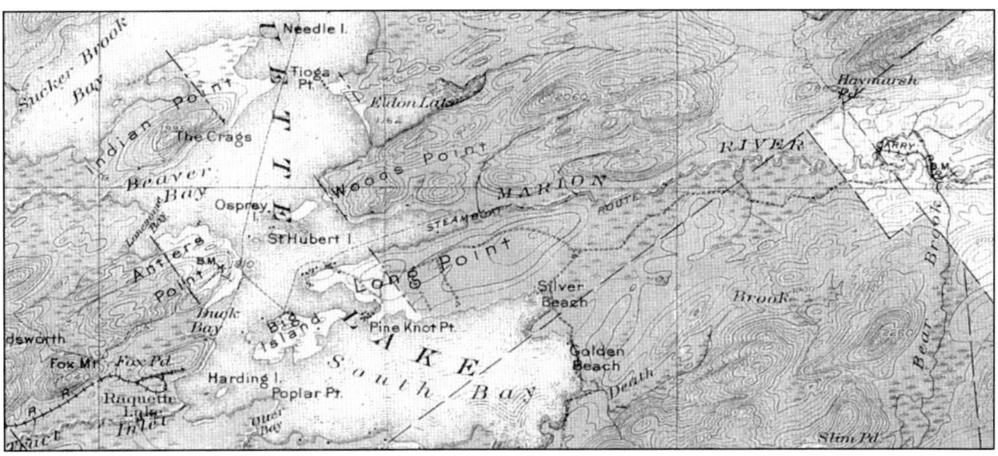

This map shows the Marion River and the central part of Raquette Lake.

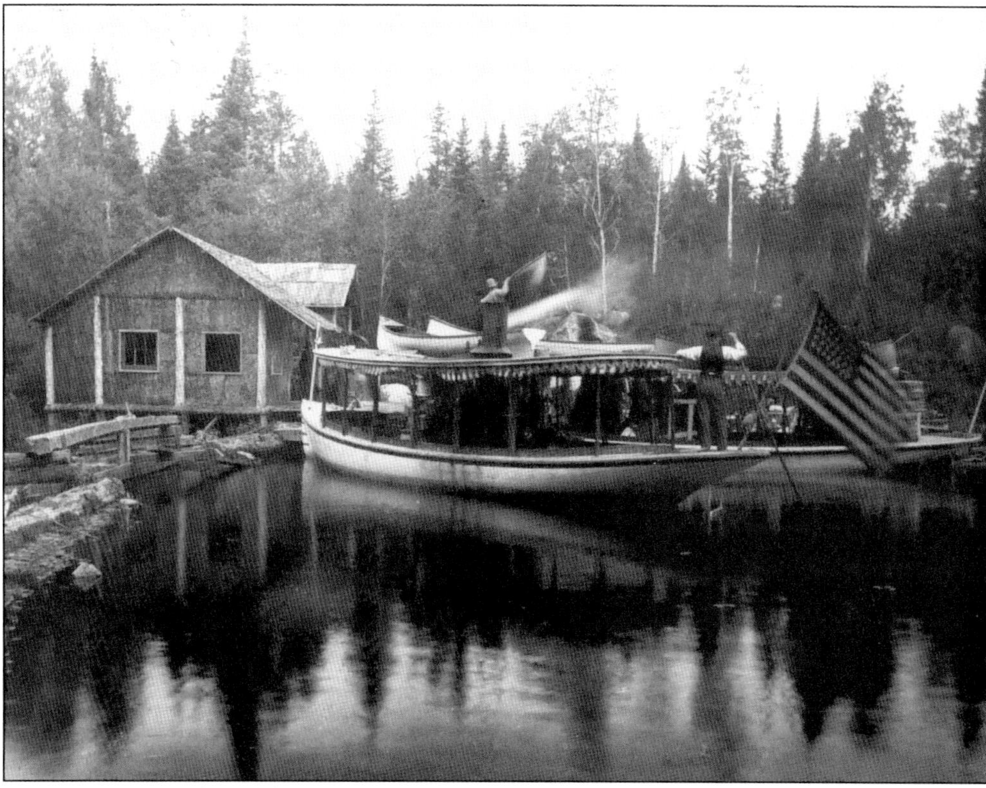

At Bassetts carry, three lakes—Blue Mountain, Eagle, and Utawana—all flow into the Marion River. This was also the location of the terminal that ended the Marion River Carry Railroad. This picture shows the early dam at left, a small store, and a boat to take passengers farther east.

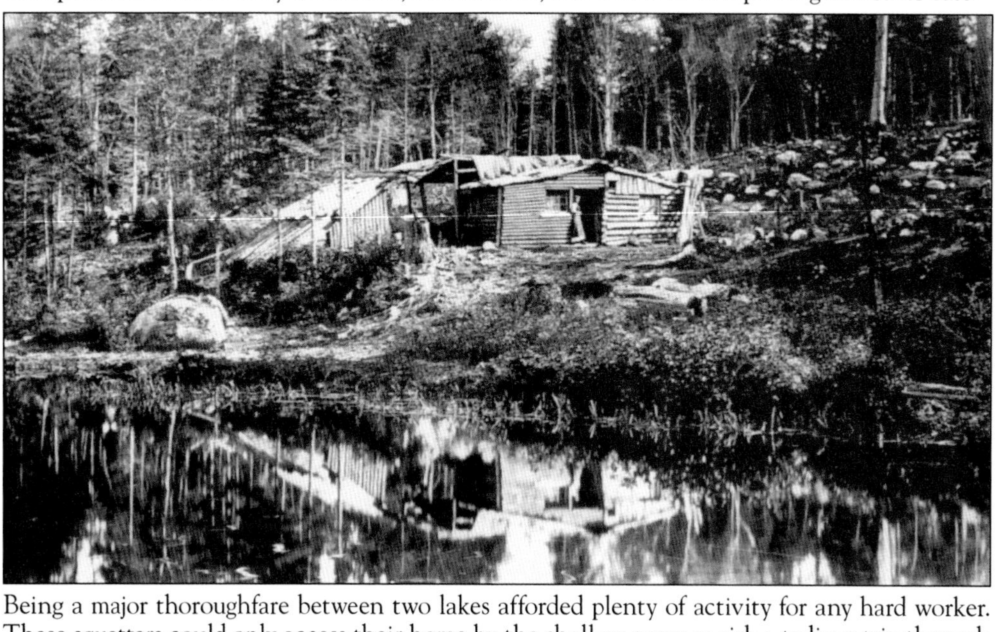

Being a major thoroughfare between two lakes afforded plenty of activity for any hard worker. These squatters could only access their home by the shallow carry or risk a tedious trip through the woods. The travelers going to and from, on the river, promised needed work.

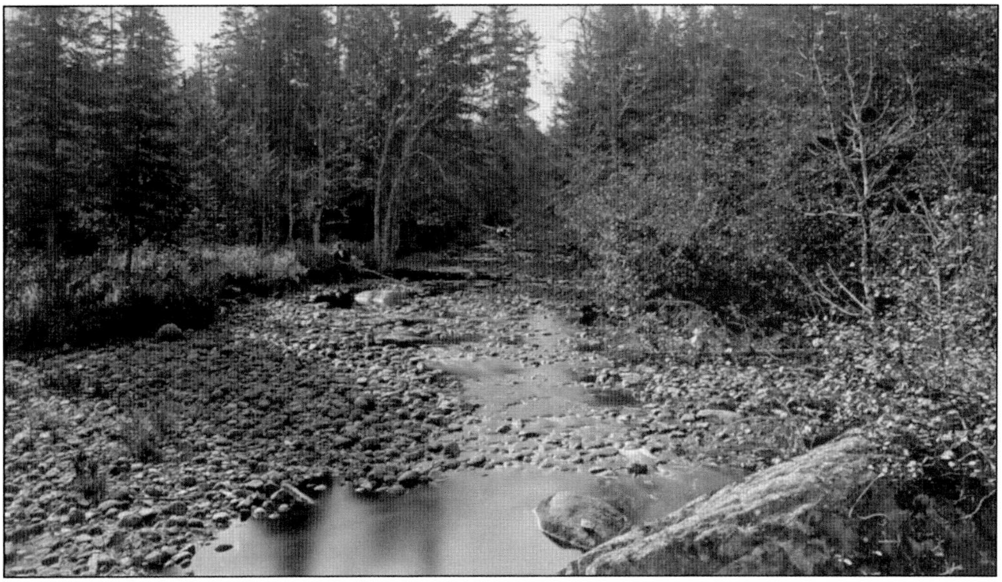

The Marion River carry, even in the wet season, was not passable for several hundred yards before arriving at the actual river. Even passage by canoe or guide boat was impossible most of the time.

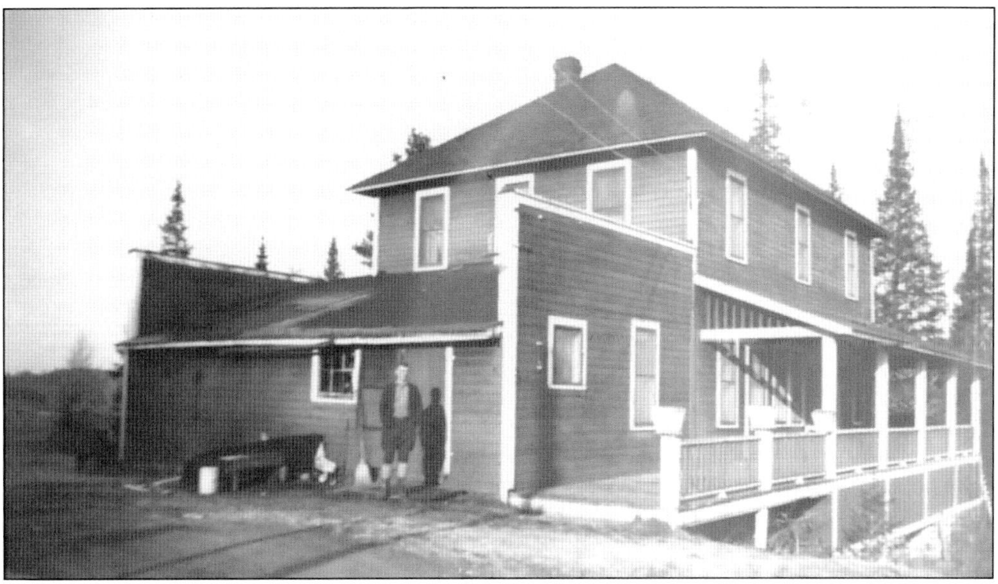

The Marion River Carry Inn was used by travelers from the boats or train who did not want to travel farther overnight. Architect William West Durant built the inn in 1890 to ensure the convenience of his customers. Also available here was a team of horses and a driver to handle baggage and goods. The Marion River Carry Inn stands to this day.

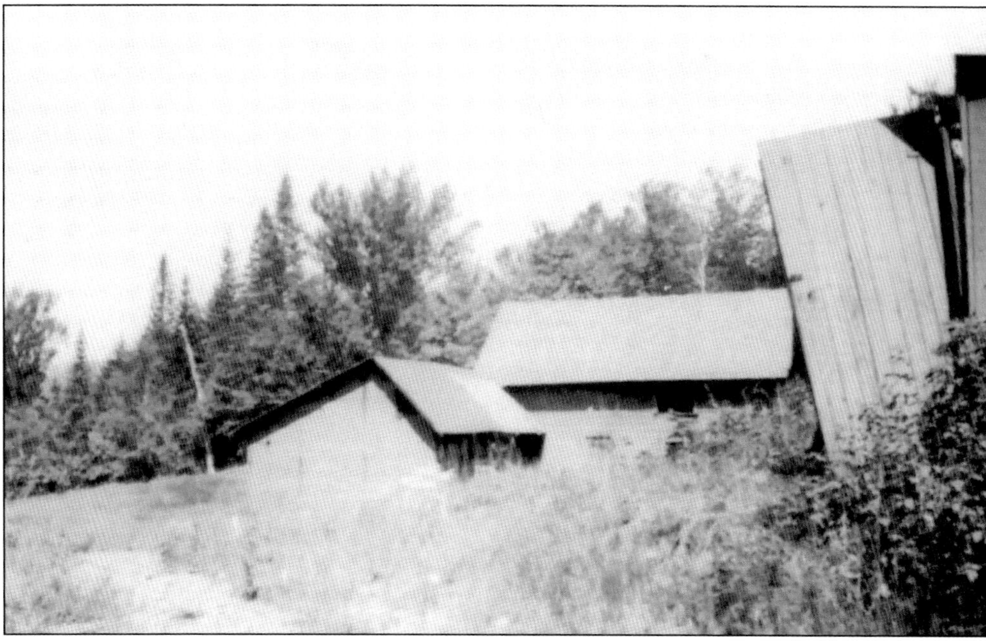

At the Marion River Carry Inn, a farm was built to provide food, services, and storage. Fresh eggs and some vegetables were always on hand. A small shop repaired wagons and farm implements. A stable housed the inn's team of horses, as well as guests' horses, and a storage building held freight.

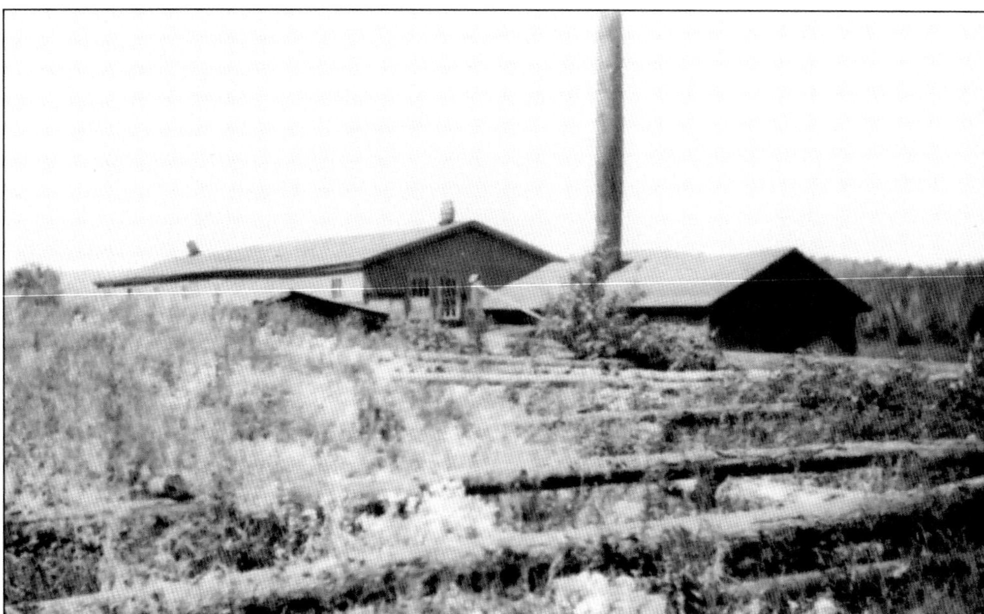

Nearer the deep area of the Marion River, but within eyeshot of the Marion River Carry Inn, William West Durant had a sawmill erected in 1892. The mill created lumber for the completion of Great Camp Uncas, Great Camp Sagamore, and the Eagles Nest Country Club and construction materials for the railroad. The mill was later moved to Raquette Lake village.

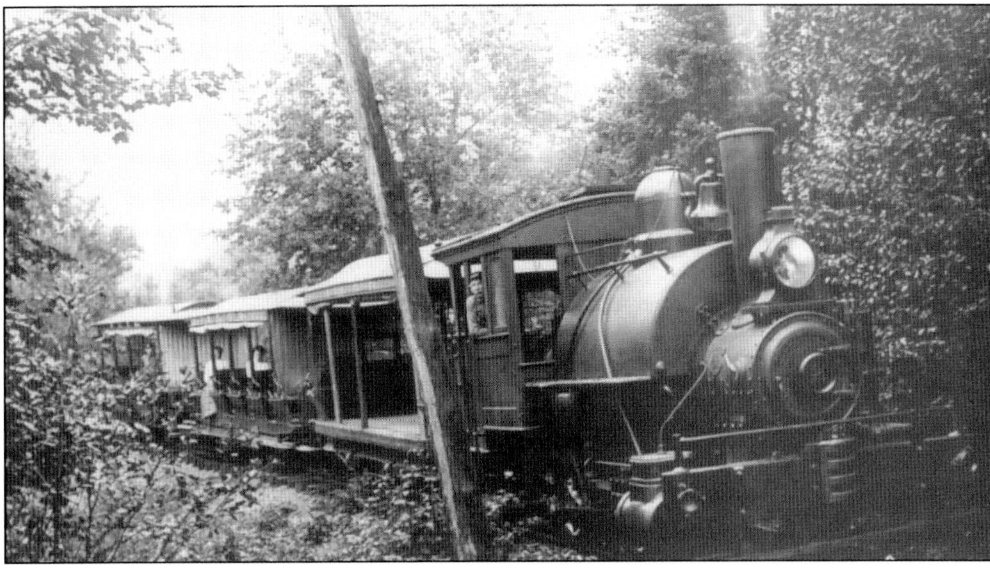

The Marion River Carry Railroad was created by William West Durant and was ready for use in the spring of 1900. The entire line was less than a mile long and had the distinction of being the shortest standard-gauge railway in the world. The railcars were old horse-drawn trolley cars adapted for use here. They were originally from Brooklyn. The railroad was abandoned in 1929.

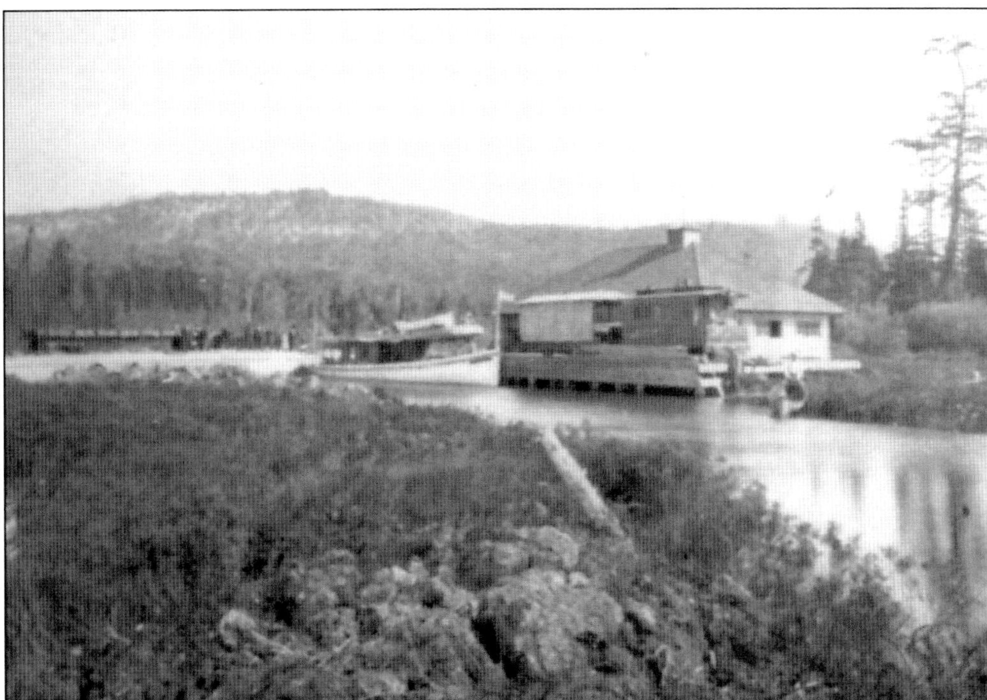

The ride on the Marion River started at a small terminal for the Marion River Carry Railroad. This was as far as baggage barges and steamships could go on the river. Shown are a barge and a railcar. The steamer is loading people onto a railcar already on the dock. The picture was taken from the turnaround in the river. This area eliminated congestion and saved time.

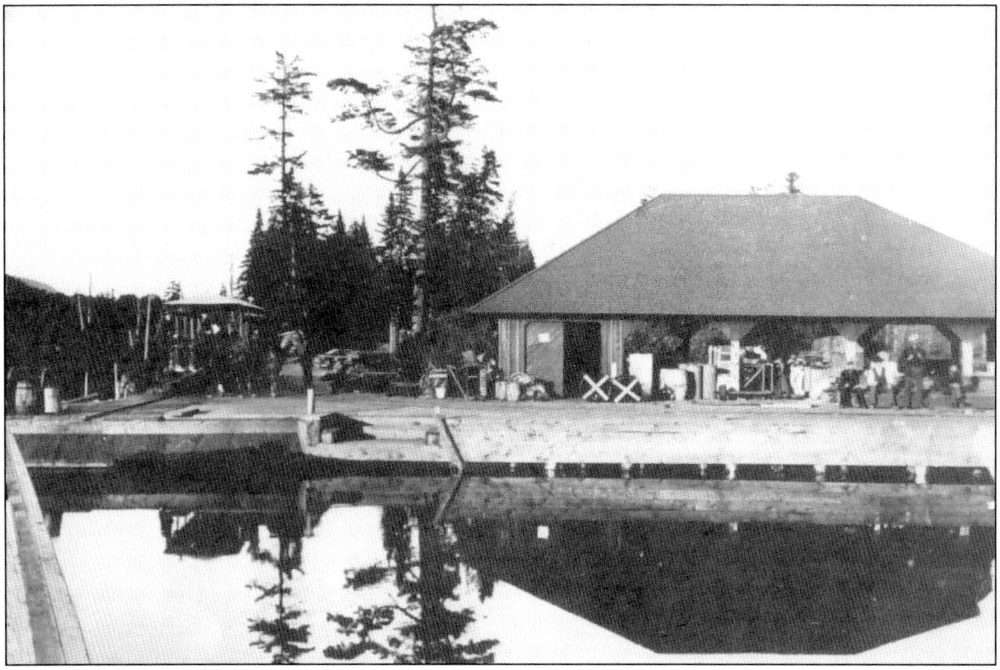

This close-up of the Marion River terminal shows the array of people and material awaiting transport. The photographer is on a barge that is lined up to be unloaded. Note the team of horses and the lone railcar to be loaded.

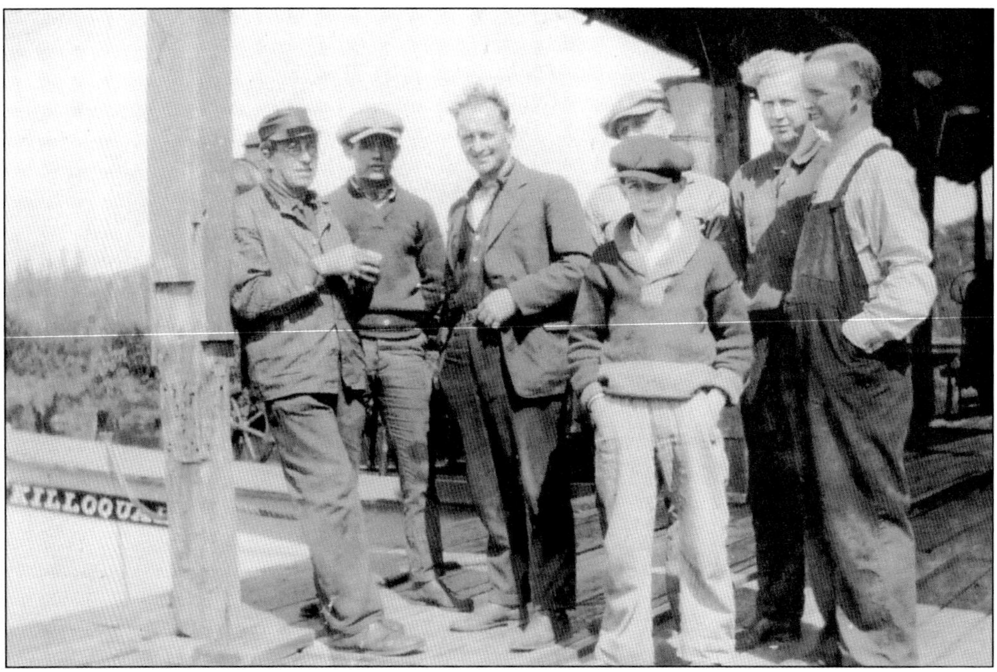

There was never a lack of help during the heyday of rail and water transportation. All ages worked at any time of day and through the week. These workers at the carry dock range in age from the young lad in front to the teenager at the rear and the seasoned firemen and pilots. The man in the center was probably the station agent; he is wearing a suit.

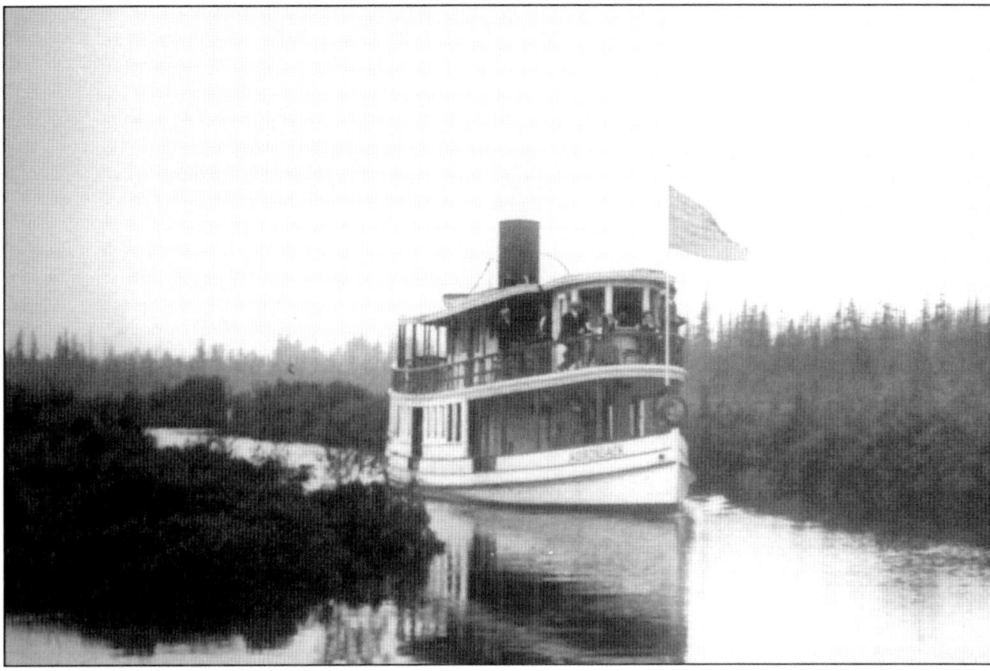

One could really arrive in style up at the carry. Shown is the double-decker steamer *Adirondack* arriving at the Marion River carry to discharge passengers and freight headed farther east. On its return, the steamer would hold passengers continuing on to Raquette Lake and points farther west.

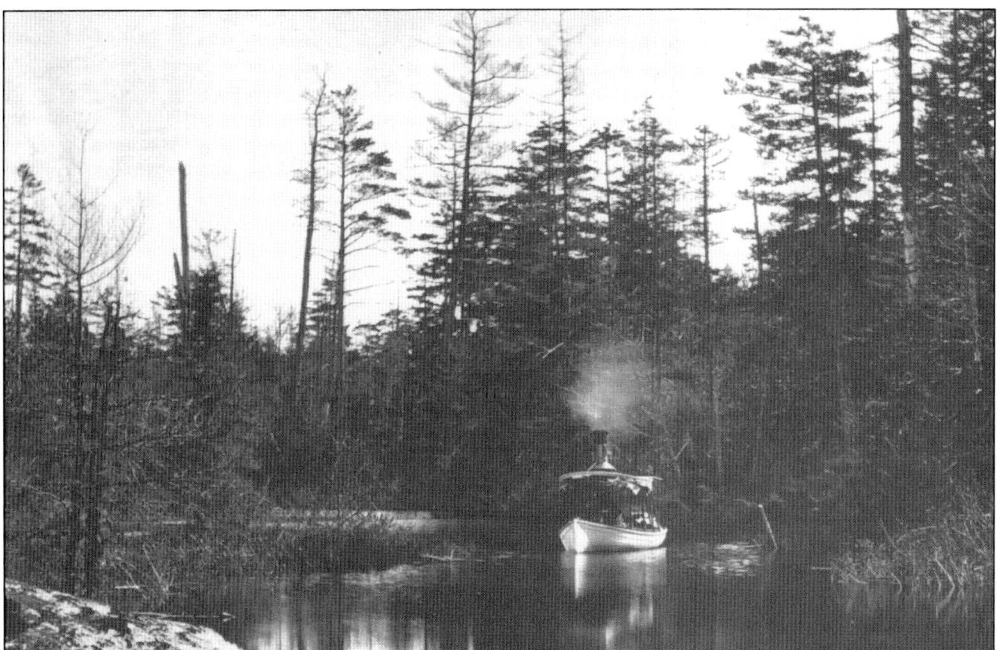

This smaller steamer rounding a turn on the Marion River may have been the private launch of one of the numerous homes or inns around the lake. Notice for the moment it is empty and has no business name on the bow.

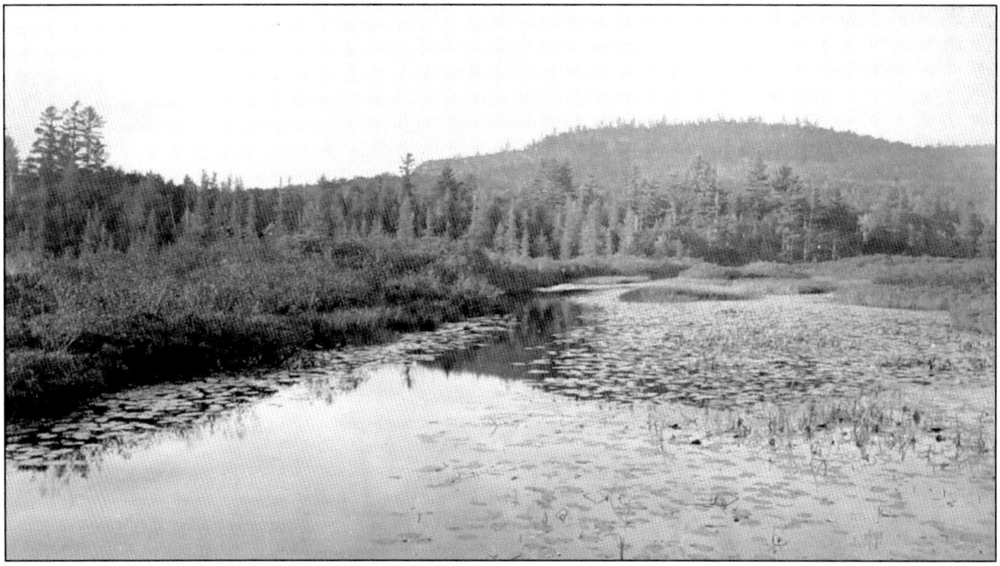

Coming down the Marion River, for even the most seasoned traveler, was a beautiful, natural experience. The flora and fauna usually were unique for the new riders. This shot shows the river where the churning of riverboats has made a path through water vegetation.

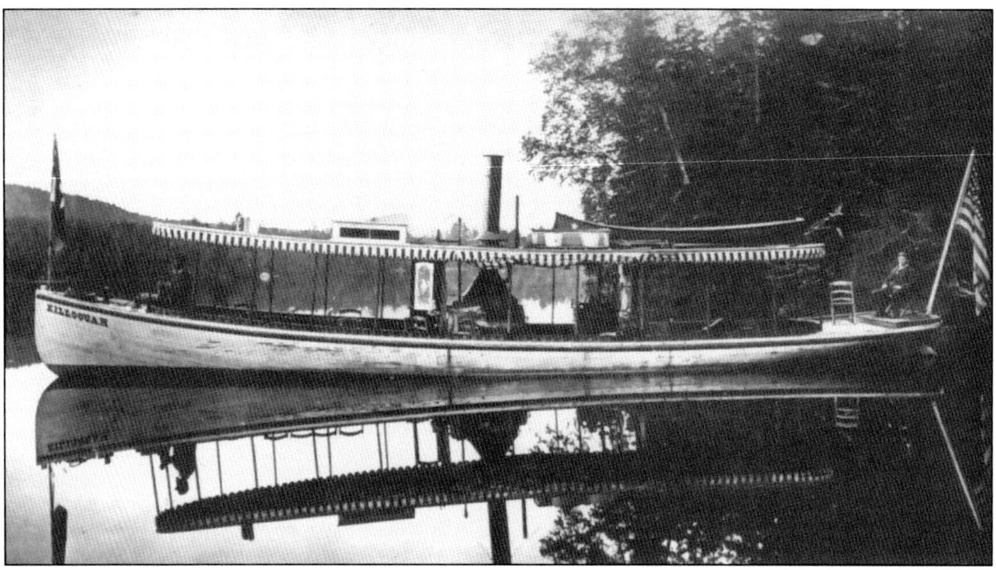

The steamer *Killoquah* waits for passengers just offshore. Note the pilot at the front and the conductor at the rear. As a precaution, most lake steamers had lifeboats on top for safety.

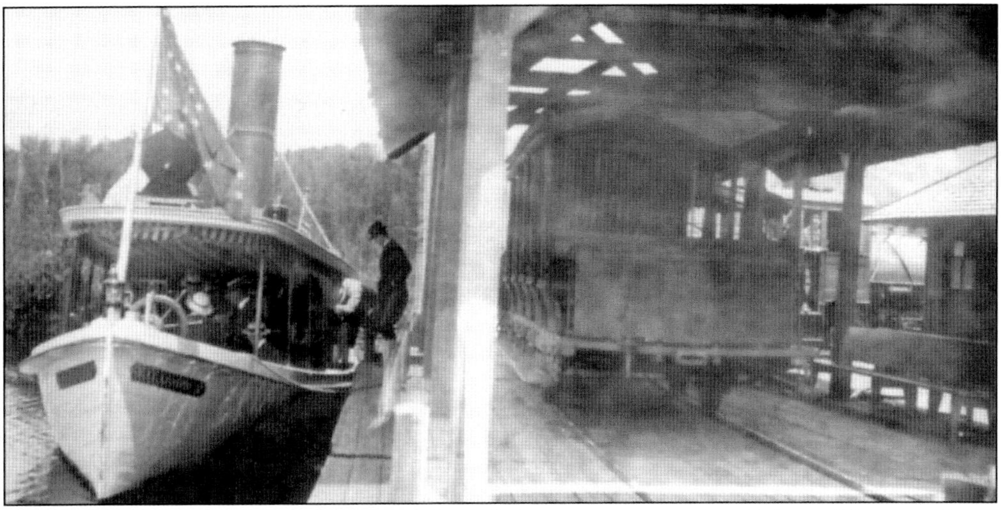

Delays were a possibility, but the train delivered the passengers within 10 feet of the steamboat, and the trunks were sure to follow on a service boat.

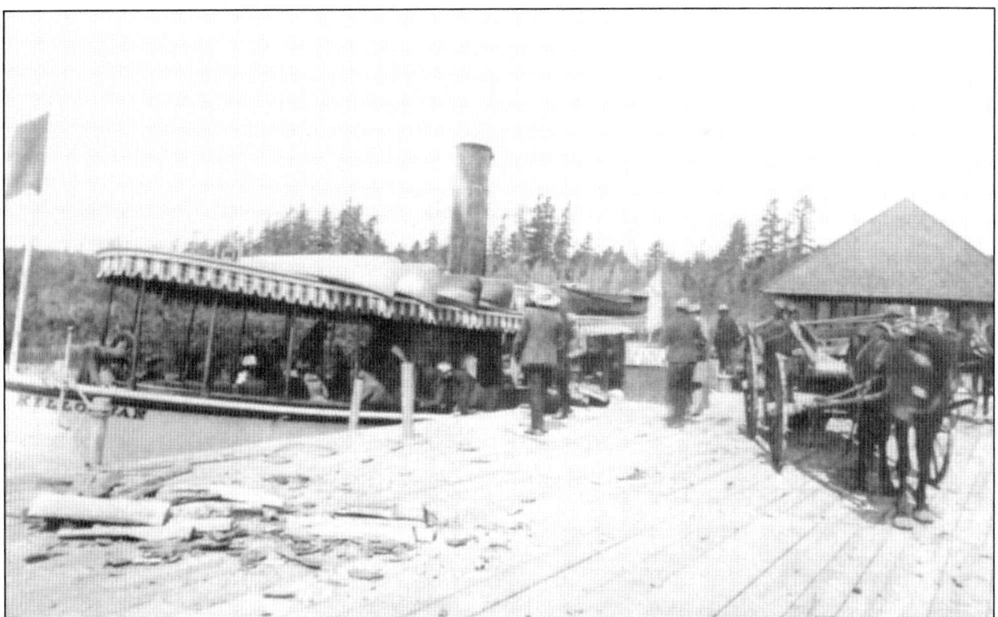

Carriages also brought passengers directly to the dock to catch a steamer. Here a horse and buckboard wait while people board the steamer. Notice the steam from the whistle; this was probably last call.

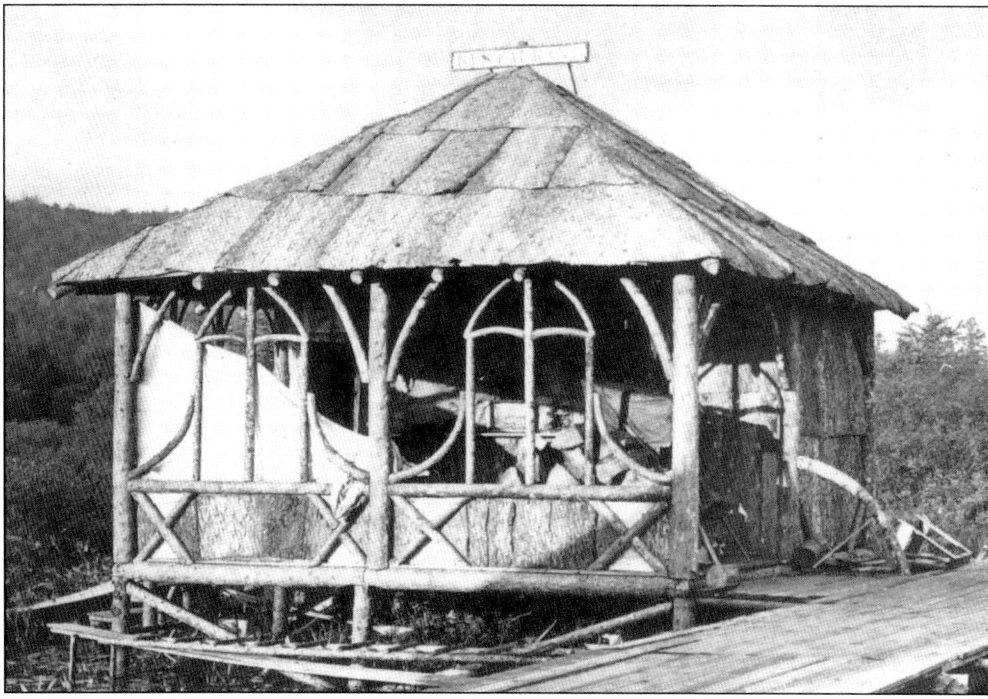

If there was a little time to spare at the carry, passengers could always catch a quick meal at a small restaurant here. Right off the dock was an open-air kitchen where the public could dine.

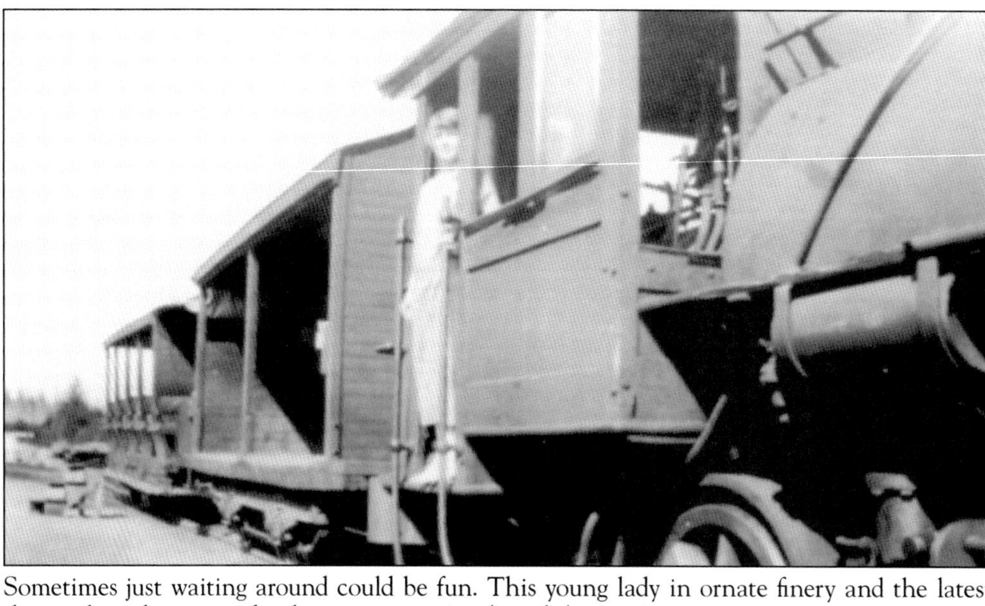

Sometimes just waiting around could be fun. This young lady in ornate finery and the latest shoes takes advantage of a photo opportunity aboard the waiting carry engine.

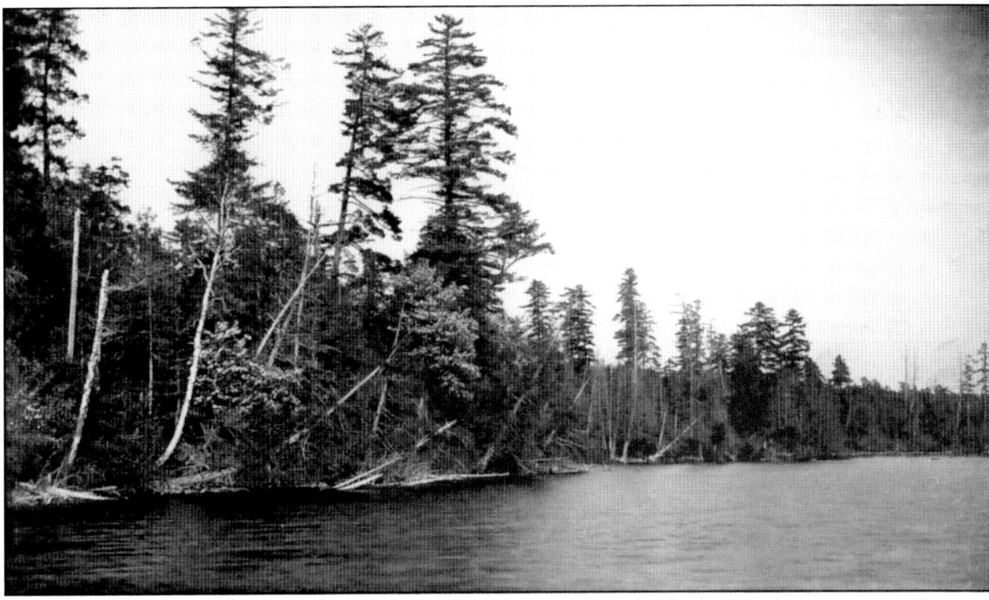

Majestic pines tower above the river. Traveling down the Marion River was a breathtaking experience.

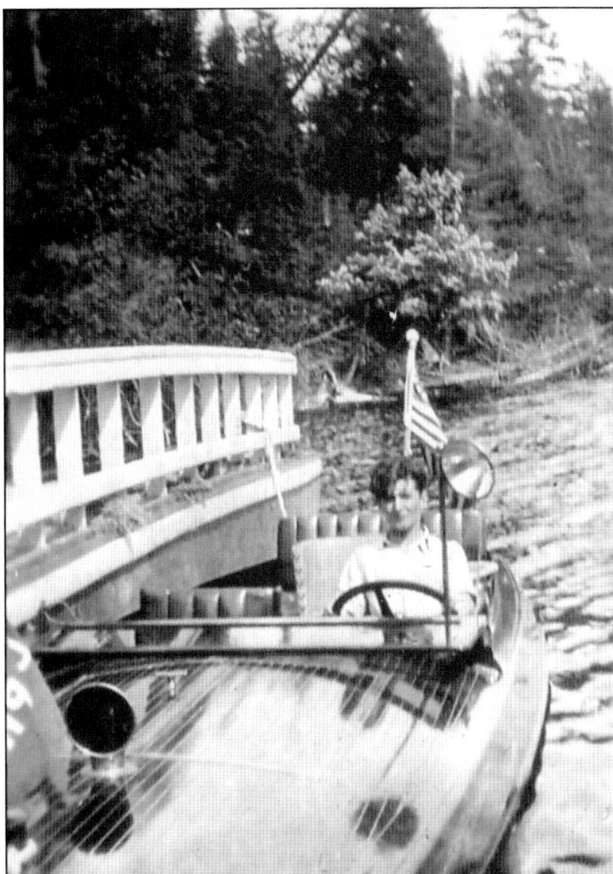

Occasionally a wealthy customer would send a personal boat for his own pickup. This young lad, sitting in a sporty gas runabout, waits for his master to show.

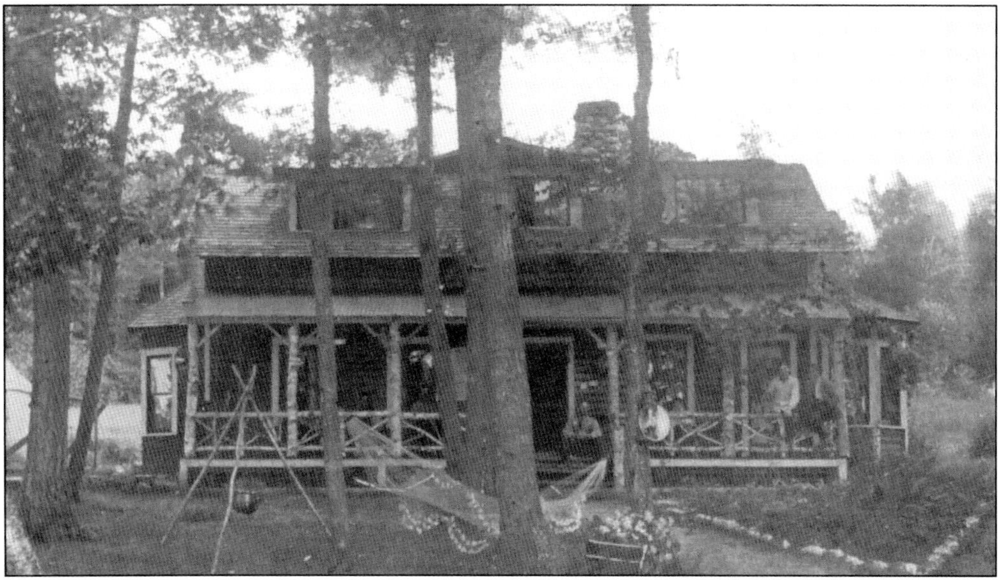

Camp Marion was one of the first establishments that came into view as boats headed west out of the Marion River and onto the central part of Raquette Lake. The main house of this complex of several camps and service buildings is pictured from the lake. Guests are resting on the front porch, but no one seems to have claimed the hammock yet. The buildings of Camp Marion no longer exist.

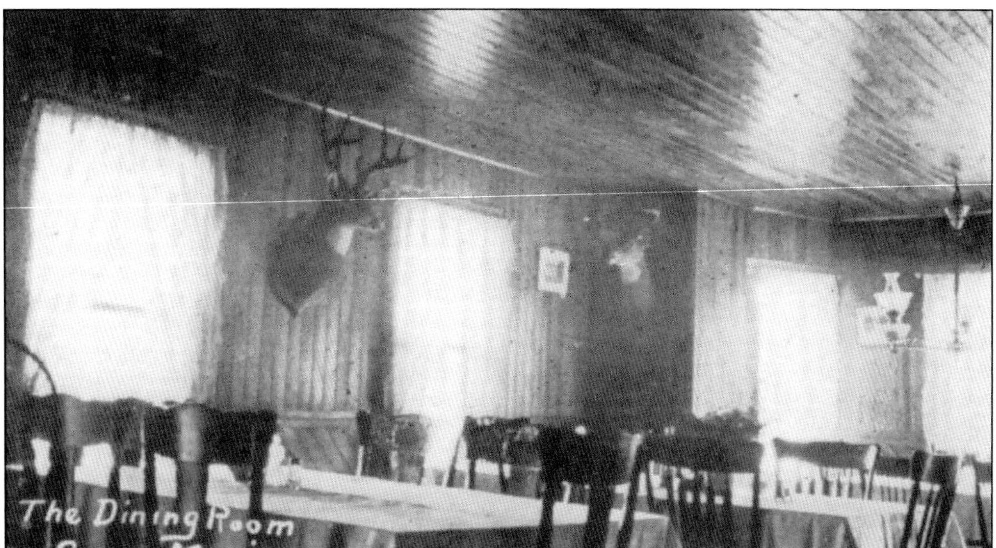

The dining hall of Camp Marion was advertised with a menu that was excellent and wholesome. It offered fresh vegetables, milk, and poultry. To work up an appetite, one could play tennis, go for a hike, or take a row in a boat. Rates were $18 and up per week.

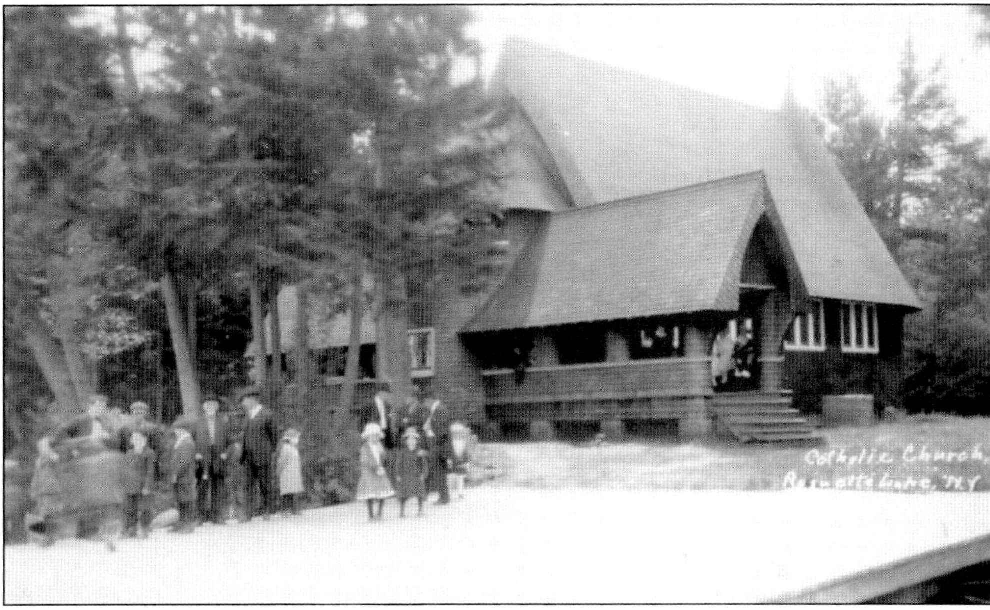

The next stop on this side of the lake was St. Williams Church. This area on Long Point developed as the original village and was designated as Durant. It had a post office, a store, and the church, built around 1890. This view shows people waiting around the dock area. In 1938, the congregation built a new church at its present site in Raquette Lake village because of convenience or the possibility of inclement weather.

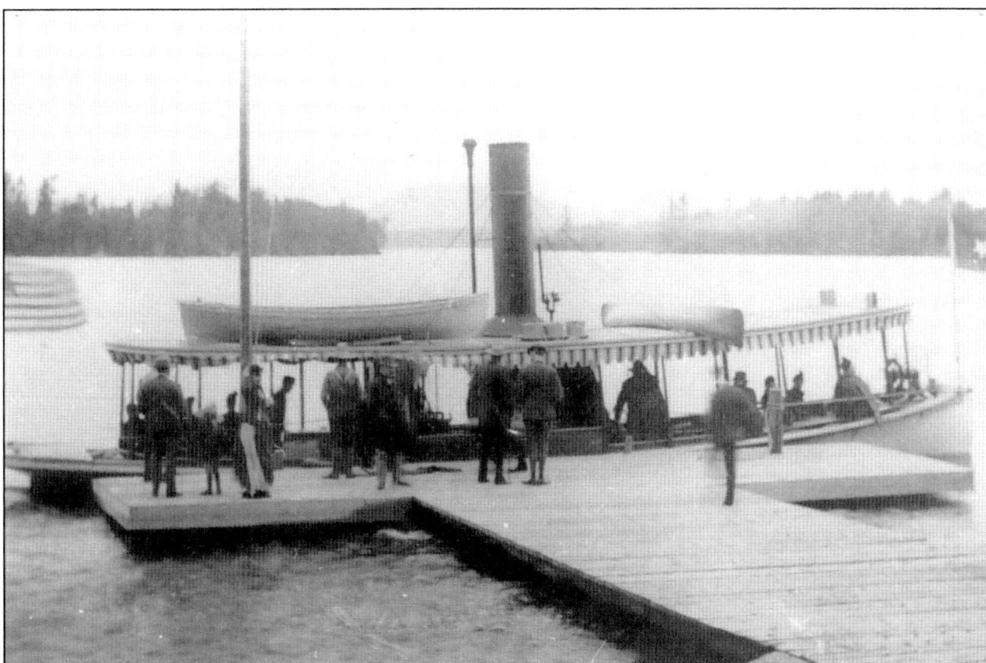

The steamer *Killoquah* is tied up at St. Williams dock in this view looking west. Passengers on and around the dock could be coming or going. Note the different stages of dress: formal, informal, and working class. St. Williams stands to this day and is designated a national historic landmark.

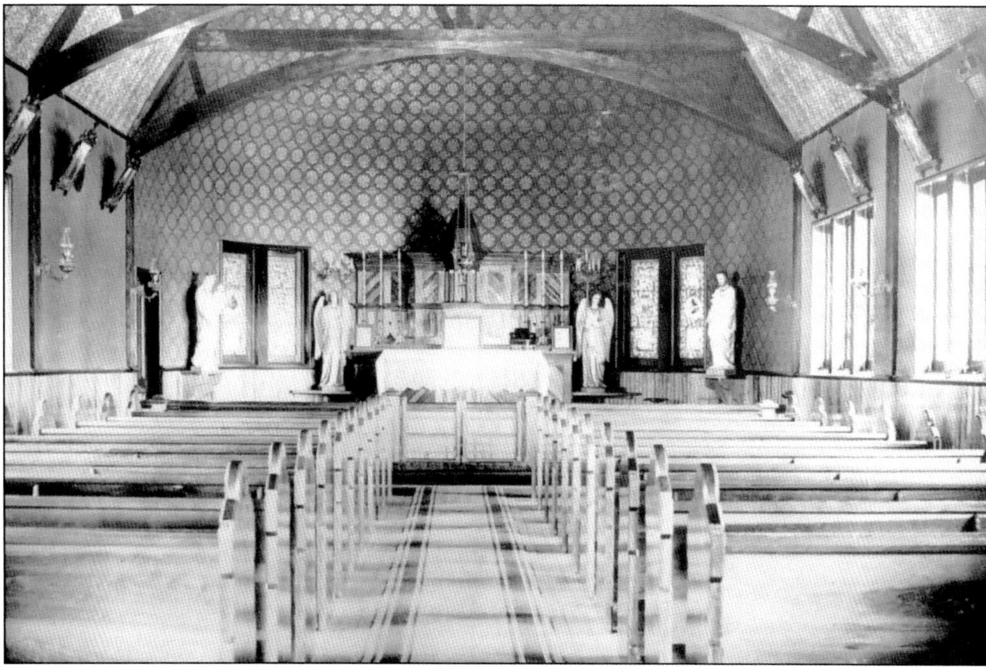

The interior of the original St. Williams was truly a sight to behold. This shot shows the incredible amount of handwork that went into the interior. Note the oil lamps lining the walls for illumination.

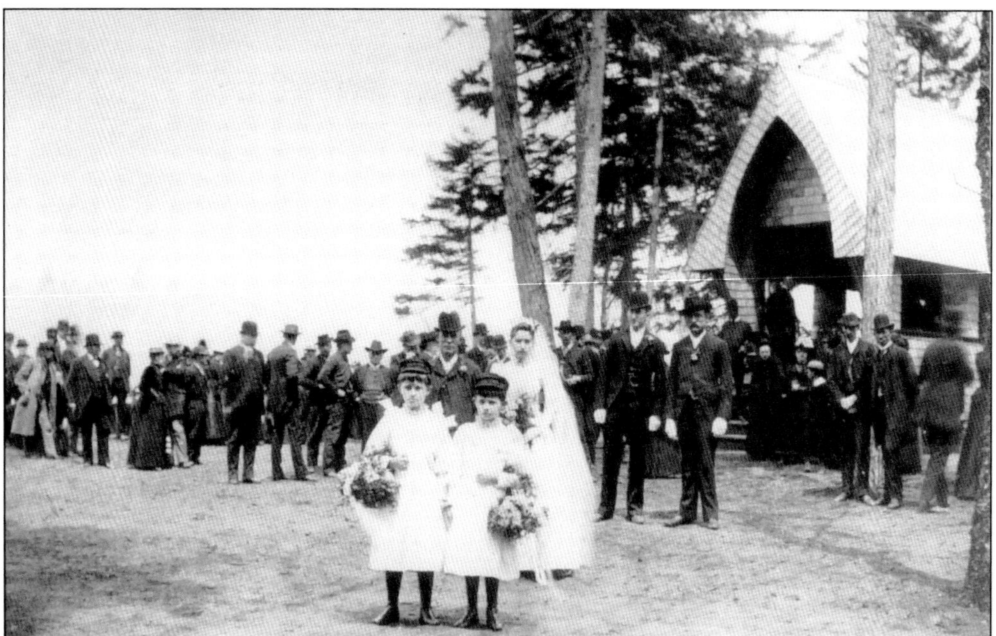

The church was used for many occasions. Here two flower girls lead the way for the bride and groom. The people involved were probably of high society, as almost everyone is dressed formally, including the servants.

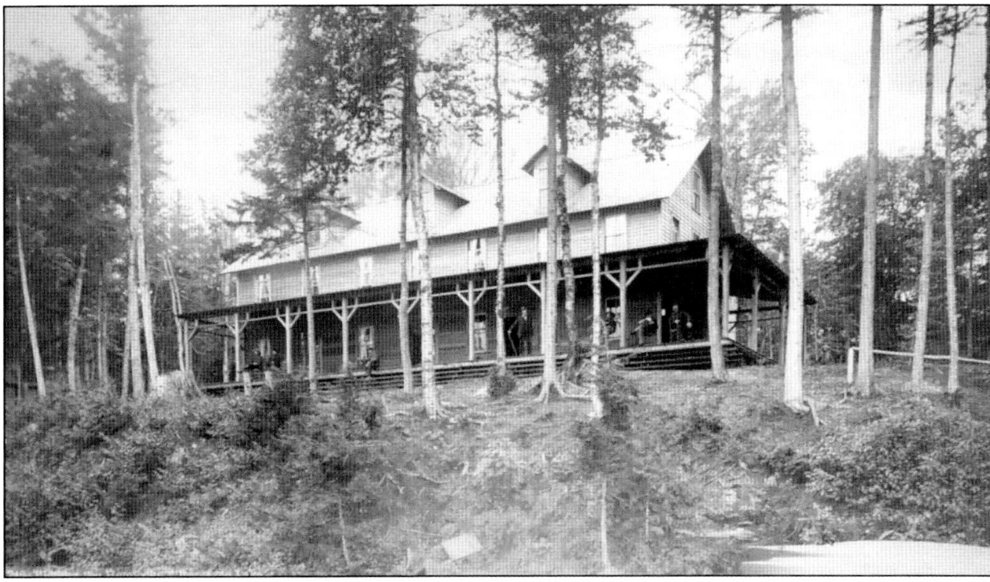

Under the Hemlocks was the name of the hotel on Long Point just below St. Williams Church. Constructed by Ed Bennett in 1883, the hotel could accommodate 45 guests. In 1889, Bennett sold the place to Eugene and Frederick Fink, who renamed it Raquette Lake House—the third time that a Raquette Lake establishment was so named. In the early 1890s, Jack Daly purchased the establishment and returned it to its original name, Under the Hemlocks. The guest book shows Ulysses S. Grant to have vacationed there with his family. The hotel was claimed by fire in 1900 and was not rebuilt.

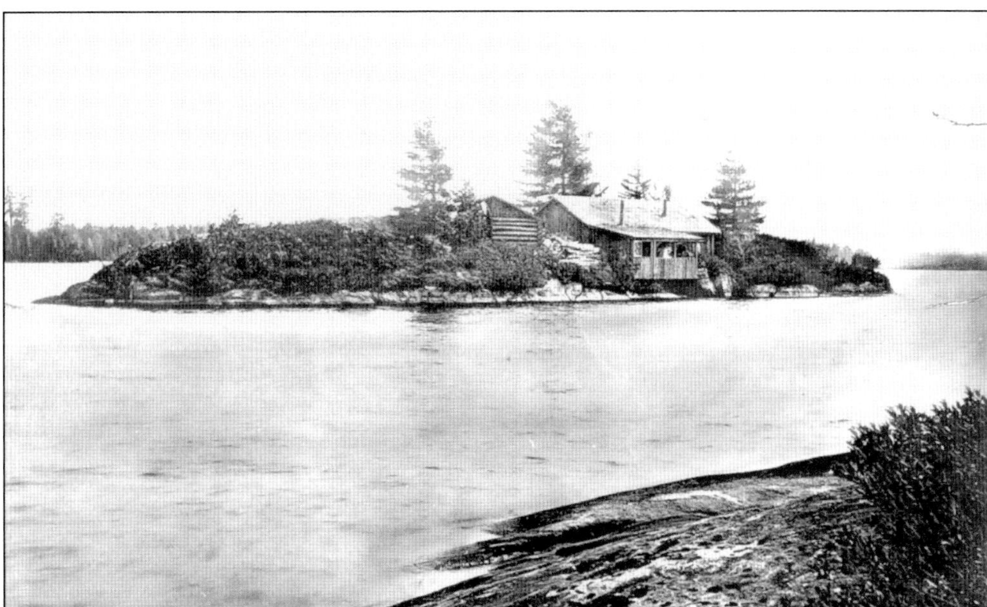

This view, looking north from St. Williams, shows an island of small stature. Mostly rock, it was named Little Rock Island. It has barely enough room for its cottage and outer buildings. The island exists today very much in its original form.

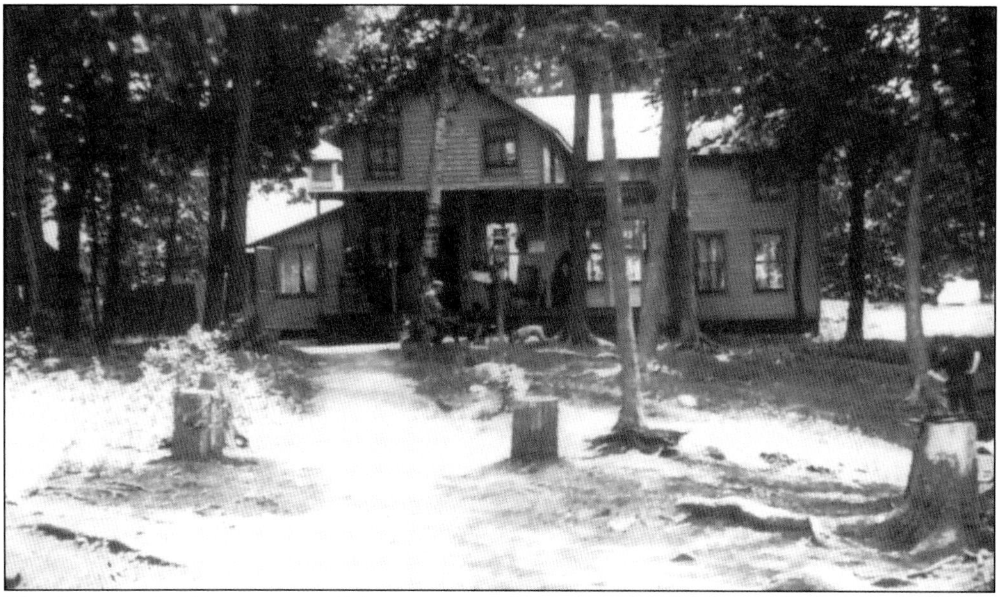

The Bennett brothers were well known around Raquette Lake. In the late 1880s, Richard Bennett built Sunset Point Camp on the south shore of Woods Point. The area consisted of a main house, a boathouse, and several lodges along the shore. Shown from the lake is the main house with its dock in the foreground.

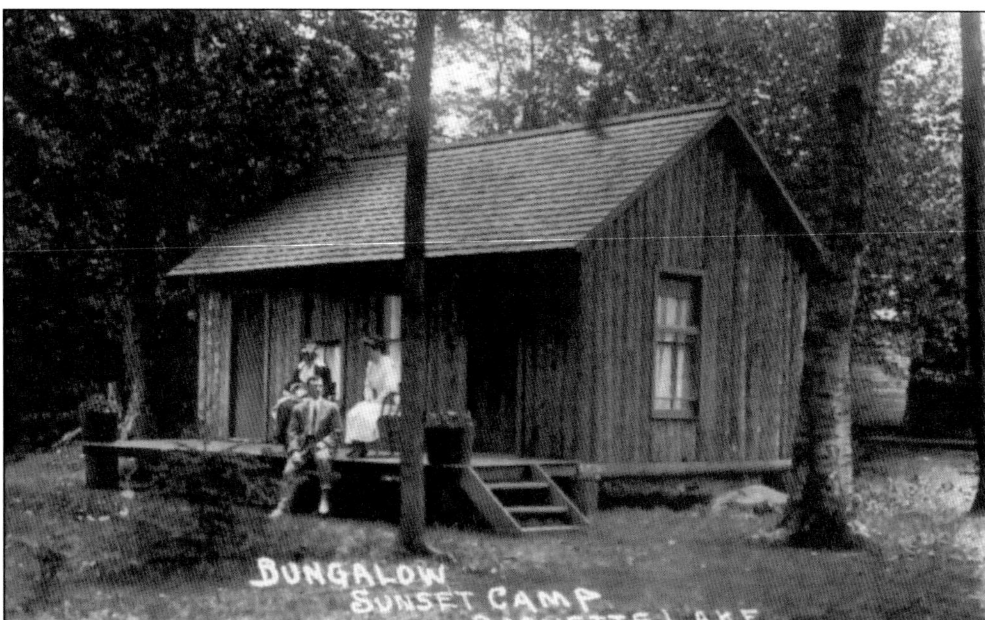

Visitors could choose anything from a room to a cottage away from everyone else. Sunset Point Camp exists today with exception of the main house and some service buildings.

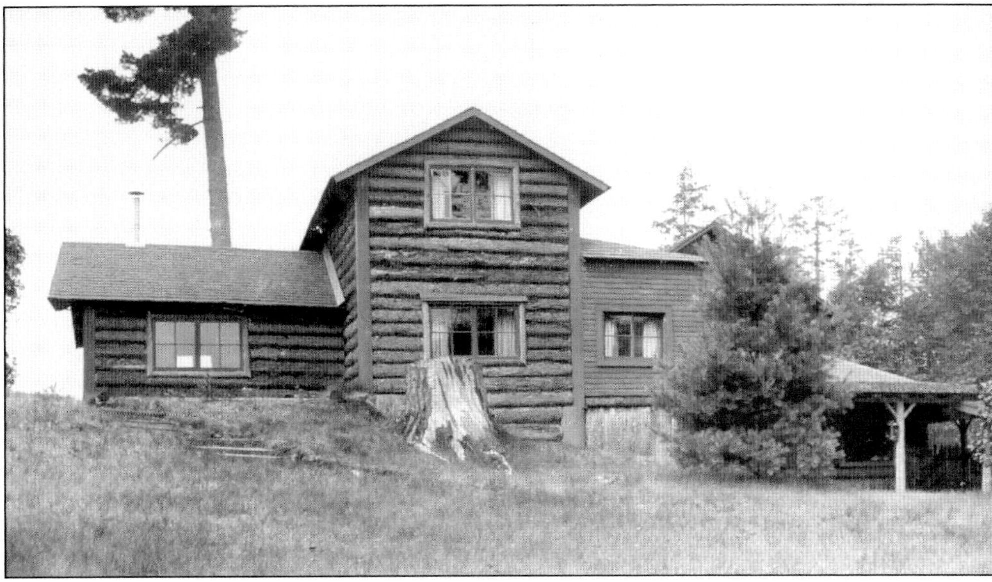

Osprey Island created a channel between itself and Woods Point. Located on the west side of Osprey Island was a complex of buildings called Camp Fairview. This picture shows the larger inn-style structure sitting on the point looking north. The majority of the buildings were of log construction in Adirondack style. Early tenants included Adirondack Murray, Alvah Dunning, Charles Durant Sr., and J. Harvey Ladew.

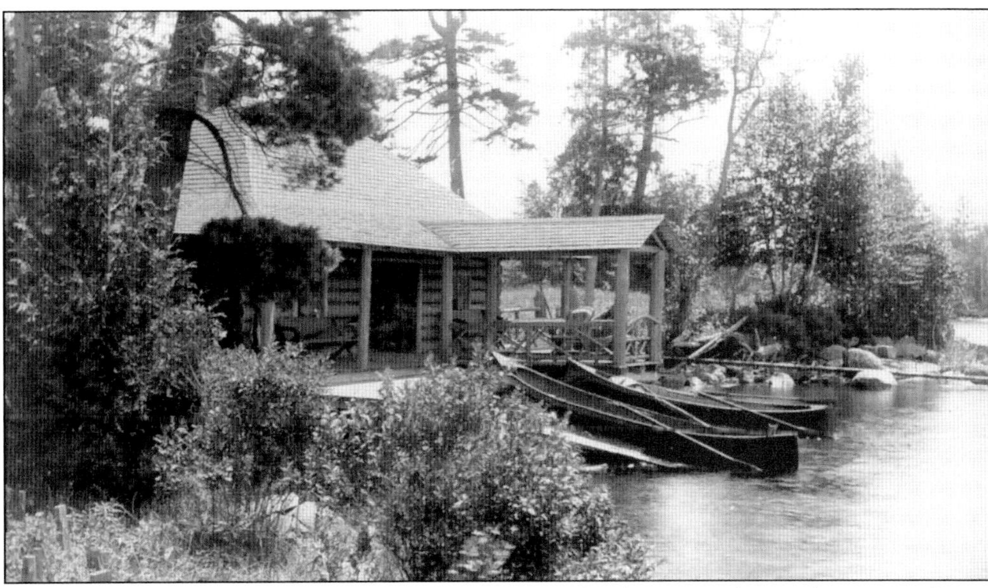

During ownership by J. Harvey Ladew, a great court battle occurred regarding ownership of the island. After a lengthy process, Ladew ultimately won. He and his family spent summers on Osprey Island after they had arrived in Raquette Lake village in their private Pullman car. They were met by their own steamer, the *Osprey*, and were transported to the island. Ladew was in the wholesale leather business. At the end of World War I, when the U.S. government flooded the market with wholesale leather, Ladew's fortune crumbled. Most of Camp Fairview was lost to fire, but this small boathouse survives to this day.

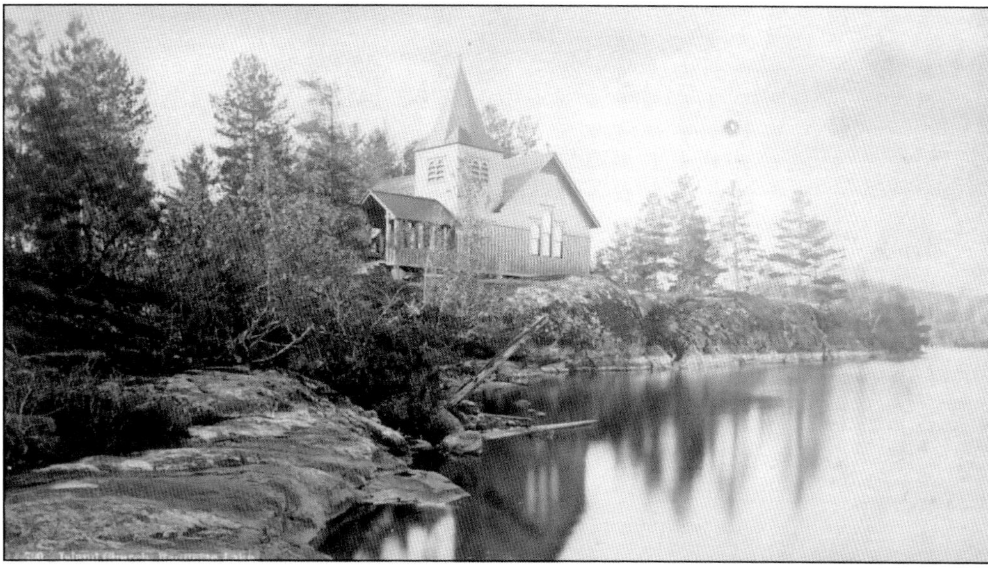

Across the channel to the south sits a chapel on a large mass of rock called St. Huberts Isle. The chapel was erected in 1882 with William West Durant's help so that workers had a choice for worship. The Episcopal Church of the Mission of the Good Shepherd was built on solid rock and has endured time's test, for it still stands today.

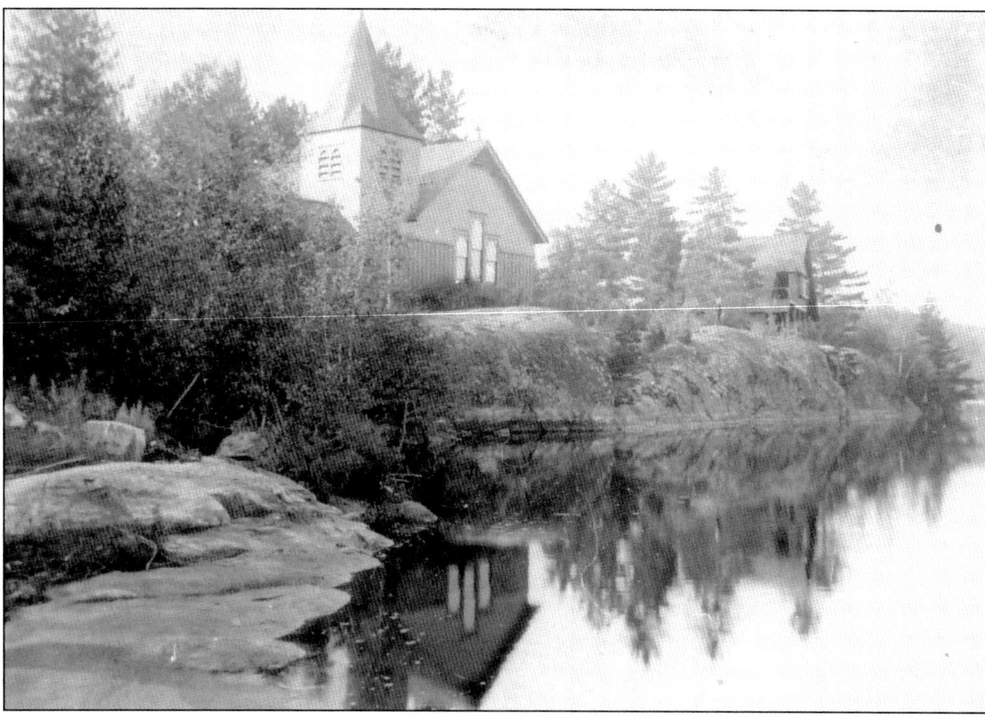

Later a rectory was also set up by Durant, west of the chapel. The rectory, in its final form, stands today, and the mission still holds a summer service.

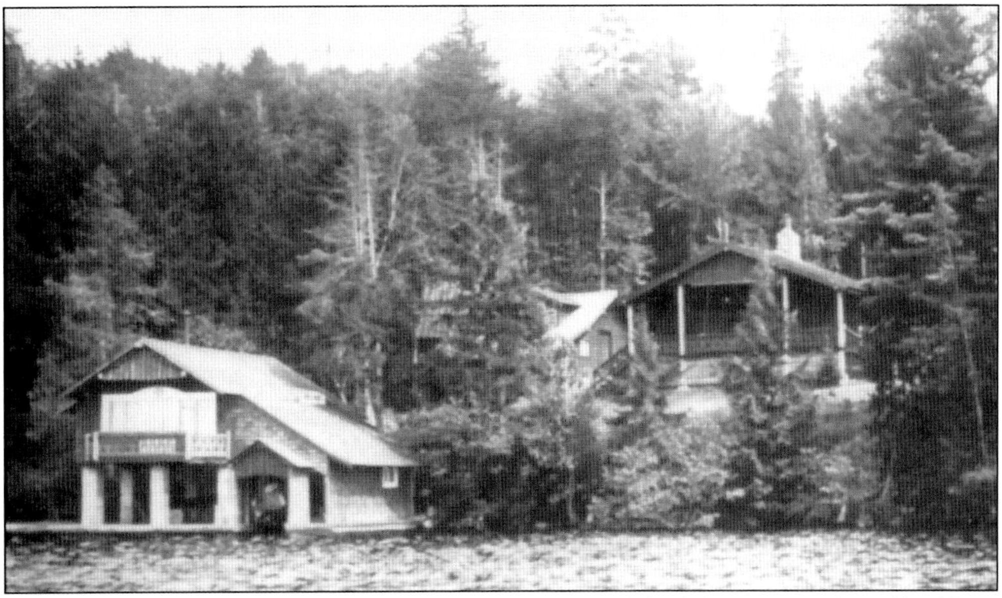

On the part of Big Island that faces the central portion of the lake is a complex of buildings once owned by Dr. Arpad G. Gerster. Gerster called this complex Oteetiwi. He and his family traveled from New York City to this site for about 22 summers. As Raquette Lake became busier and more hectic, Gerster sold his complex to a sculptor named Carl Bitter. After the main house burned down in 1907, Bitter rebuilt it, and the complex remains on the site to this day.

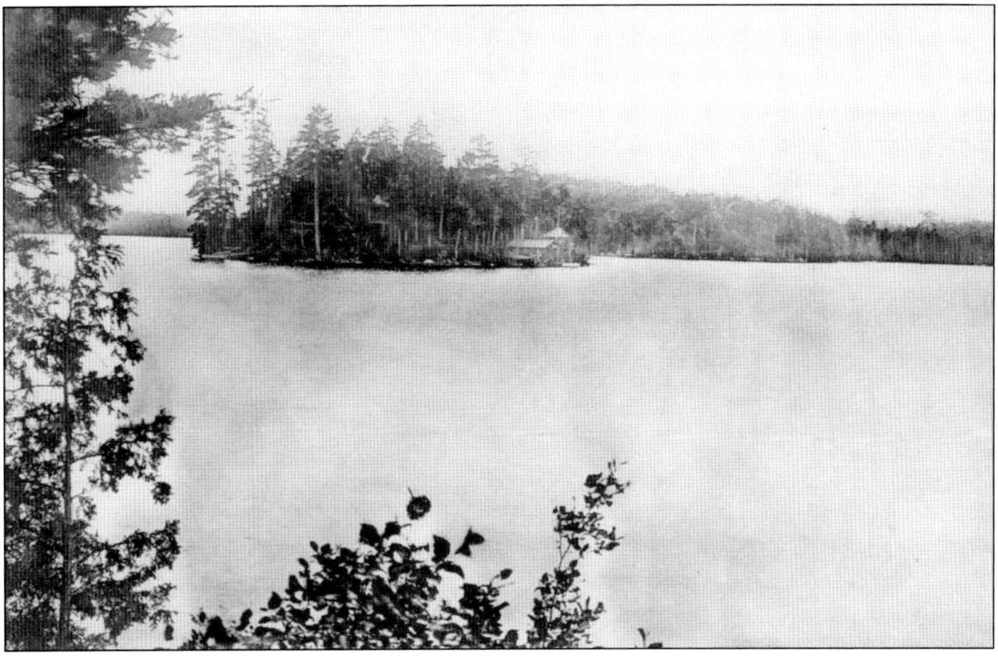

Just south of Big Island is Inman Island, or originally, Round Island. Here Horace Inman, a container manufacturer, set up a complex of buildings. Inman was known for his love of the tropics. Situated around his homes were numerous gardens. The inside of one of the buildings was set up with steam heat. This enabled the growth of plants and flowers not common to the Adirondacks and provided a haven for some of the tropical animals that Inman kept as pets.

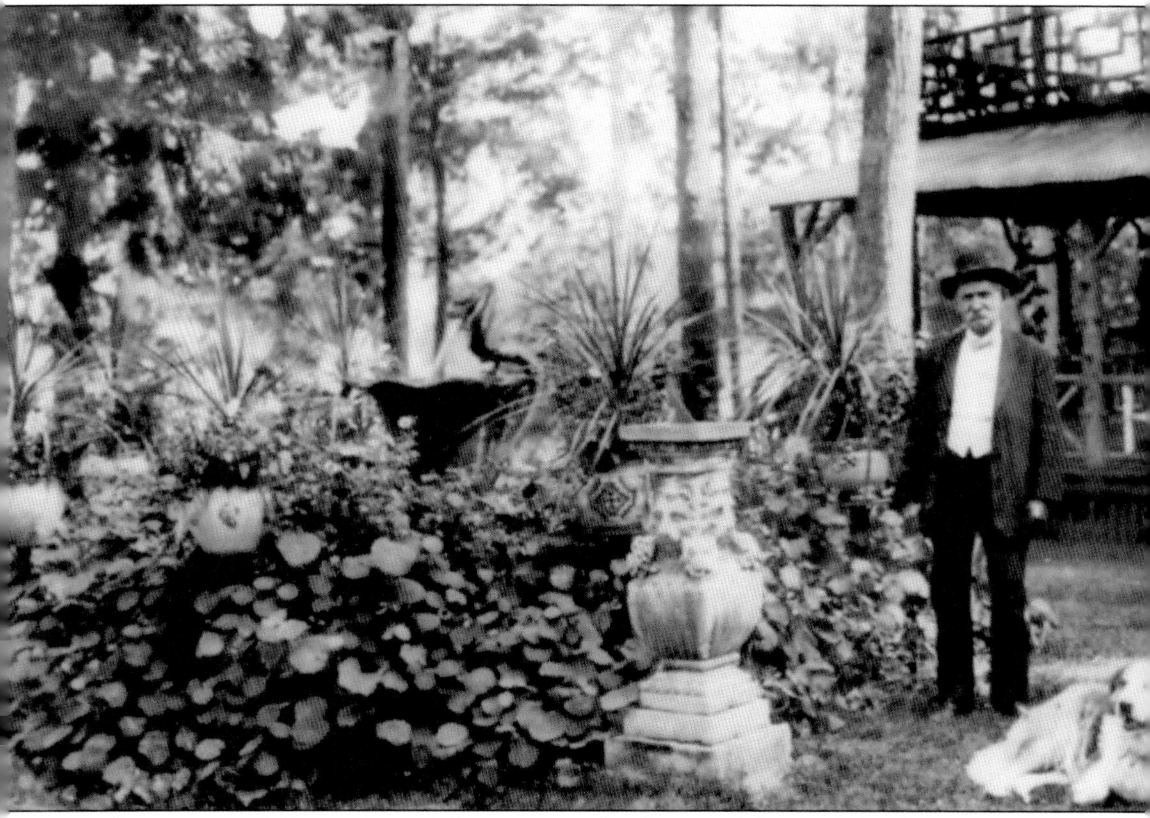

The exteriors of Horace Inman's homes were also decorated, but with local flora and fauna. Here Inman, with one of his dogs, stands in one of the numerous outside gardens. Inman was friends with former president Benjamin Harrison, who visited while he was at his own estate in Old Forge. Many construction styles were visible in Inman's buildings. One of his boathouses showed touches of not only the great camp style but also some Chinese heritage, which was glimpsed in other Raquette Lake structures.

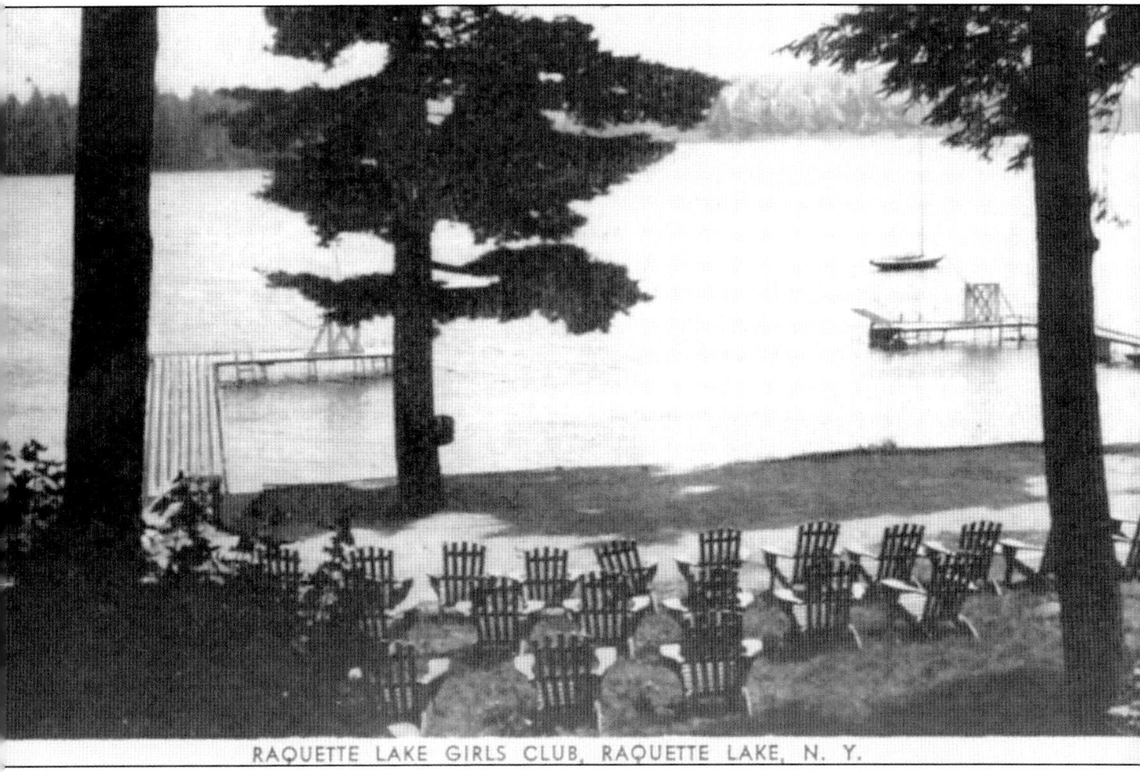

The Raquette Lake Girls Camp, in its final location, is seen across the bay from Inman Island. The beautiful beachfront was used for aquatic activities of all sorts, from diving to sailing to, perhaps, learning to swim for the first time. Girls could also play baseball, kickball, hockey, basketball, and tennis. The camp is still in operation today.

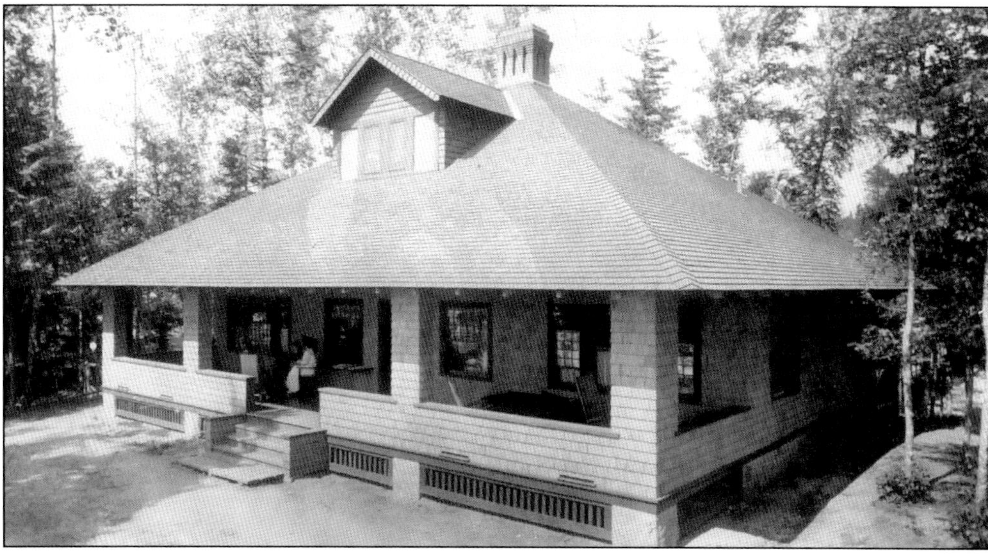

Northward along the western shore from the girls' camp lie the boundaries of the Antlers Hotel. This collection of buildings was established by Charlie Bennett on what was known over the years as Sand Point, Constable Point, and then finally Antlers Point, around 1887. Birch Cottage was the southernmost point of the Antlers Hotel. The cottage was typical of an Antlers rental, as it had a central lobby with bedrooms that could be accessed from the lobby. It still stands today in this form.

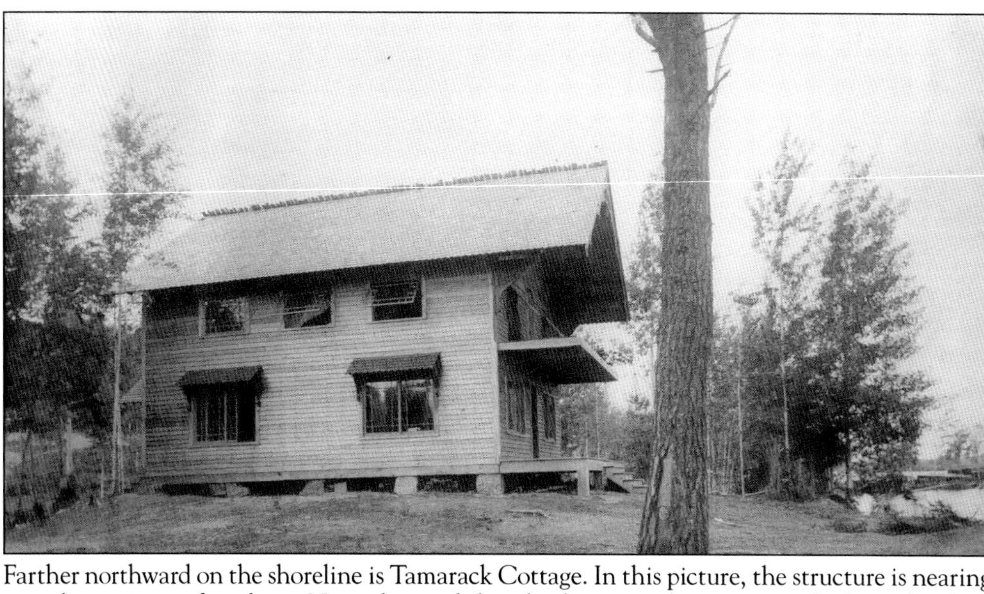

Farther northward on the shoreline is Tamarack Cottage. In this picture, the structure is nearing completion in its first form. Note the roof shingles have not been trimmed. As technology improved, inside plumbing was added to all these buildings.

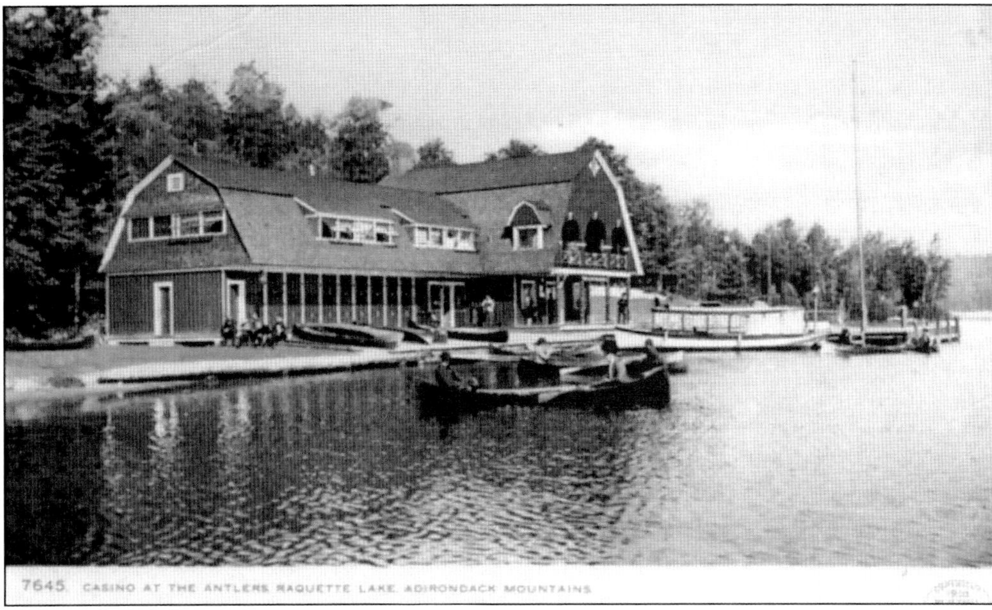

Still farther northward along the shore, past the Antlers Beach, is the Antlers Casino. Here guests checked in, ate, played, or were entertained. They could also rent a canoe or a guide boat to view the lake. In the early days, wire service and mail pickup were available here. Today an Antlers postal cancellation is a collectible item.

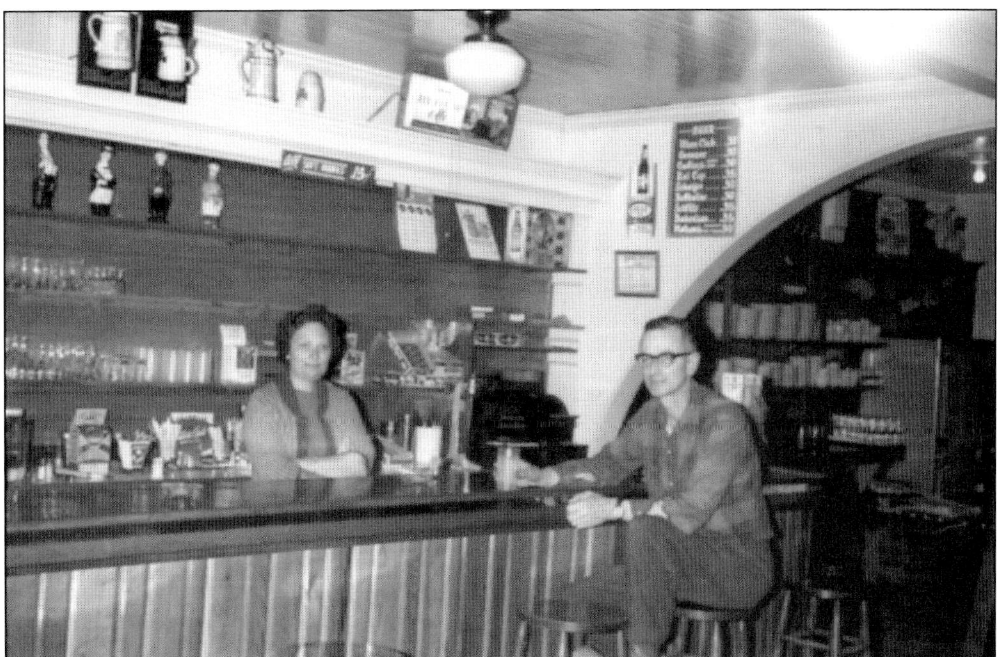

The Antlers Hotel was sold and divided in 1957. Don and Betty Langham purchased the casino. This picture shows these owners sitting at the bar awaiting the rush of customers. In the mid-1960s, the casino, the remaining cabins, and the main house were purchased by the State University of New York at Cortland, which still utilizes them.

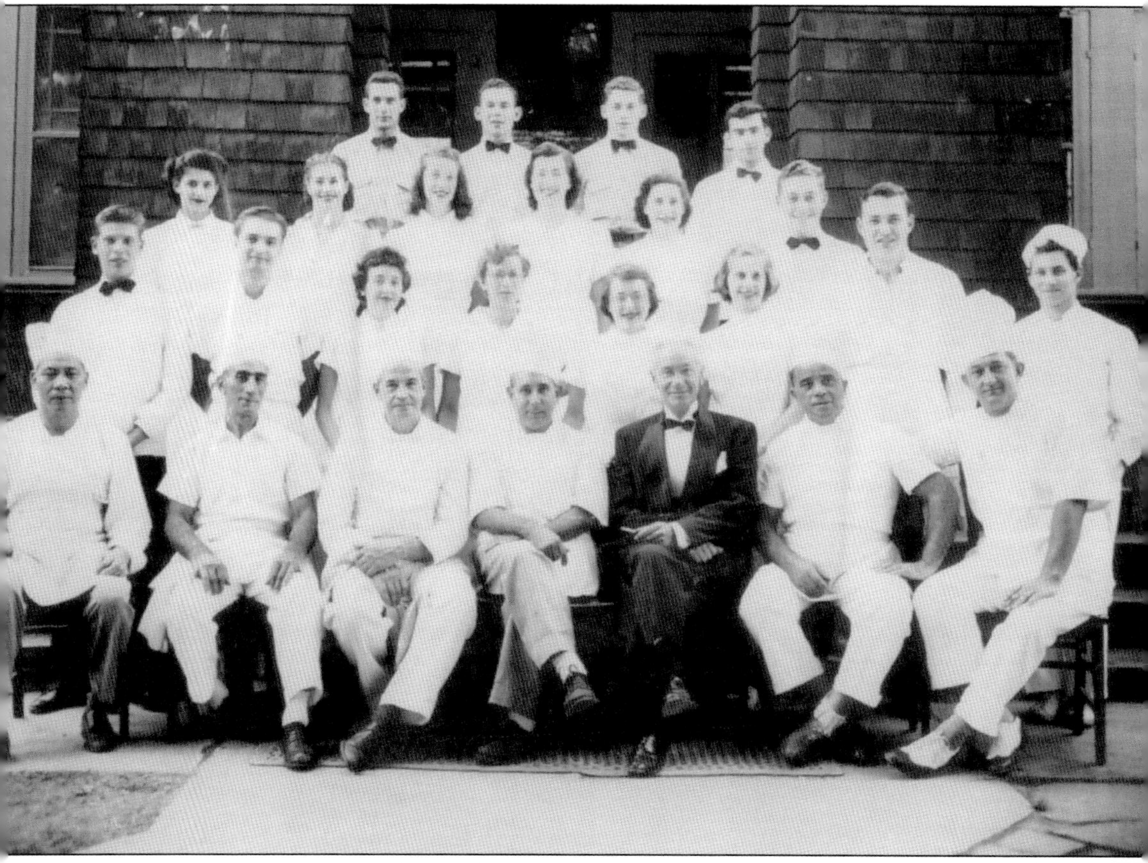

Guests at the Antlers Hotel had a choice of single rooms or whole cottages. The staff of the Antlers was always ready to wait on guests hand and foot. On the steps of the Antlers dining room are staff members, starting with the tuxedo-clad host and the cooks, then the waitresses, and finally the busboys.

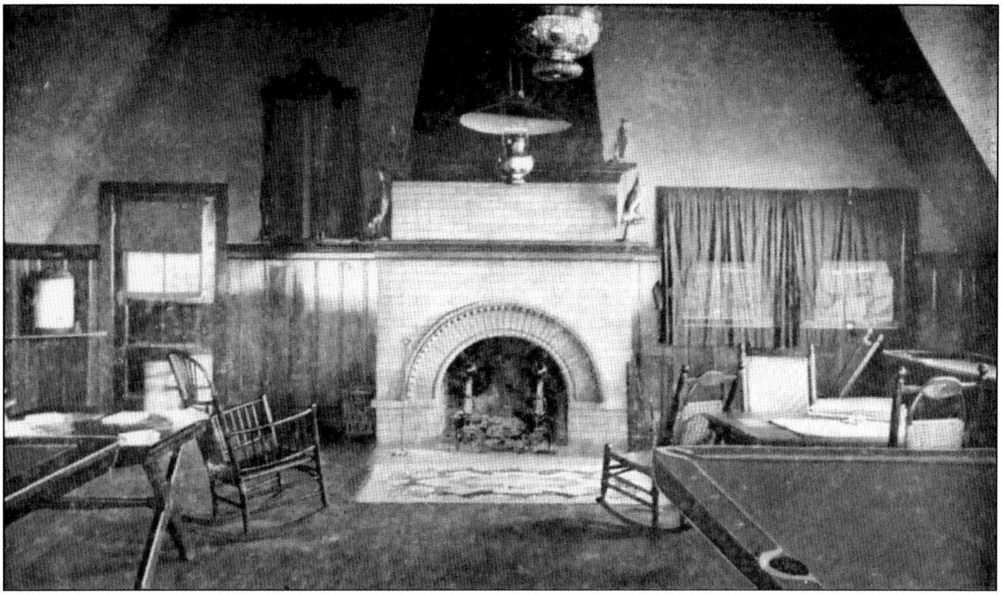

Activities and pastimes were plentiful at the Antlers. The upstairs of the casino's social hall, pictured here, offered Ping-Pong, billiards, and card tables. On special evenings, the upper porch of the casino was home to the occasional orchestra or band, which allowed people to dance to the music on a roll-up parquet floor on the waterfront.

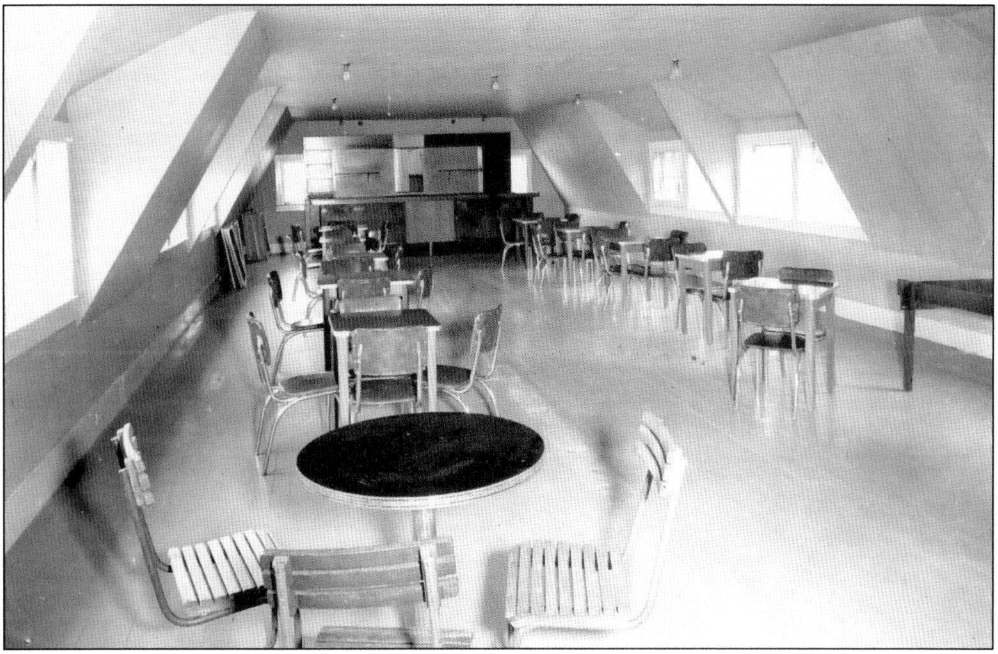

For guests who preferred less-active pursuits, the Antlers provided a small café on the second floor, away from the bustle of the mainstream bar.

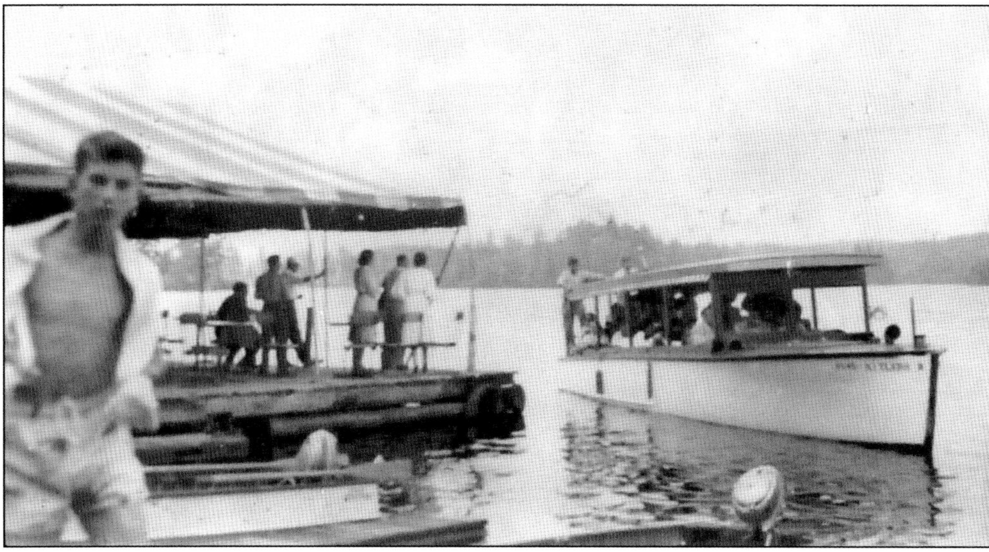

There was plenty to do outside at the Antlers: swimming, sunning, or renting a canoe or rowboat. But the ultimate experience was to ride the hotel launch.

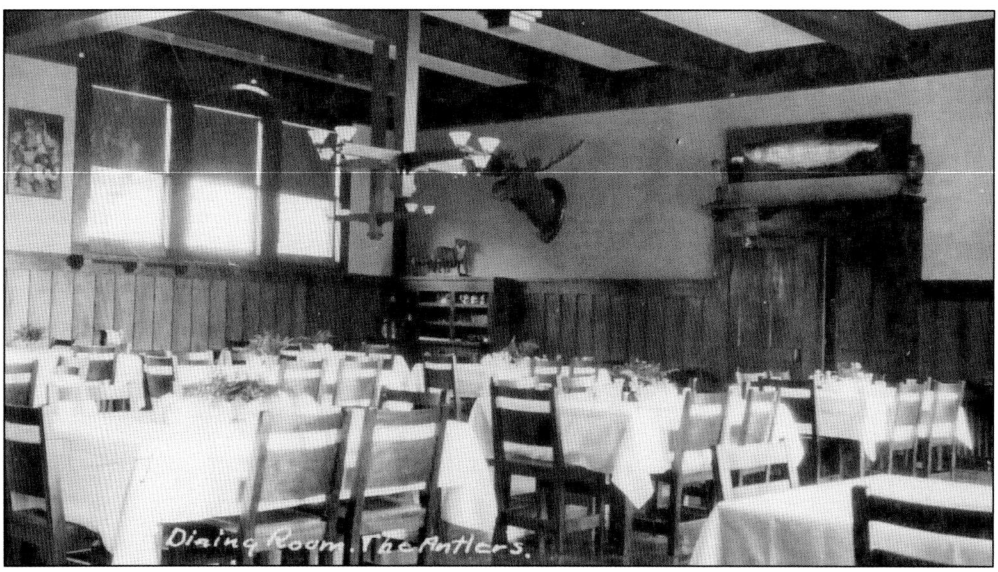

After an energetic day at the Antlers, one was always rewarded with top-notch meals in the spacious dining hall.

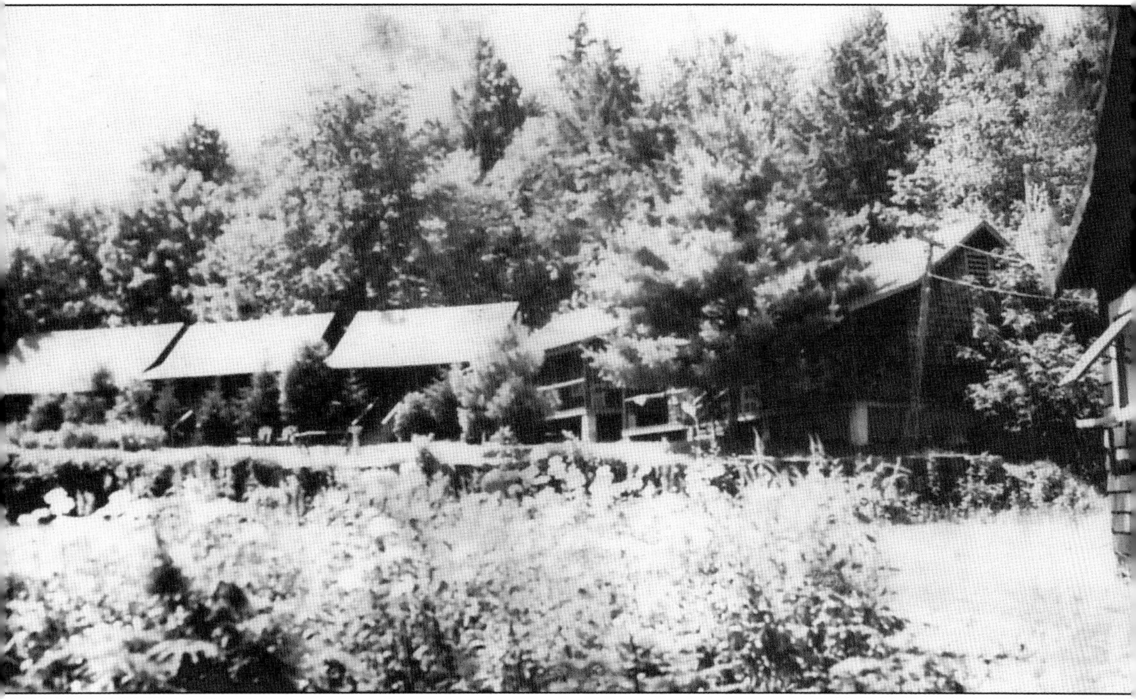

Accommodations varied, with the different terraces at the Antlers providing cottages with one, two, three, or even six bedrooms. This enabled the individual traveler to have his privacy and the family to stay together.

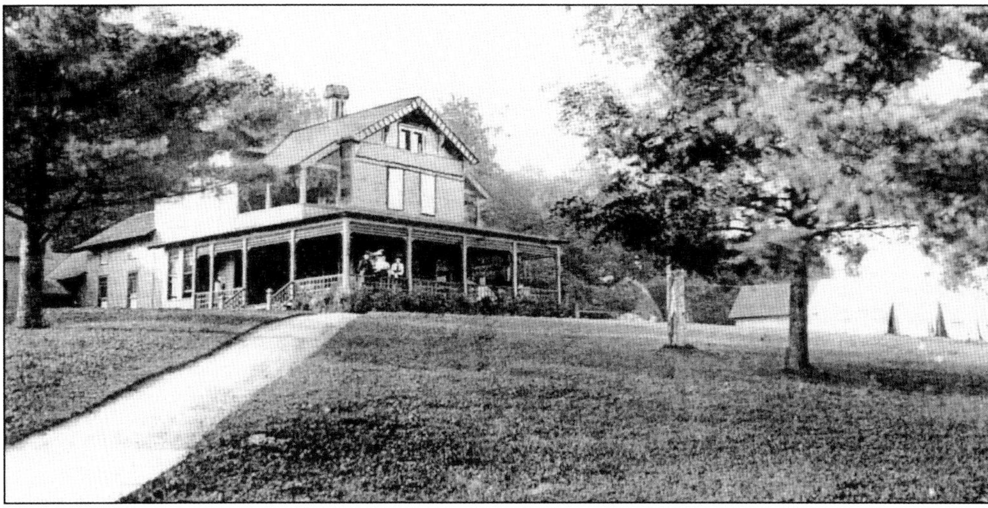

Standing majestically on a hill at the Antlers was the main house. Inside, guests could rent a room, enjoy the spacious main-floor lobby, and send mail or a telegraph to friends. Those who preferred to rough it could book one of the tent platforms and still take in the fine meals at the dining hall.

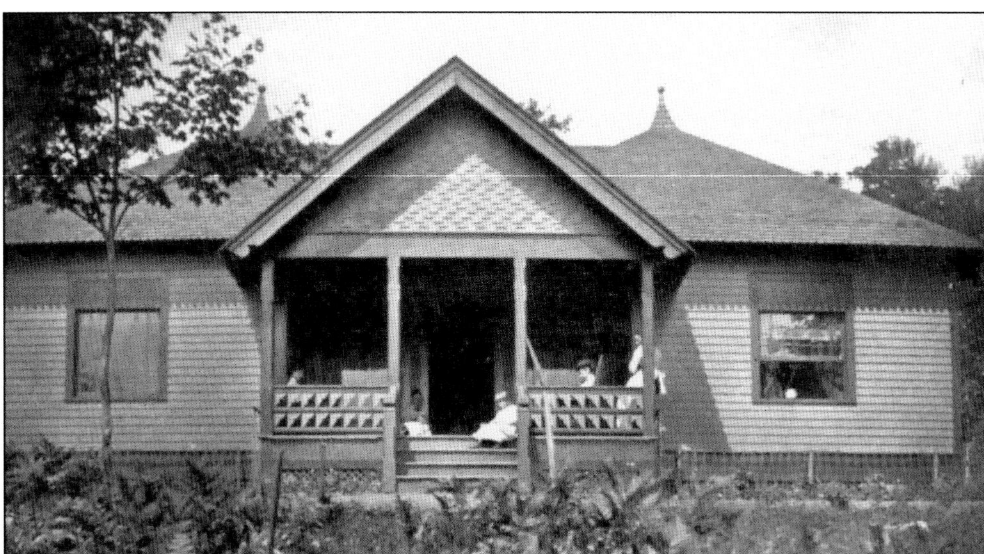

Larger cottages for whole families could also be rented. This unit provided four bedrooms, a lobby with a fireplace, and a large porch.

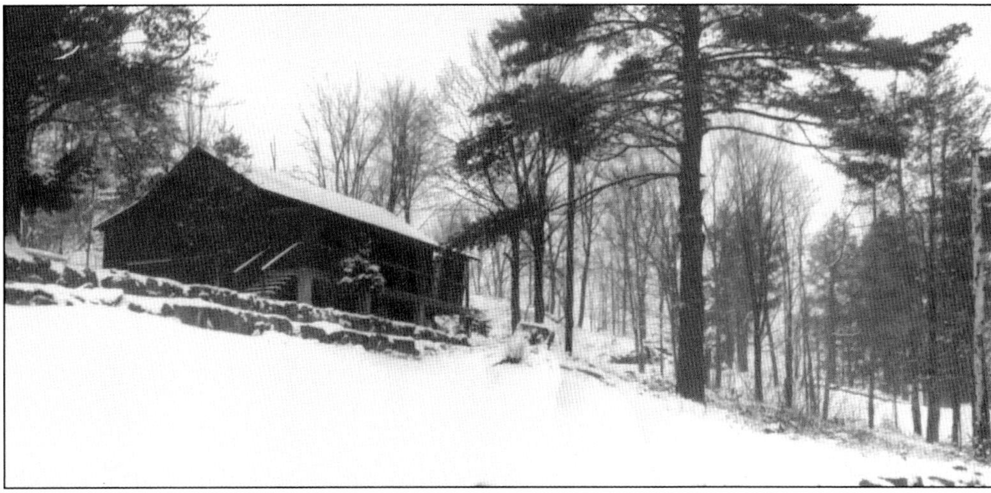

The last cottage built at the Antlers was the Lake Cottage. This was a three-bedroom unit that bordered the Antlers' private nine-hole golf course. Adjacent were private showers where golfers could clean up after playing the course.

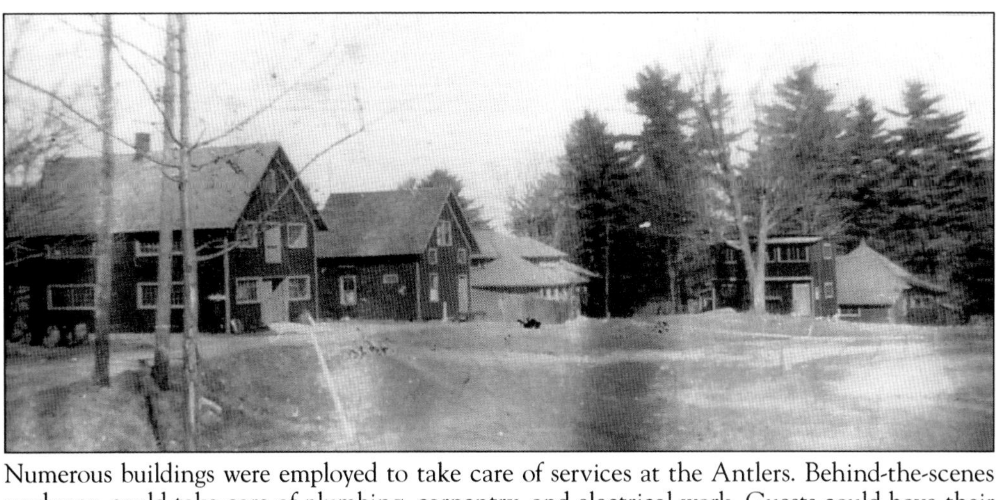

Numerous buildings were employed to take care of services at the Antlers. Behind-the-scenes workmen could take care of plumbing, carpentry, and electrical work. Guests could have their personal car washed and waxed, or they could employ one of the Antlers' two limousines.

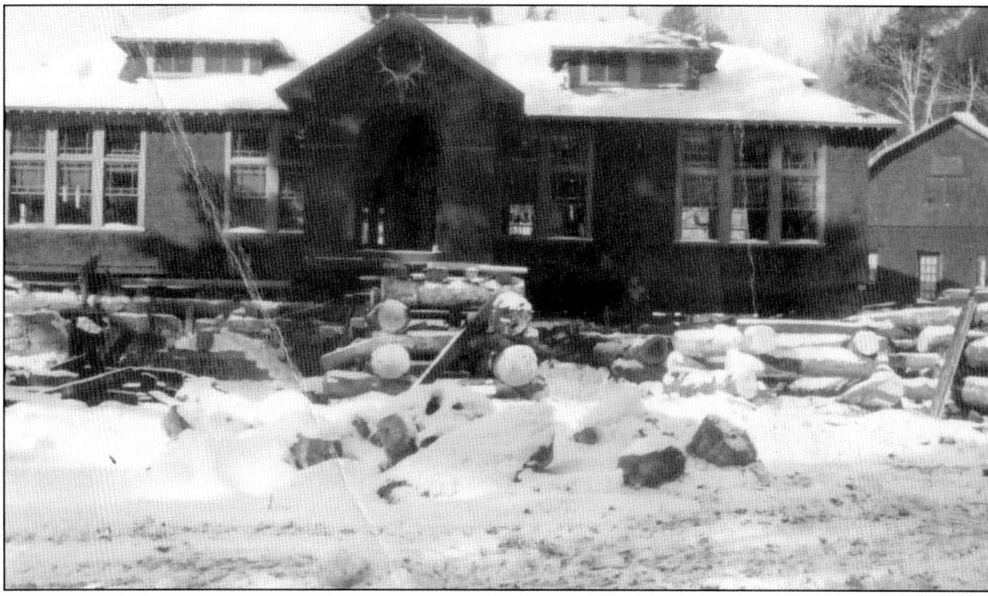

When the Antlers was sold, some buildings were moved for other uses. In this picture, the Antlers dining hall is jacked up and being moved to its current location at the Raquette Lake Girls Camp. The majestic dining hall was soon to be a gymnasium.

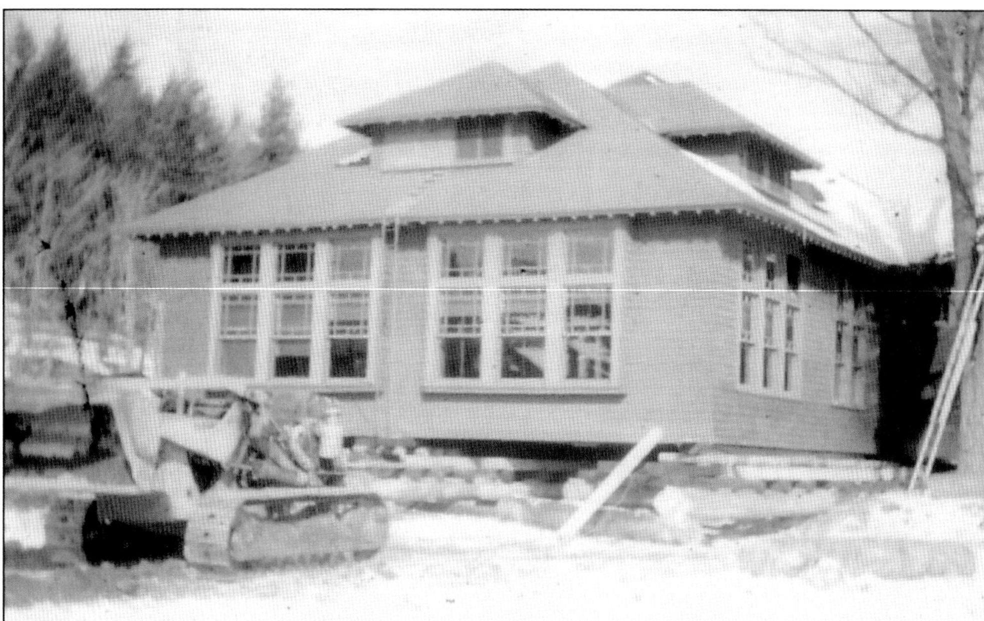

Some barriers had to be overcome. Note the tree in the right-hand corner of the picture. It was in the way and, thus, had to be cut down so that the dining hall could be moved to its future location.

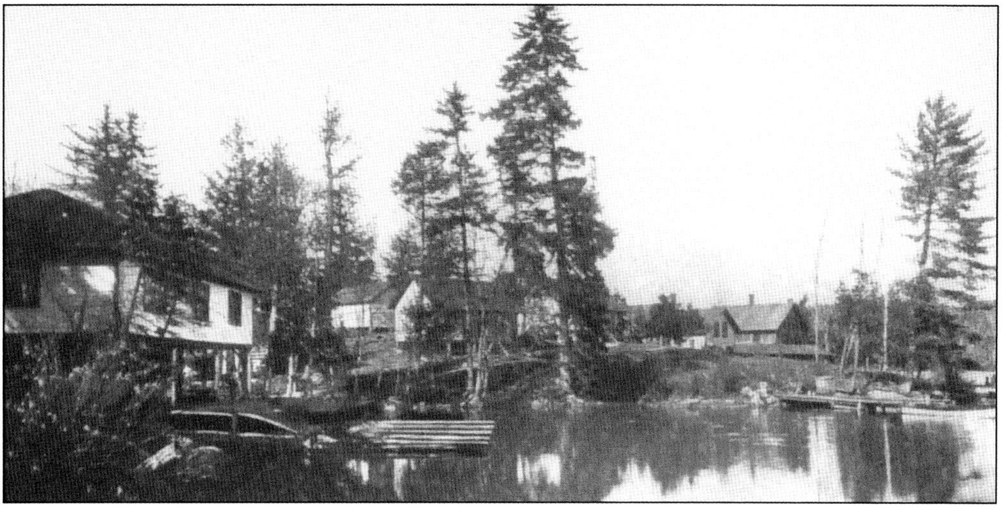

Around Antlers Point beyond the golf course are a cove and a point that used to hold Hunters Rest, an establishment built by George Carlin around 1894. The first building, situated in the cove, was a boathouse used for storing canoes and guide boats.

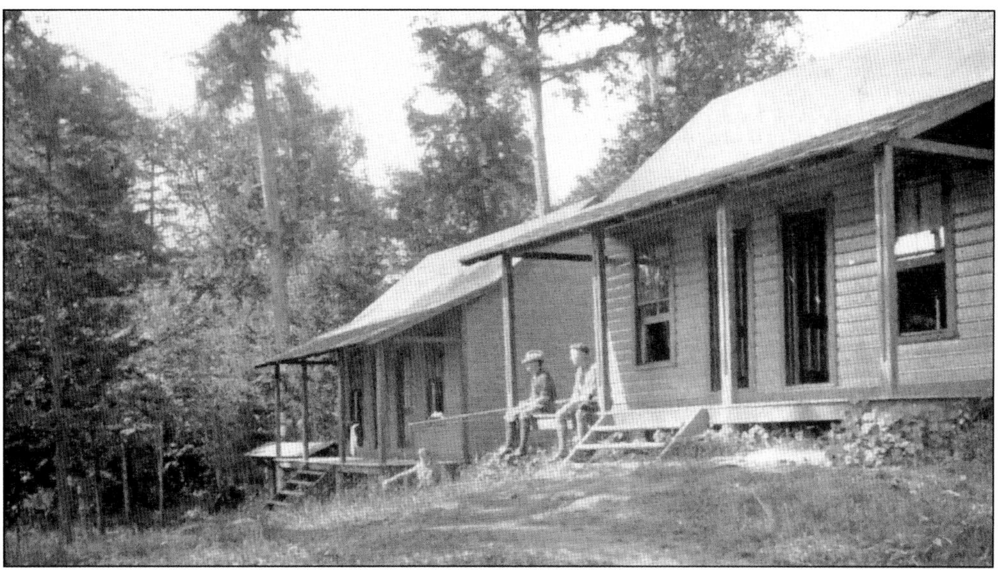

Cabins stood on the hill next to the boathouse. These units could be rented by the day, the week, or the season.

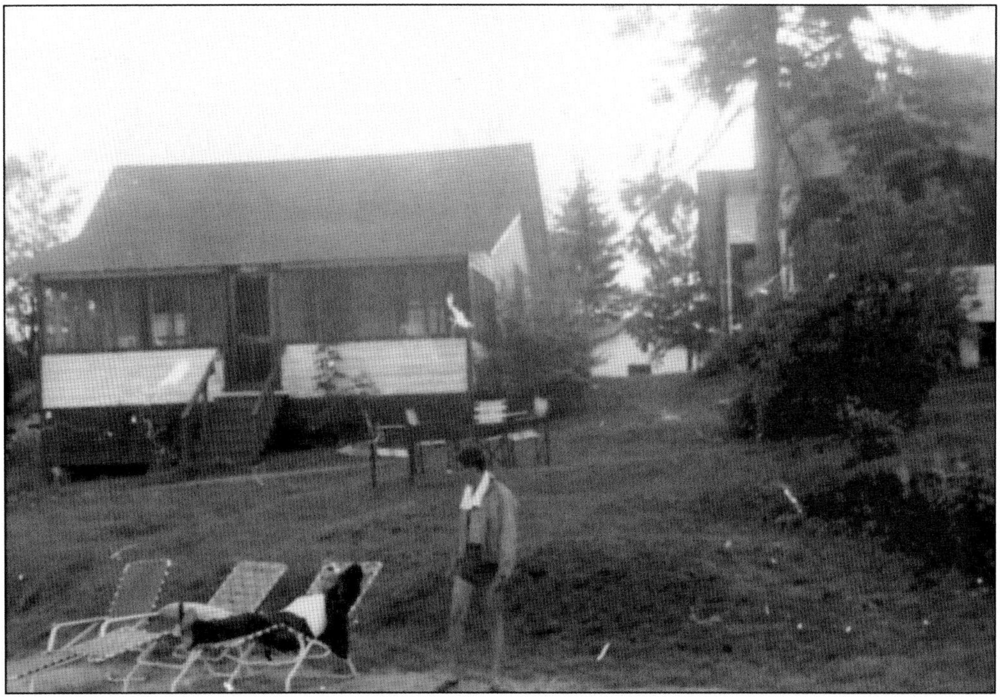

As the years progressed, the cabins were upgraded and improved with inside plumbing, heat, and screened porches. Some were close to the lake so that guests could use the sandy beach.

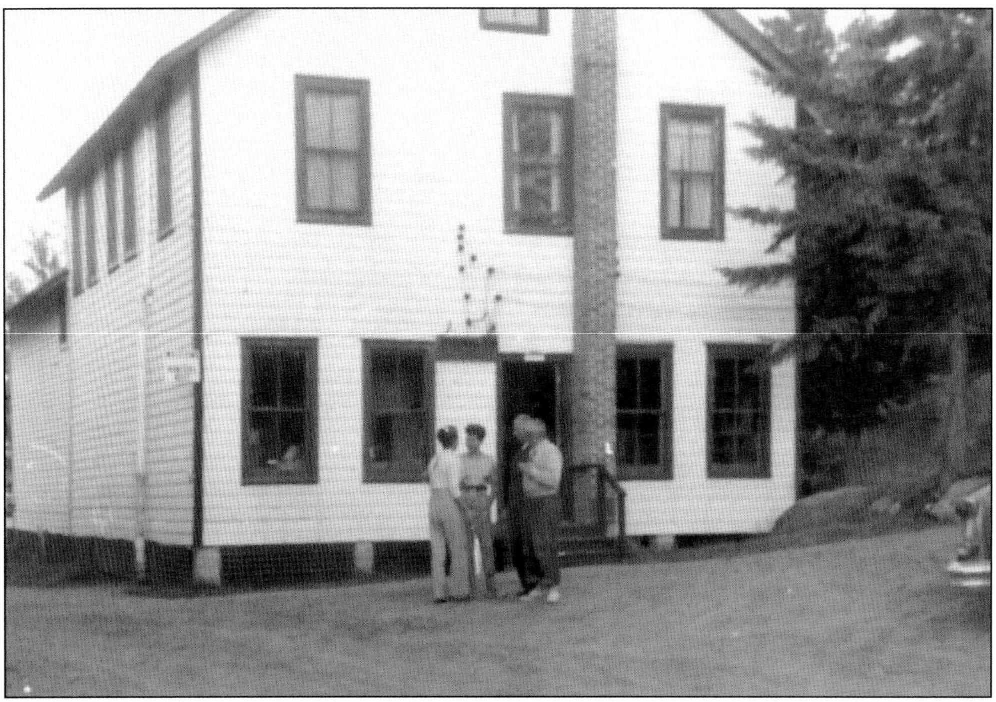

Down the hill stood a small casino with a post office. Guests could walk in the front of the building and enjoy a game of cards or Ping-Pong, or they could try their luck at the slot machine. Near the rear door of the building were mail slots designated for individual rooms and cabins.

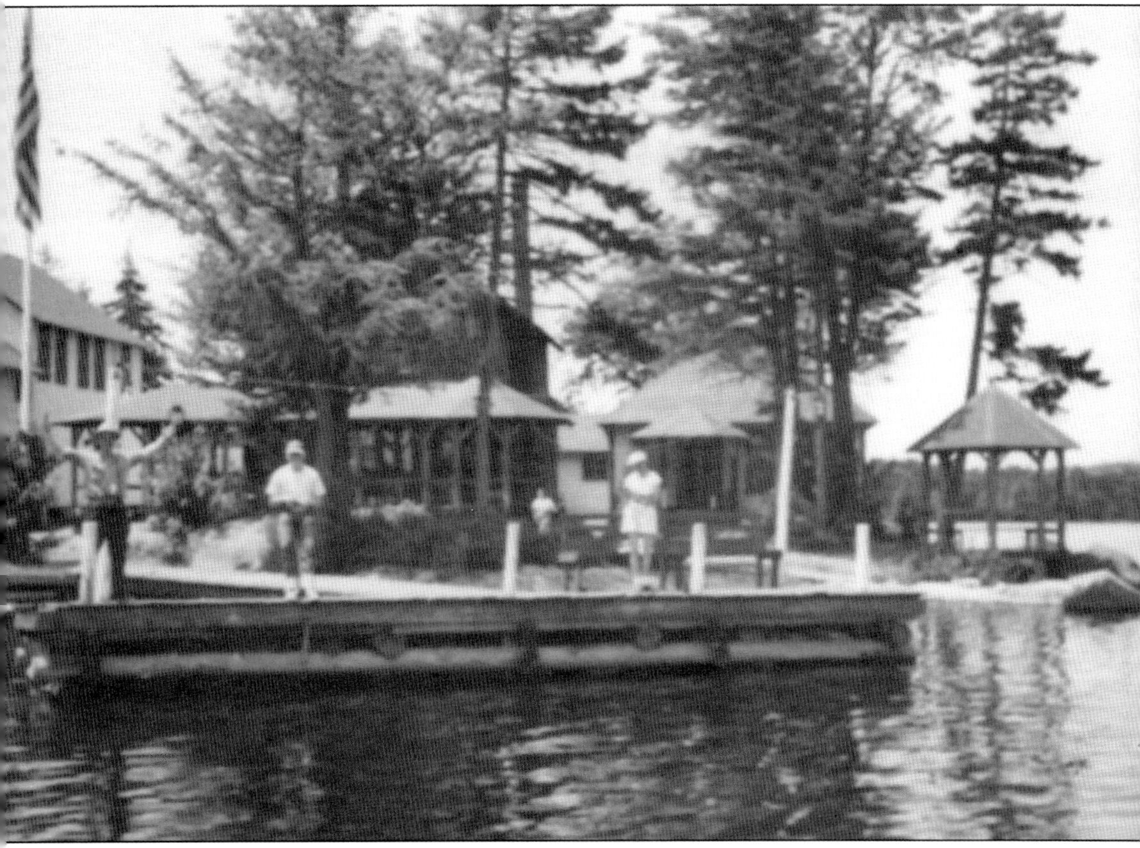

Next door to the post office was the main building, which housed the kitchen and a front lobby that was connected to the dining room. Upstairs were individual guest rooms. The dining room was built on pilings over the water, so when guests ate dinner, they felt as if they were floating on the lake. Hunters Rest employed a private launch to transport guests around the lake or to create a floating picnic.

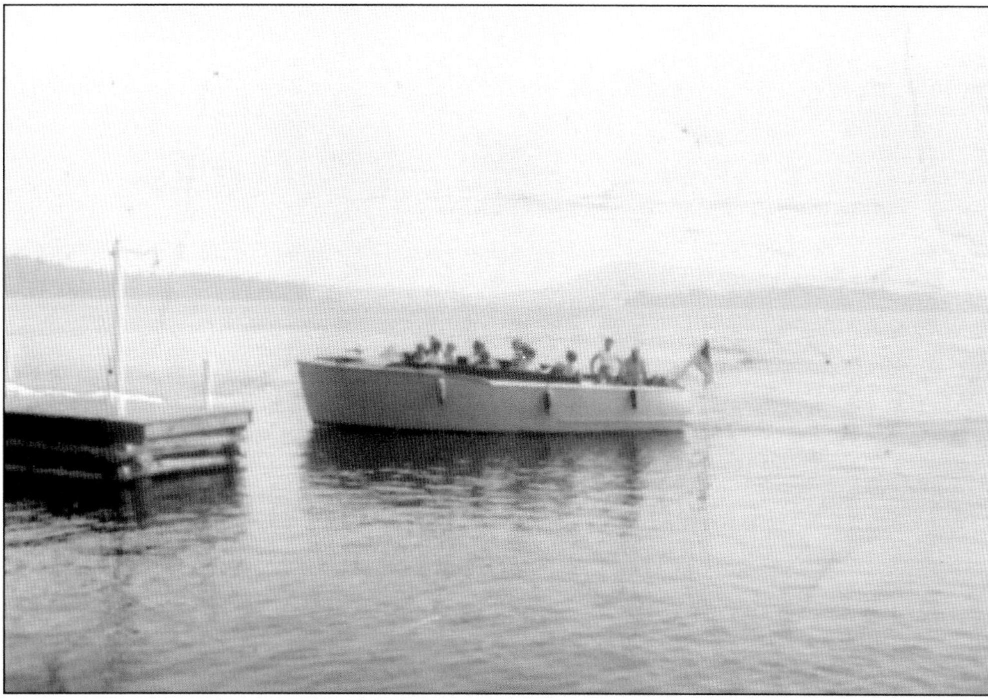

By 1948, George Carlin retired and full ownership fell to Marion and Jim Bird, who ran Hunters Rest until 1962. The Birds continued to offer top-rated service, but some things never changed. Here the mail boat *Carol* pulls into the Hunters Rest dock to drop off and pick up the mail.

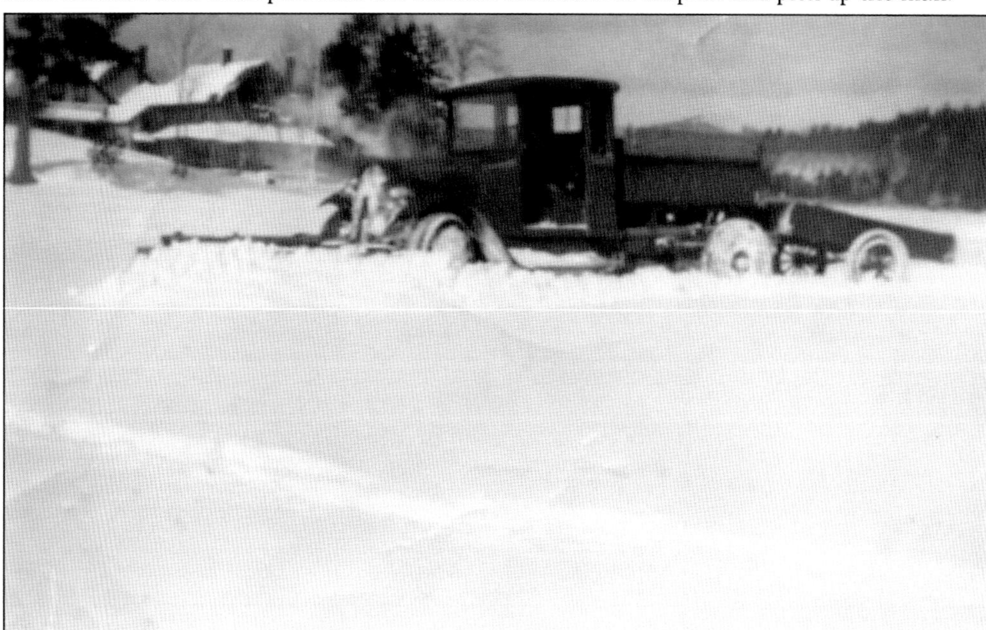

Although many of Raquette's tourist spots closed in winter, there was still activity to maintain the summer season. Icehouses had to be stocked for later refrigeration in the kitchens. Here an old truck is viewed in front of Hunters Rest, ready to plow an area for ice cutting to load up the icehouse for summer.

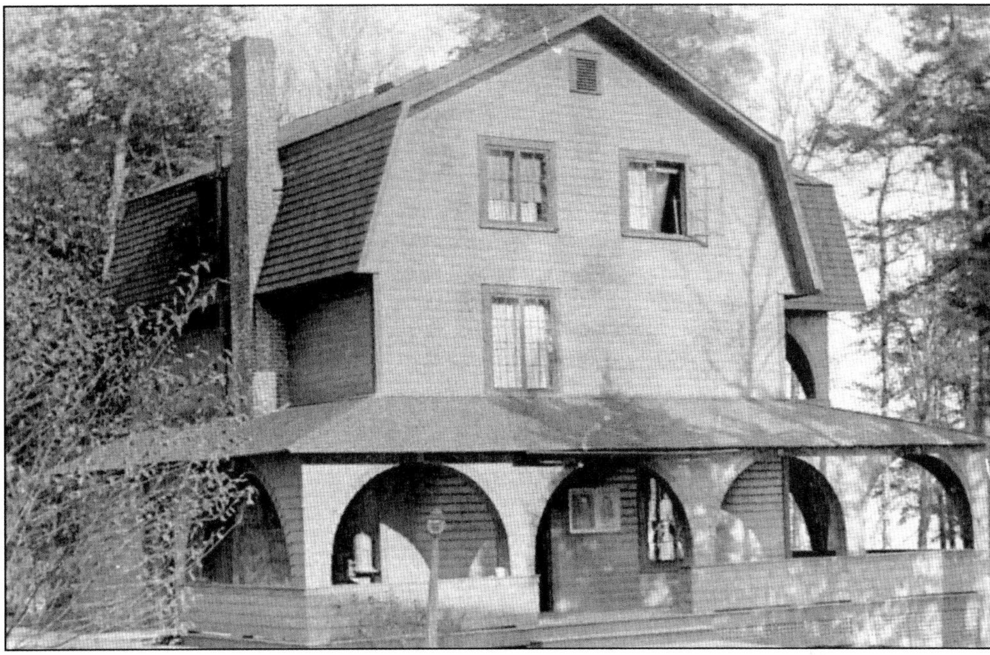

Situated on Indian Point, across from Hunters Rest, is Joe Bryere's Brightside Camp. Bryere and his wife, Mary, built the first Brightside House in 1891. They expanded the main building to include an 11-room addition. The buildings were connected by covered walkways as a convenience to the guests. This picture shows the surviving building, saved from a 1905 fire.

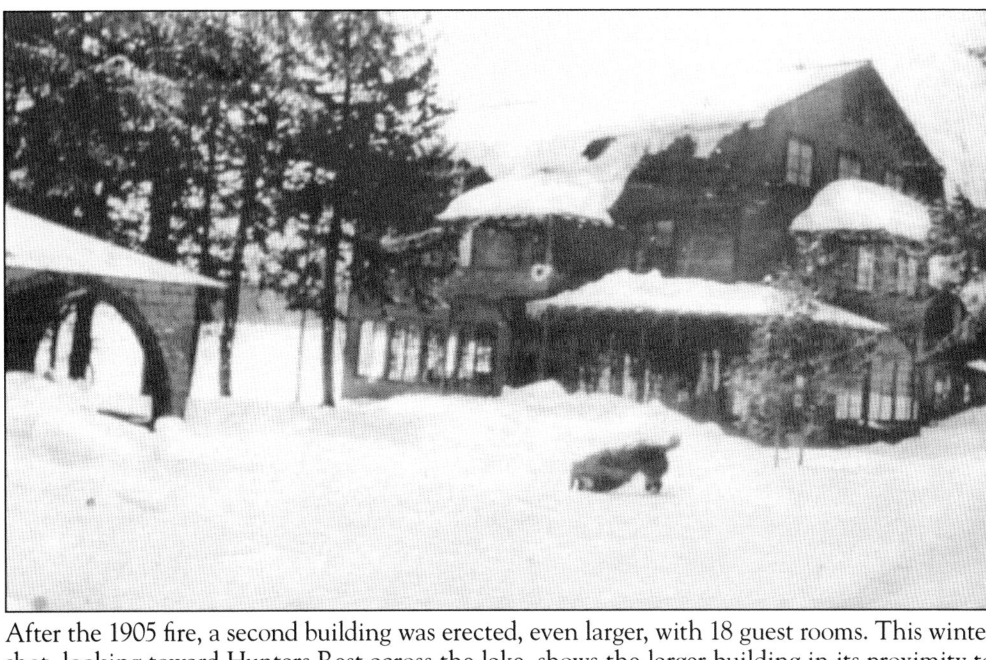

After the 1905 fire, a second building was erected, even larger, with 18 guest rooms. This winter shot, looking toward Hunters Rest across the lake, shows the larger building in its proximity to the other building. Both of these structures survive to this day.

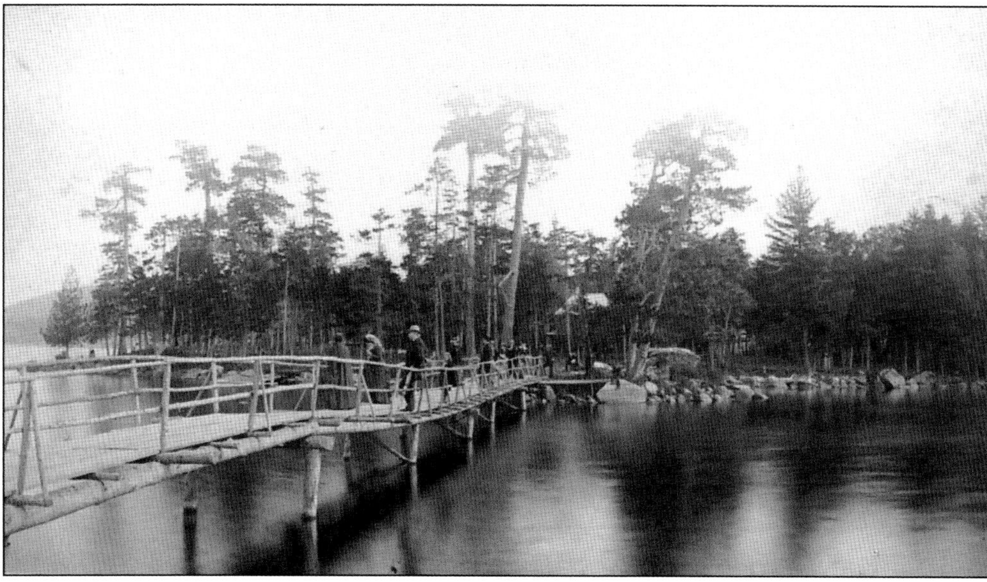

Eastward from Indian Point is Tioga Point. Ike Kenwell built one of the first Raquette Lake Houses here in 1877. Because of the rocky shores and shallows, it was necessary to build a dock out into the water for the traveling steamships. Here customers wait on the dock prepared for the steamer to arrive.

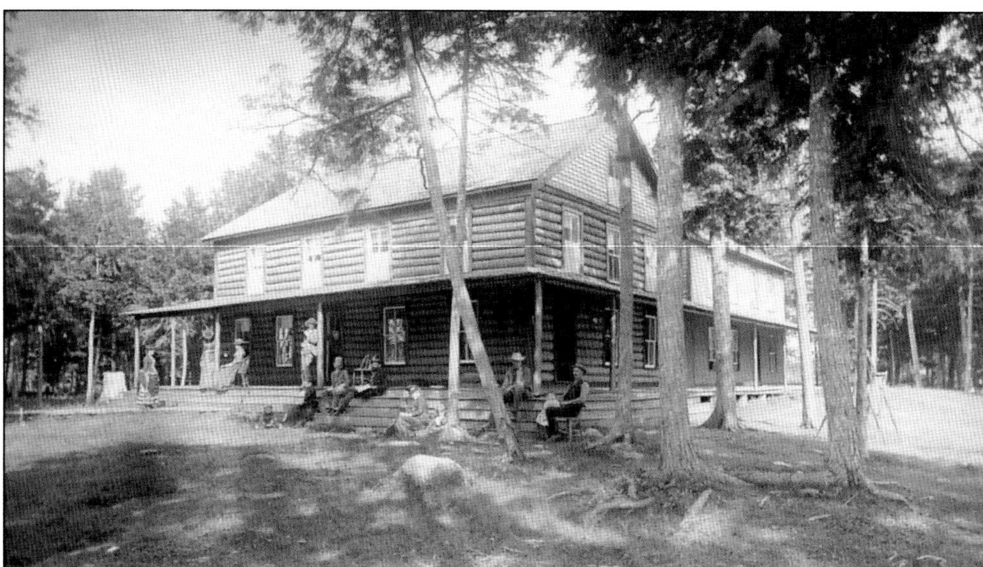

Walking into the clearing on Tioga Point, guests were greeted by a log structure, surrounded by vast porches. A fenced garden up in the woods supplied the table with fresh vegetables and fruit, and Ike Kenwell's hunting skills provided meat for the menu. The establishment burned in 1877.

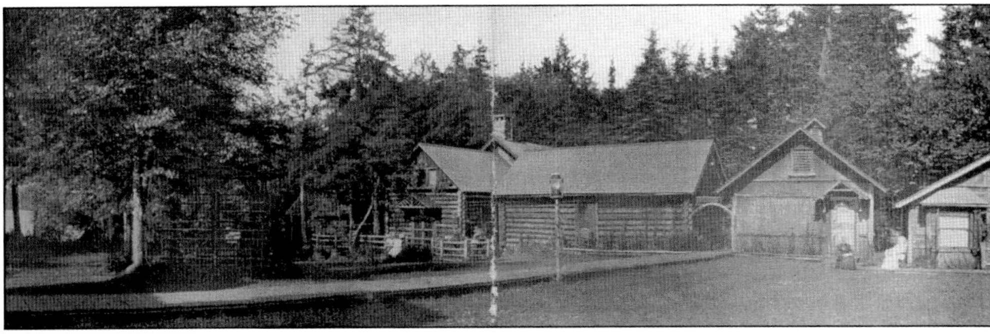

Ike Kenwell never rebuilt the Raquette Lake House on Tioga Point. He sold the property to William Strange, who in turn sold it to Frank Platt. Platt started to build a great camp with all the services for himself and for guests. Shown on the site of the former Raquette Lake House are, from left to right, a kitchen, a dining room, and two guest cottages.

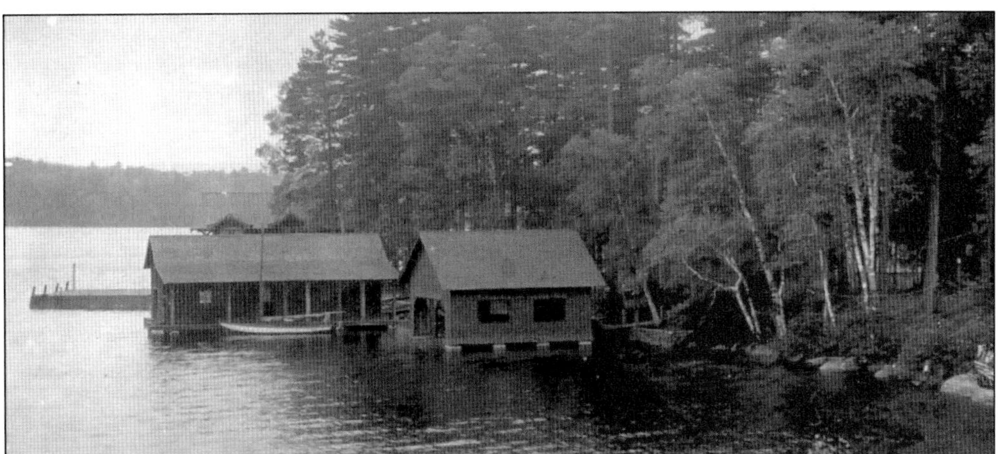

Samuel Evans, a physician, was the next owner of Tioga Point. Evans expanded on the great camp theme. Visible from the central portion of the lake were three boathouses. Both Evans and his two sons were interested in speed, and at one time there were as many as six speedboats at Tioga.

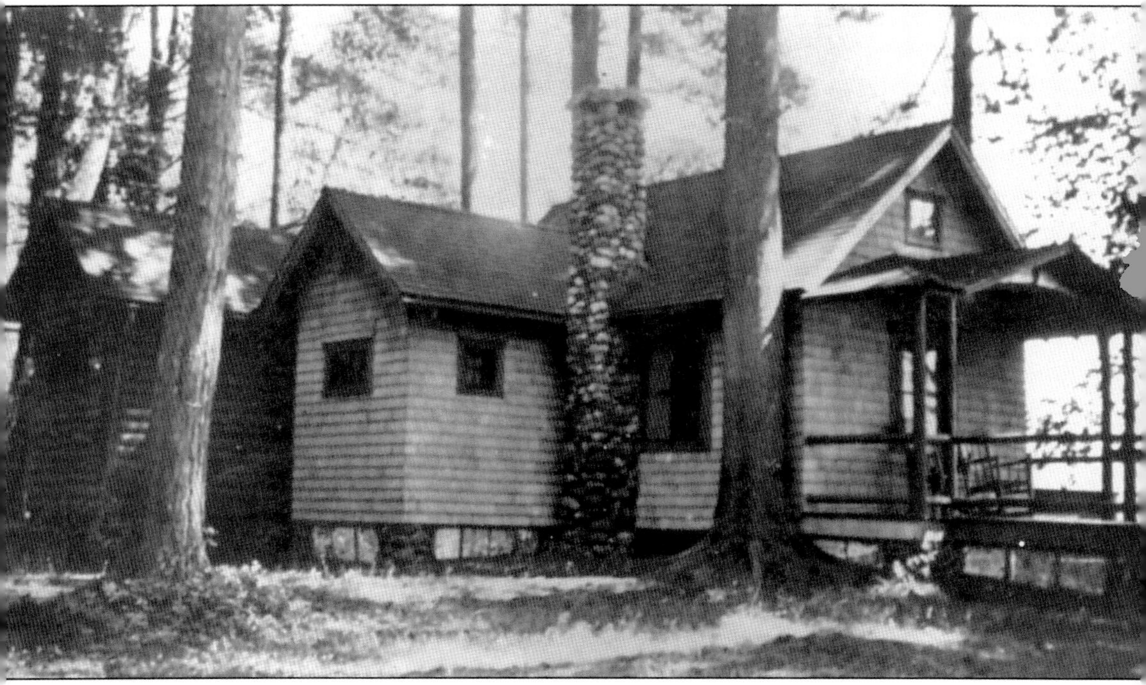

Near the boathouses was a structure that was called the Doctor's House, so named because a physician was always on the premises. This home of Samuel Evans doubled as an infirmary. Along the shore behind the boathouses was the caretaker's house (not shown). It had bedrooms upstairs that provided lodging for other staff, and next door to it was a cabin for the guides, who shared the local secrets of hunting and fishing with Evans's guests.

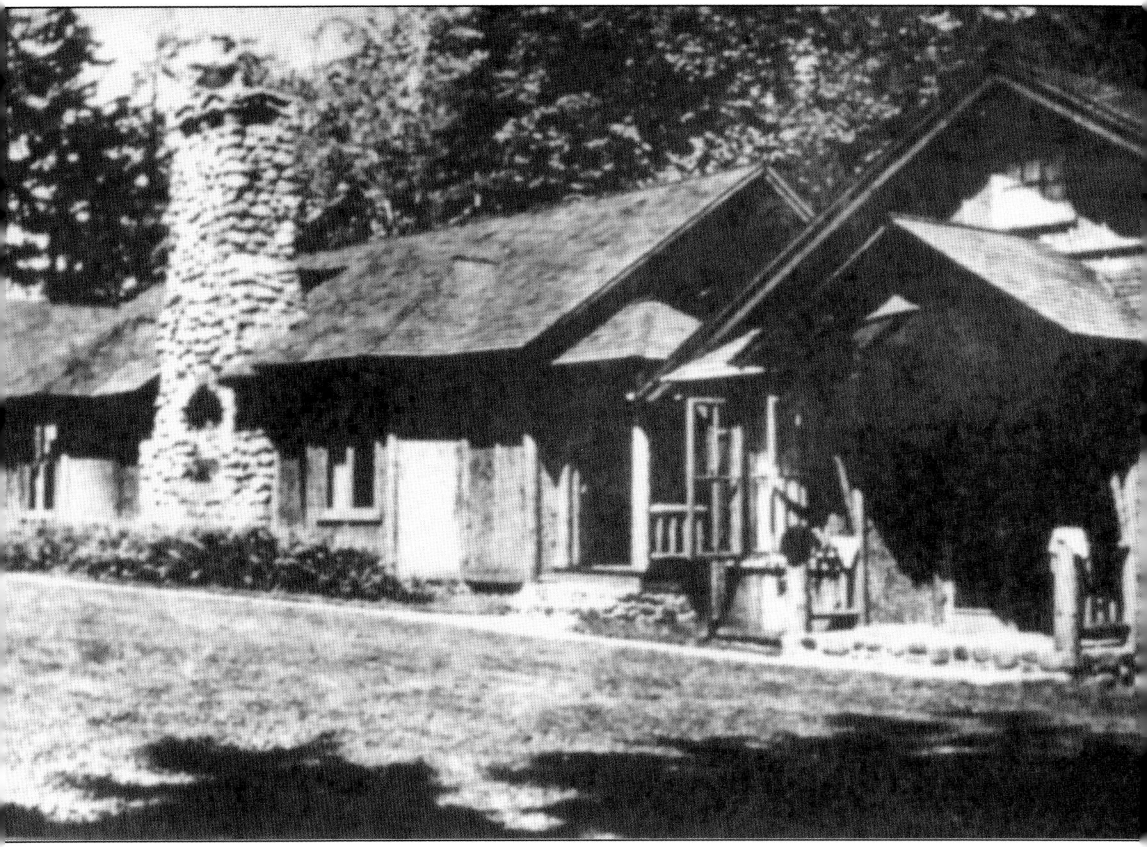

In the center of the complex, using some of Frank Platt's structures, stood the main house and guest rooms. These buildings were connected by covered walkways in the great camp style. Farther out on the point was the dining hall (not shown). It too was connected by covered walkways. It was purposely located far enough away from the main house so as not to bother guests with the noise and fuss of meal preparation.

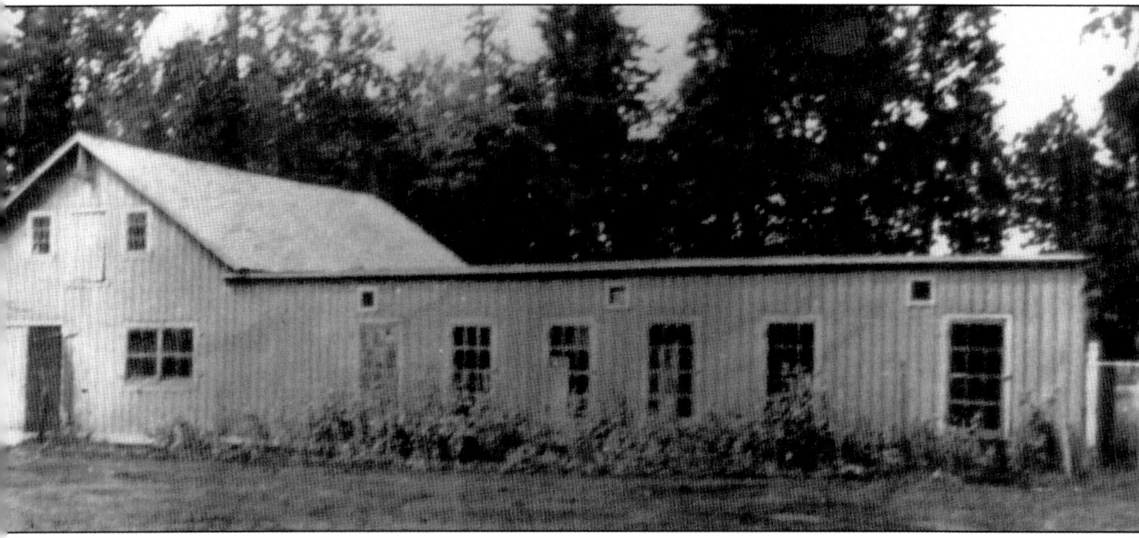

In great camp style, Samuel Evans cultivated gardens and a greenhouse in the proximity of the area set up by Ike Kenwell. Evans also added a small barn, in which he kept fowl and swine for fresh table meat. In addition, Evans's staff ran a complete laundry—not only were the guests pampered but so were their clothes. In later years, Tioga Point was used as a state conservation camp, until it was dismantled completely and turned into a state camping site. All that remains are foundations and the chimneys of the main building.

Two

The North End and Raquette Shores

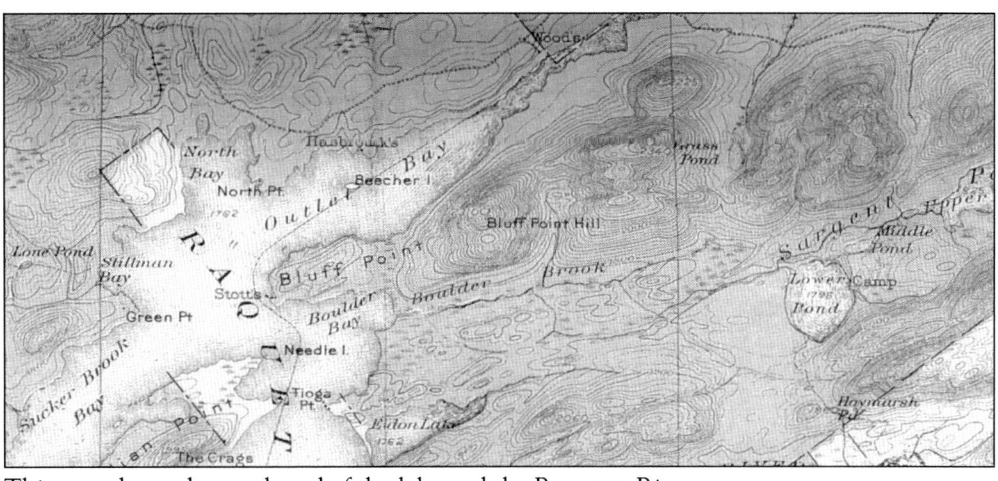

This map shows the north end of the lake and the Raquette River.

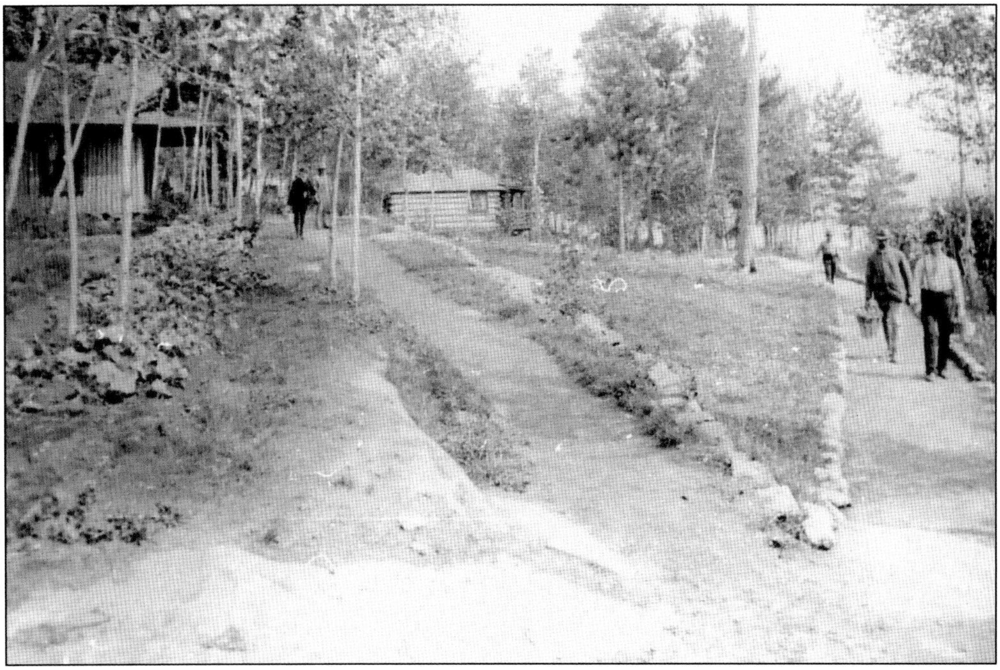

Bluff Point is reached by going through the Needle Island narrows or taking the steamship route through Boulder Bay. Frank Stott, a textile merchant, built a complex of homes on Bluff Point. From the docks, a selection of paths led to small guest camps, a kitchen building, and a main house.

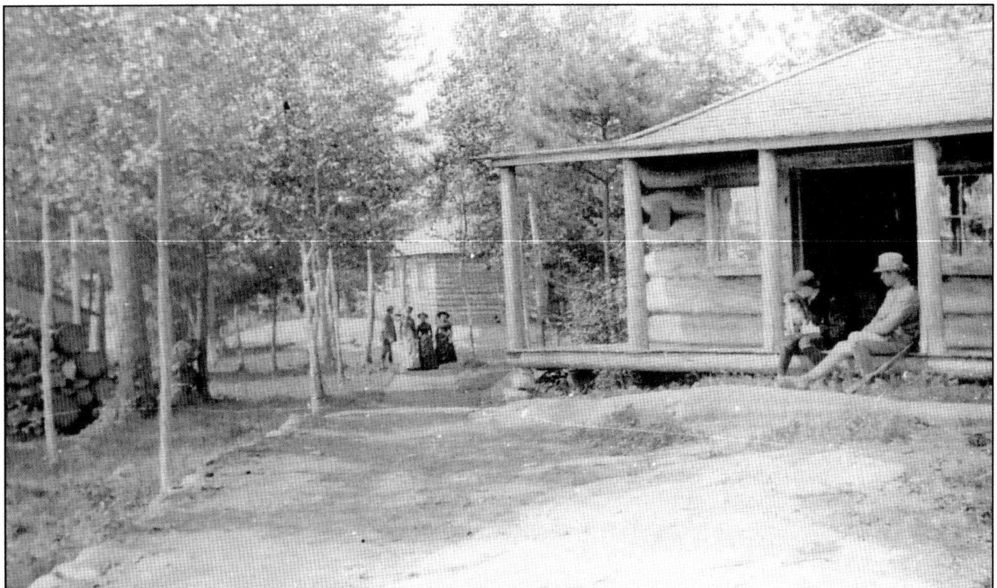

Stott servants tended these guesthouses, making the visitor's stay as enjoyable as being part of the Stott family. Notice that even in the middle of the Adirondacks, the women coming up the walk are in their Sunday best.

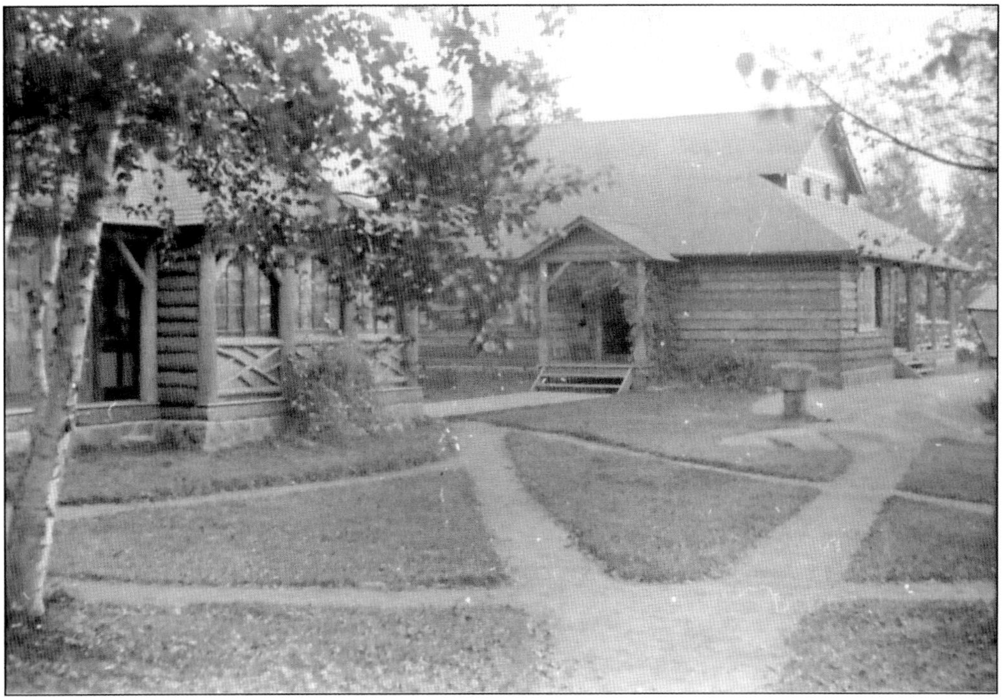

Stott's main house was closest to the kitchen building. The manicured paths ensured that guests got to the correct buildings without error. Notice the upper story of the main house. Even on the darkest days, natural light could come in the upper windows to illuminate the parlor.

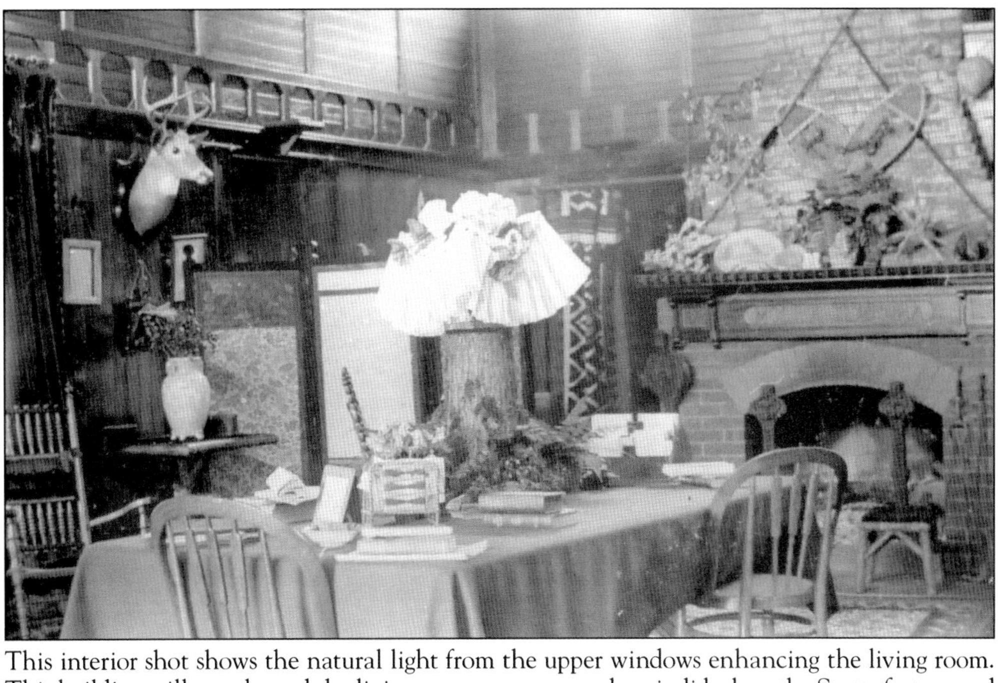

This interior shot shows the natural light from the upper windows enhancing the living room. This building still stands, and the living room appears much as it did when the Stotts first owned Bluff Point.

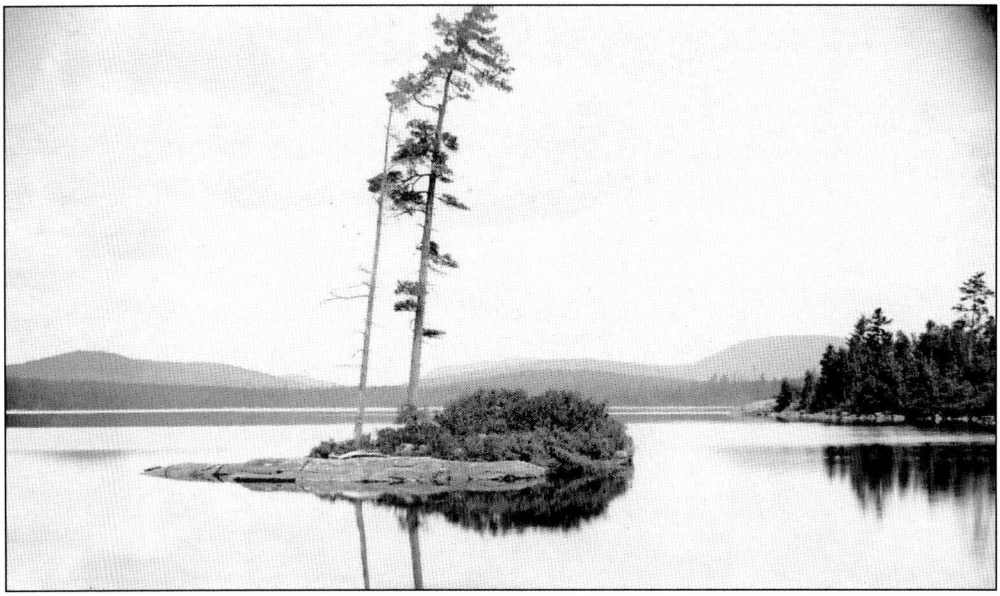

In this view, facing northwest, a small cove is visible from the Stott main house. A single rock island guards the entrance to the cove. At the base of this cove is a game room.

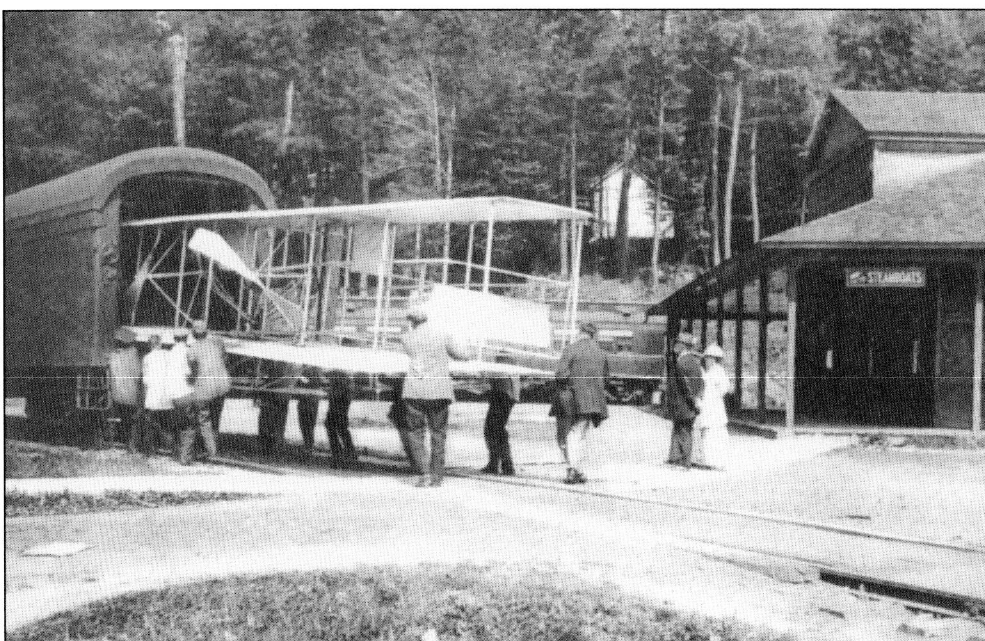

One of the few changes Robert Collier, the publisher of *Collier's* magazine, made at Bluff Point was to erect an airplane hangar on the site of the game room. Because of his friendship with Alexander Graham Bell, Collier was interested in aircraft, as well as being a fan of technology and speed with a collection of powerboats. This picture shows a Wright brothers' aircraft being unloaded from a train for Collier in Raquette Lake village. When Collier passed away, the hangar once again became a game room.

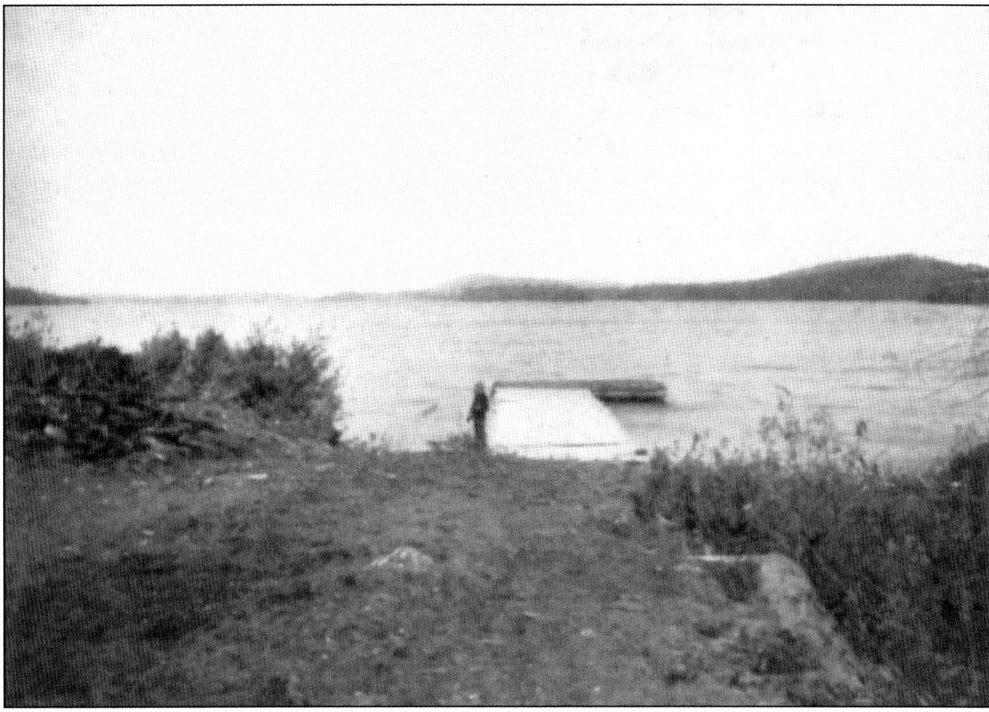

West from Bluff Point lies the end of Sucker Brook Bay. When rail travel was at its peak, it was thought that a spur line could be brought out here. After careful thought, the plan was dropped, although a road, dock, and breakwater had already been constructed.

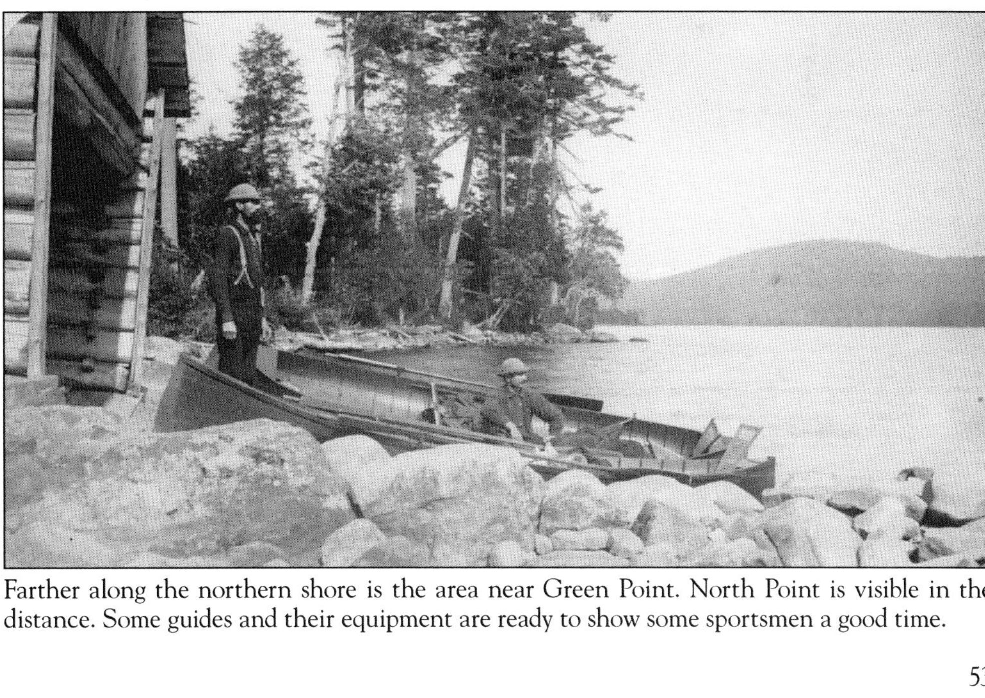

Farther along the northern shore is the area near Green Point. North Point is visible in the distance. Some guides and their equipment are ready to show some sportsmen a good time.

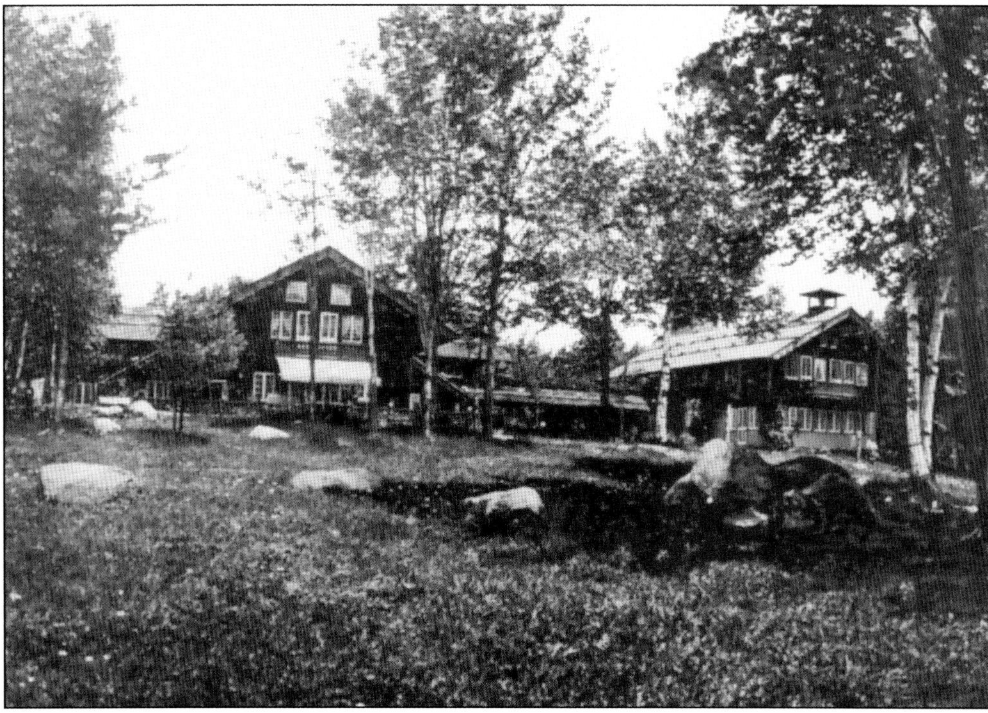

At North Point stood the summer home of industrialist Andrew Carnegie's sister-in-law. Lucy Carnegie bought this cottage complex from James Ten Eyck around 1902. She took on the job of remodeling the buildings and turned the main house into a chalet-like structure with living quarters on one side connected by a breezeway to the kitchen and dining room.

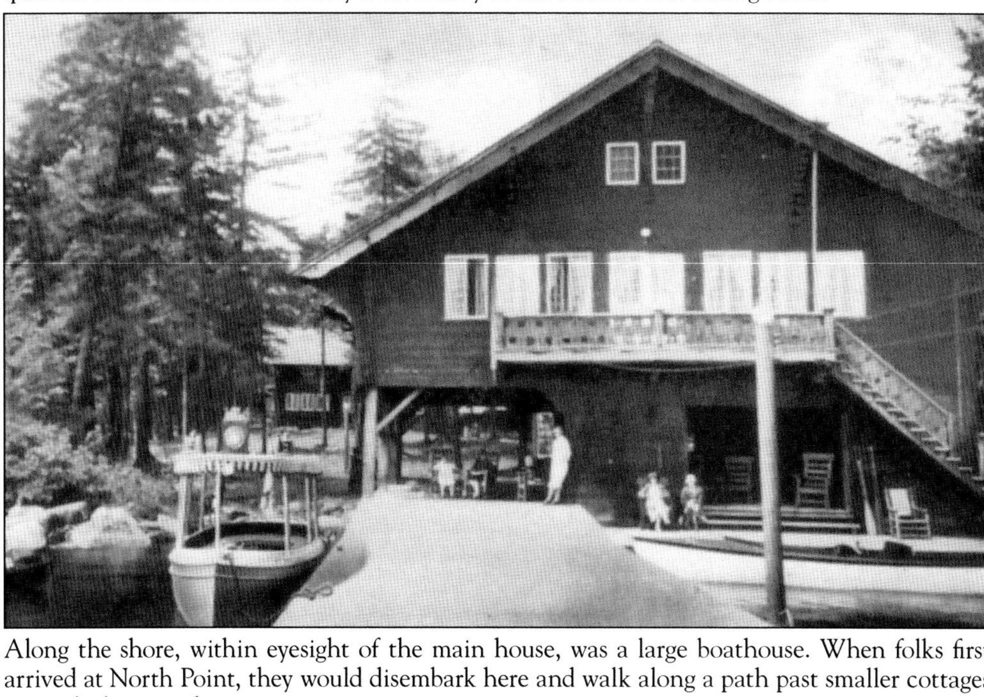

Along the shore, within eyesight of the main house, was a large boathouse. When folks first arrived at North Point, they would disembark here and walk along a path past smaller cottages to reach the main house.

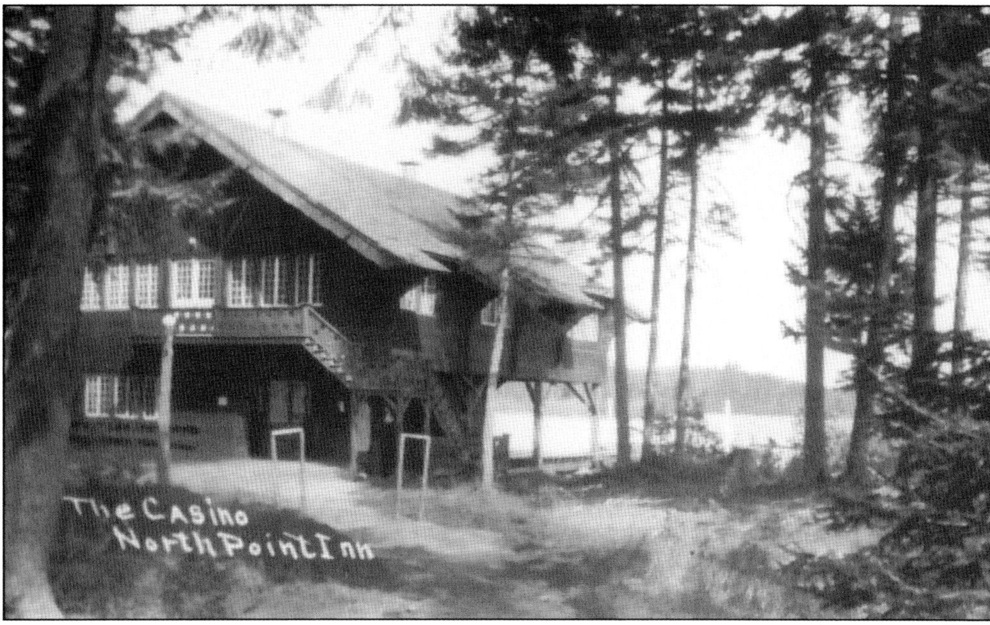

The boathouse was eastward along the shoreline from the main house. The upstairs was used as a small casino.

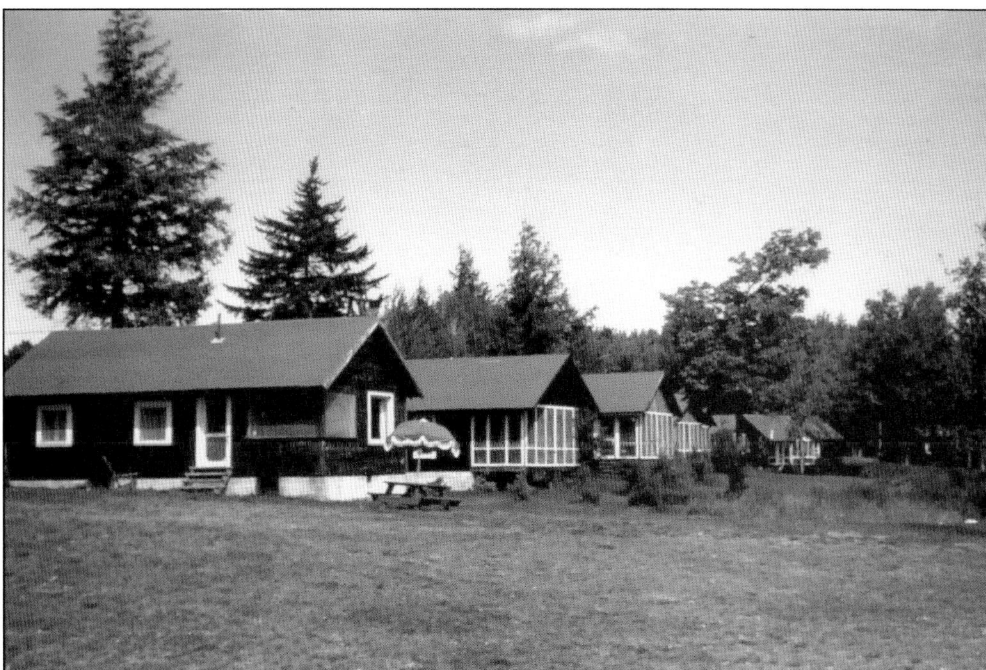

In later years, many of the cottages were set in a row onshore near the boathouse. The boathouse itself was cut up and became the basis for two other homes and some cabins that were sold individually. Lucy Carnegie built some homes farther up the shoreline. Some of these buildings became the basis for Camp Greylock girls' camp in later years.

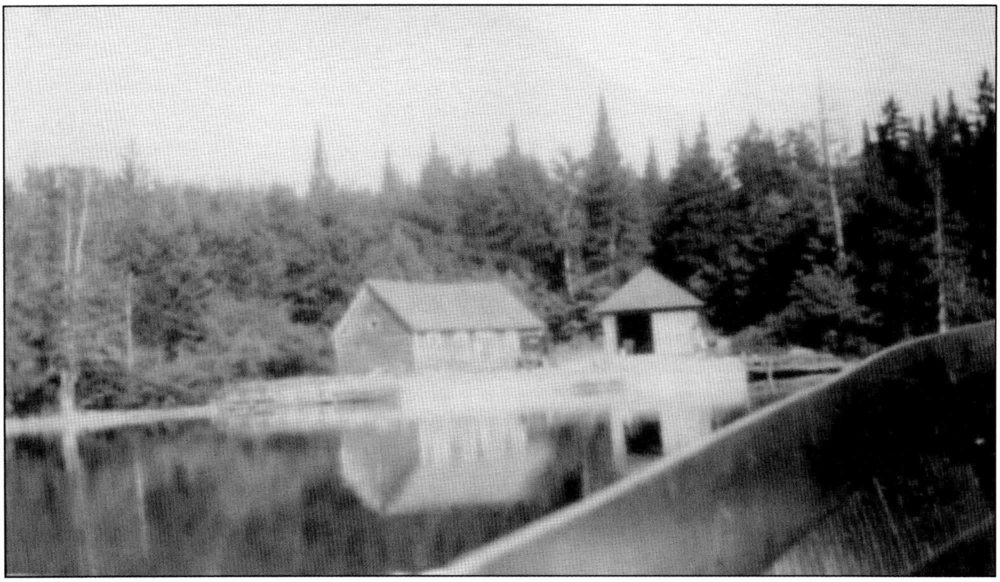

In the late 1800s until about the time Route 28 was constructed, access was also available to Raquette Lake from Long Lake on the Deerland Road. At that time, the Raquette Lake Supply Company had a small outpost at the Forked Lake carry. Visitors could come to this spot and again avail themselves of a boat ride or ship their goods by barge or have a teamster do the shipping. Transportation was first class. Pictured is the freshly painted *Killoquah* ready to disembark from the Forked Lake carry dock.

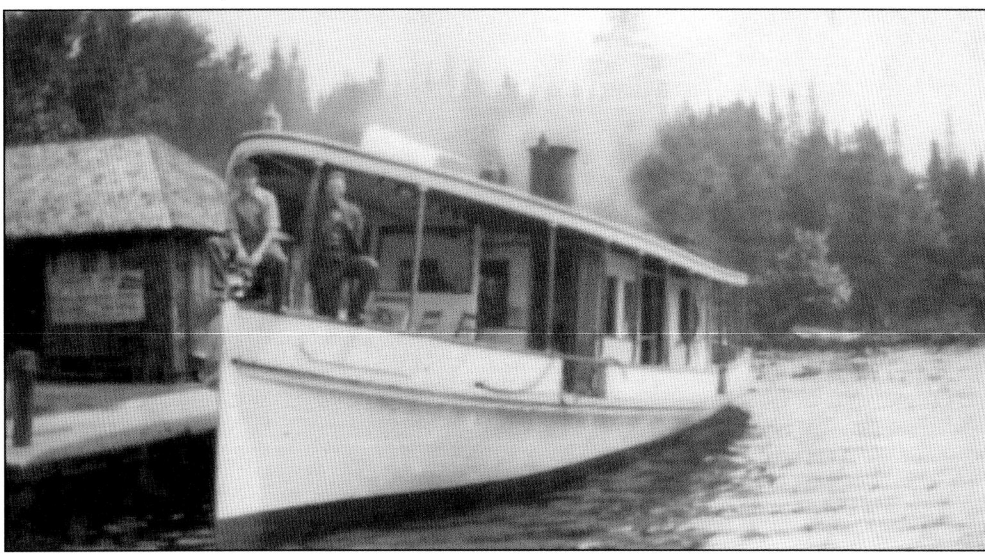

If needed, teamsters or hired truck drivers were on duty here to help with moving or shipping belongings. Next to the carry store, some trucks await their next job.

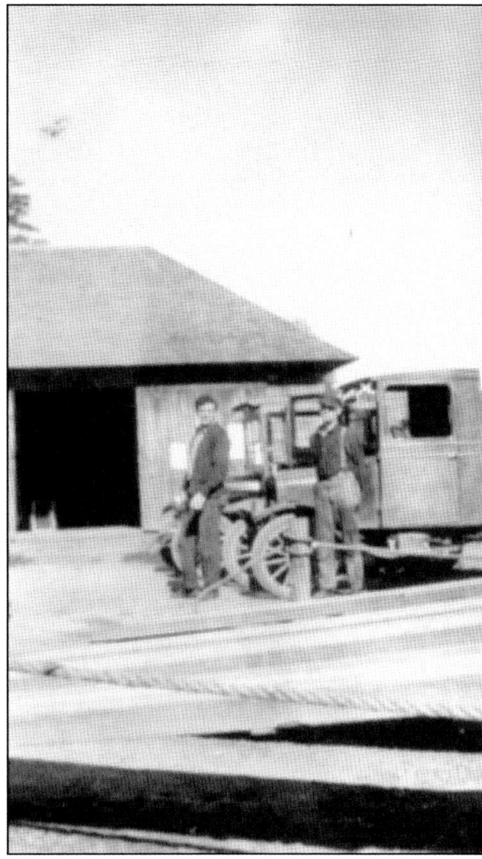

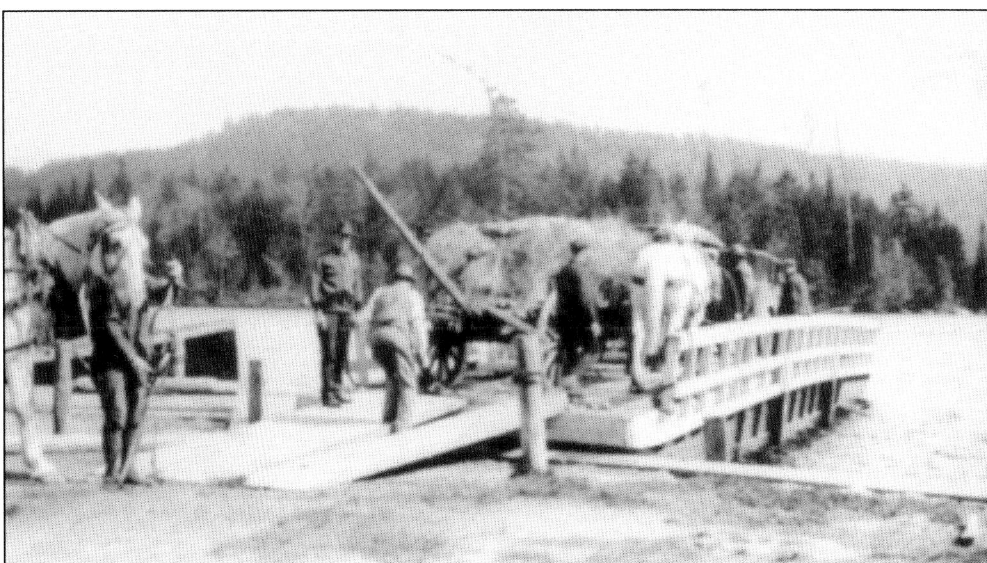

Since the mechanized era was still in its infancy, it was not unusual to still see the use of teams of horses and wagons. This picture shows a cargo barge being loaded with wagons, horses, and hay destined for somewhere around Raquette.

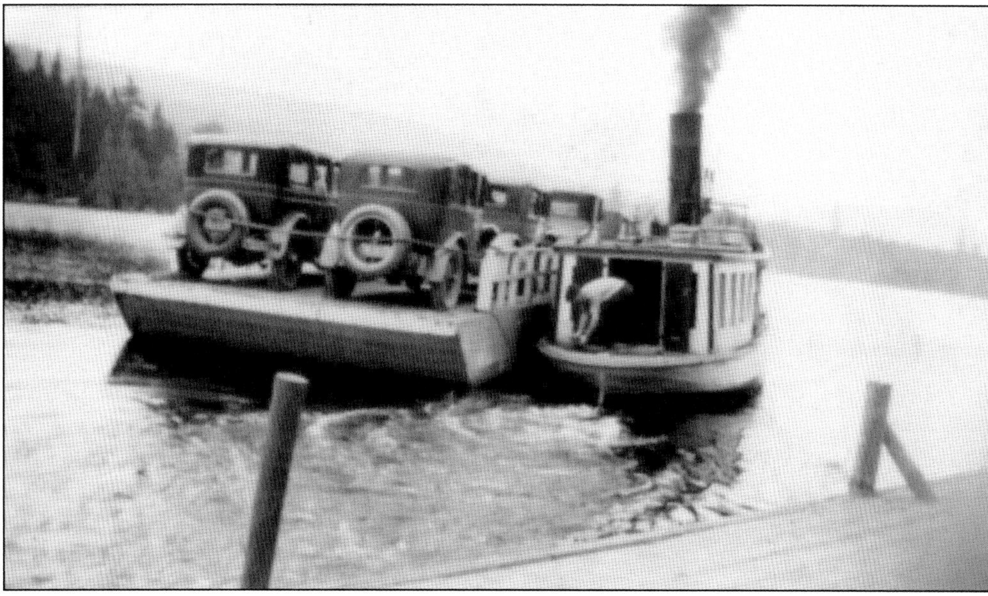

Once a cargo barge was fully loaded, a steamer would attach itself alongside to aid the barge in its movement. This barge holds about eight cars loaded for the trip down the Raquette River to the lake.

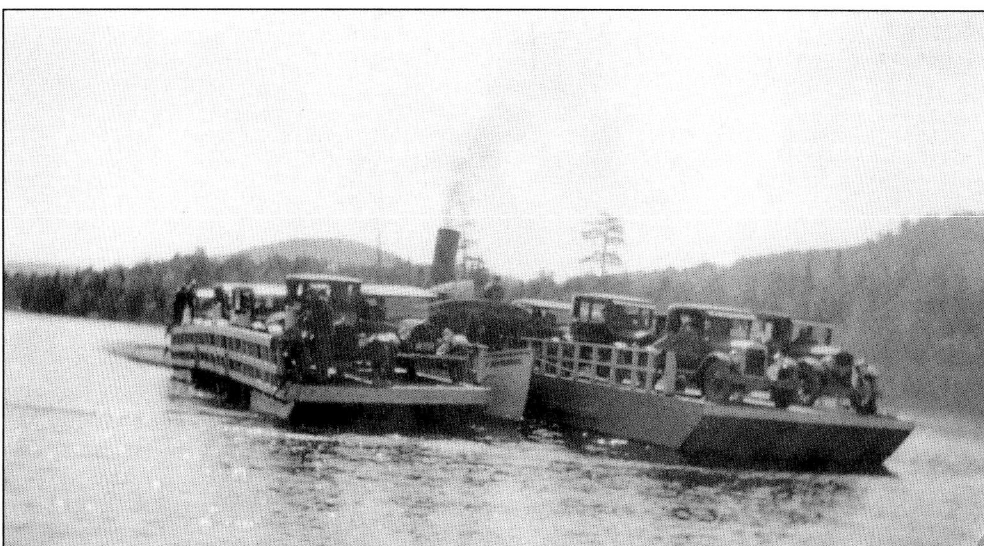

After the barge and transport steamer were free of the river area, it was full steam ahead to the next destination. This barge and cars are in front of Bluff Point and are probably on their way to Raquette Lake village. Beecher Island can be seen in the left corner of the picture.

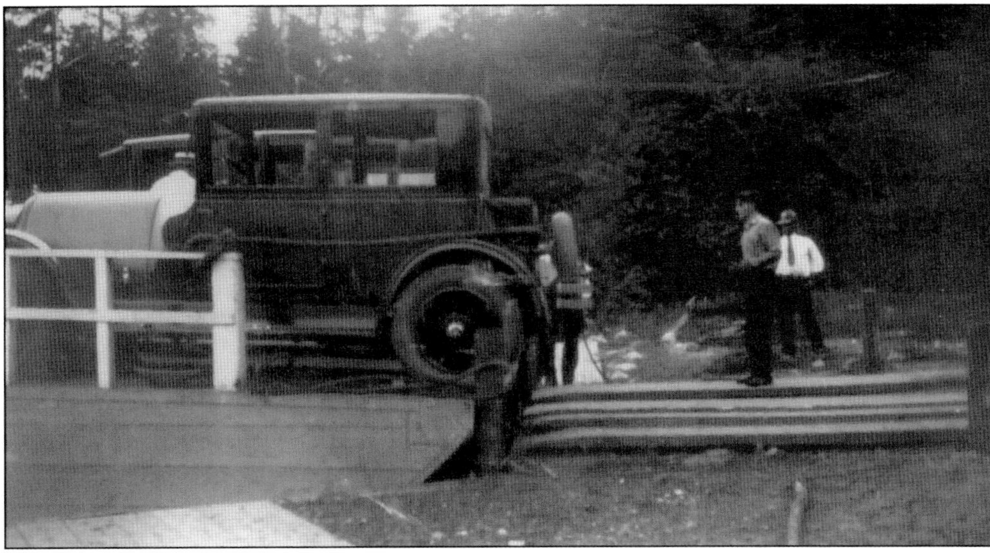

Sometimes traffic came from the direction of the village. Summer people would ship their cars across the lake to use at their homes. Here at the Forked Lake carry, the barge is ready to be unloaded.

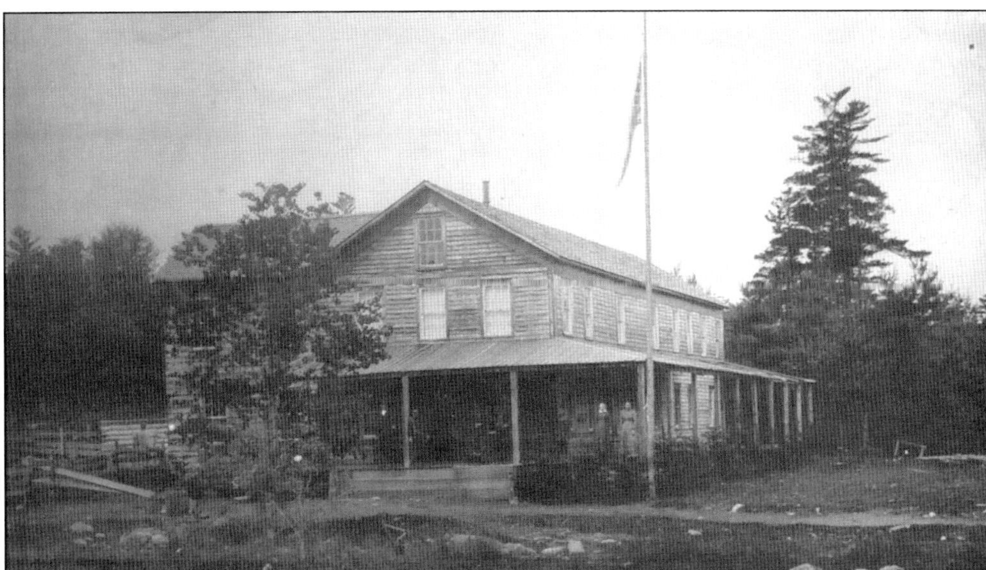

One of the first Raquette Lake Houses was built near the site of the Forked Lake carry. It was disassembled and moved to construct the Forked Lake Hotel. Shown is the hotel around 1889.

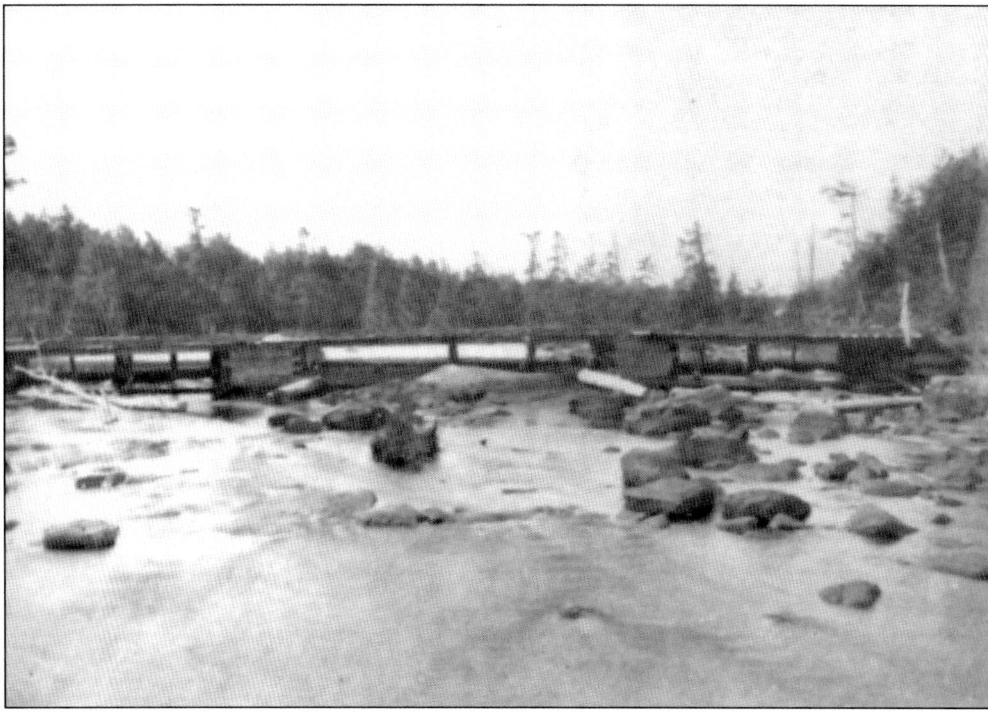

Well beyond the carry toward Forked Lake lies the Deerland Bridge. This bridge connected North Point with Long Lake. Later a steel girder bridge replaced the crude log bridge.

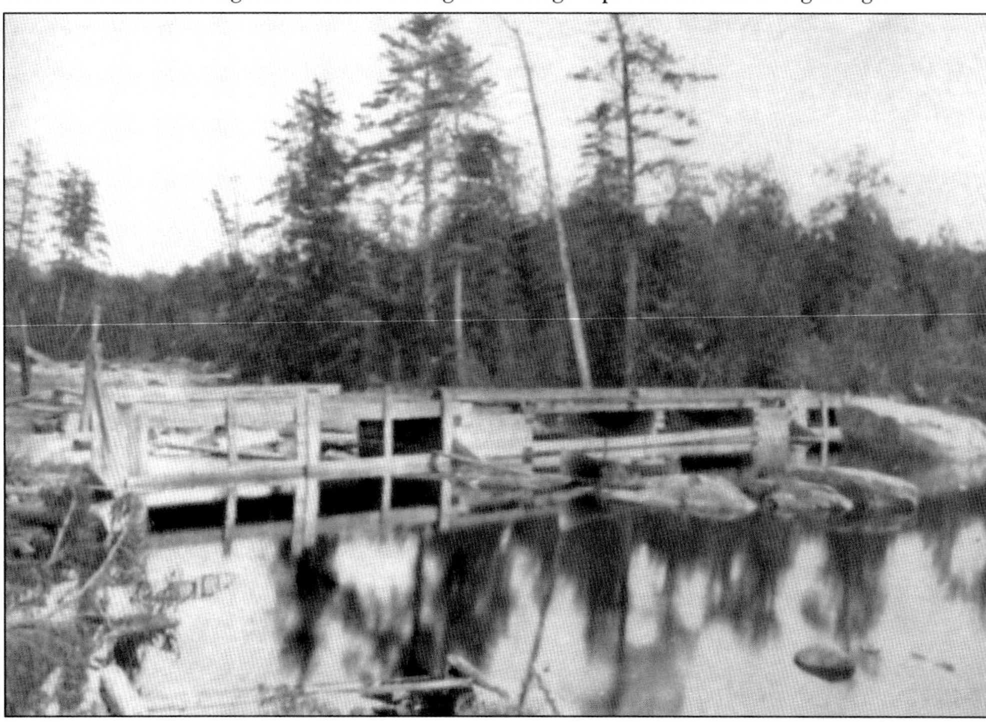

Beyond the bridge was a makeshift dam. Because of steamship transportation, the lake was kept at a safe height to avoid accidents with sandbars or rocks.

Three

The South End and Village Area

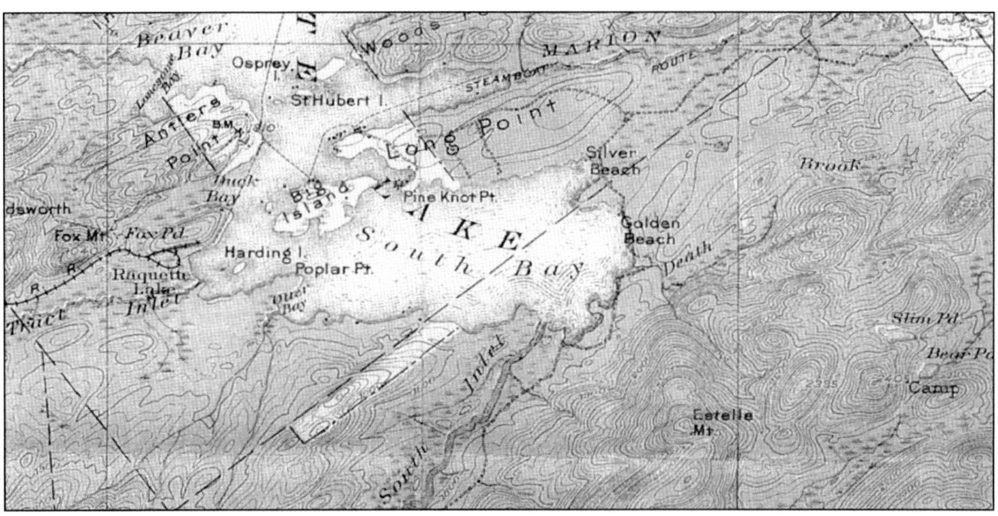

This is a map of the south end of Raquette Lake.

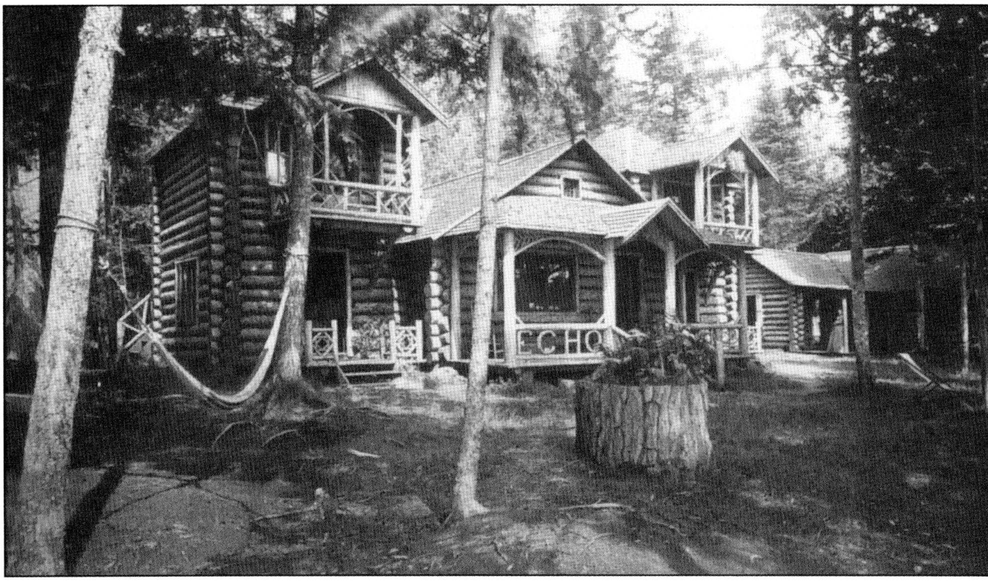

Along the channel from the central to the southern portion of the lake stood the summer home of former Connecticut governor Phineas C. Lounsbury. The great camp was built around 1885 and had numerous buildings and cottages to house family and friends. This view shows the main house. Francis "Skipper" Clough bought the complex in 1946 and ran it as a camp for girls.

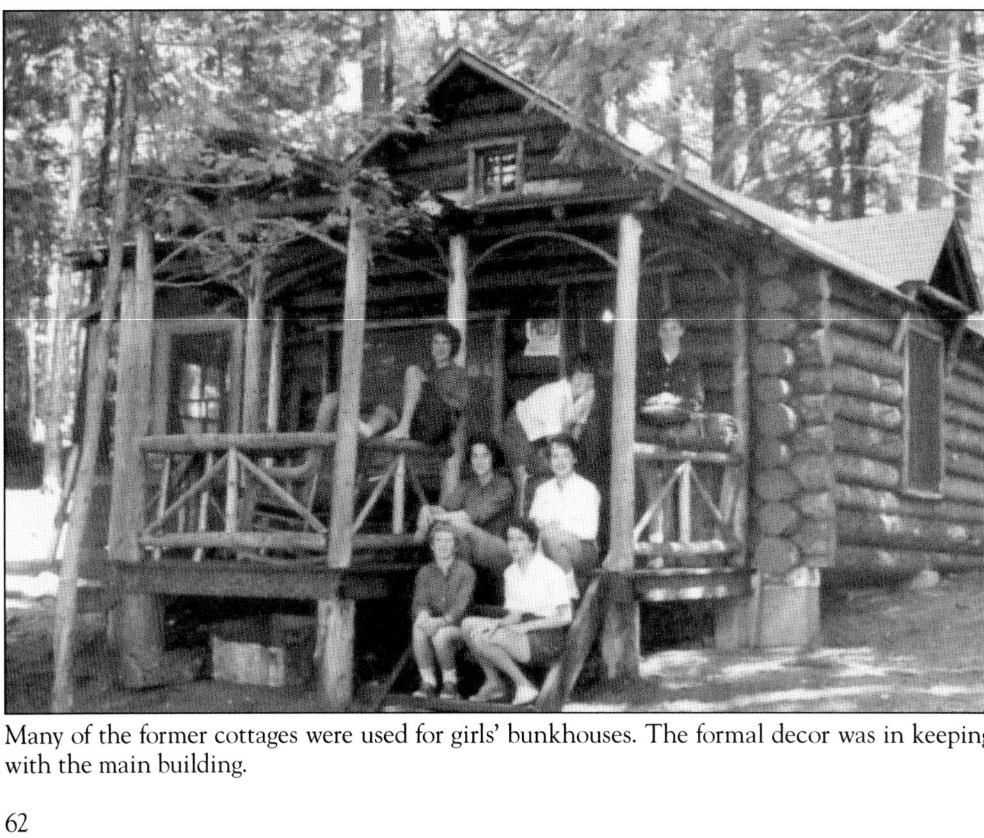

Many of the former cottages were used for girls' bunkhouses. The formal decor was in keeping with the main building.

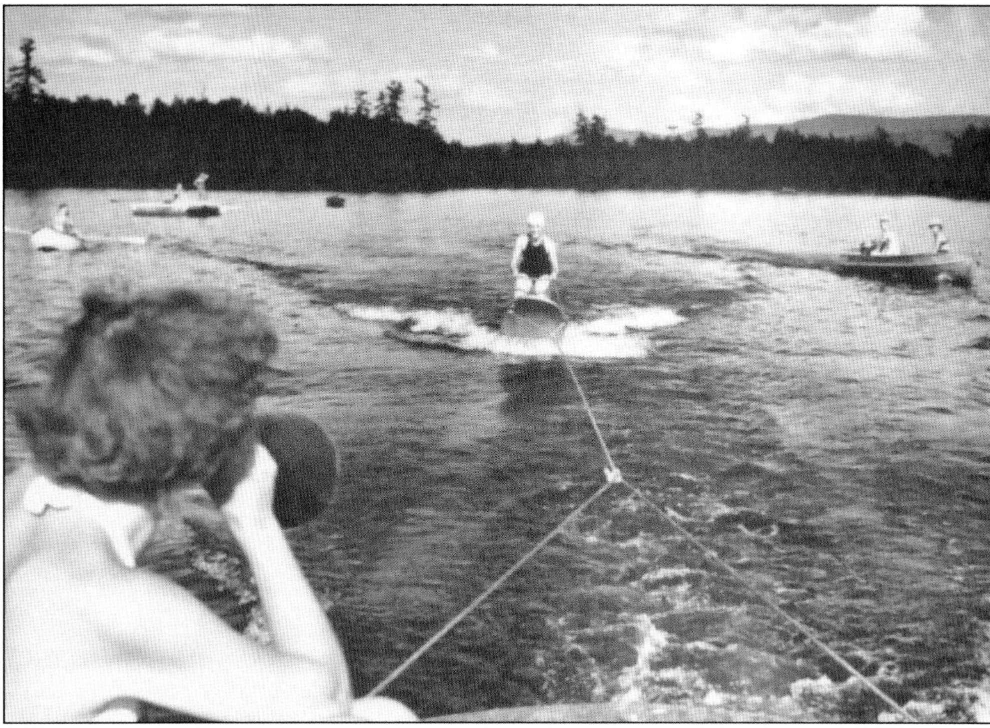

Due to the natural shelter of the channel, the calmness of the water led to a more relaxed nature for water sports. Here a camper is towed behind the camp boat. Note the smoothness of the water.

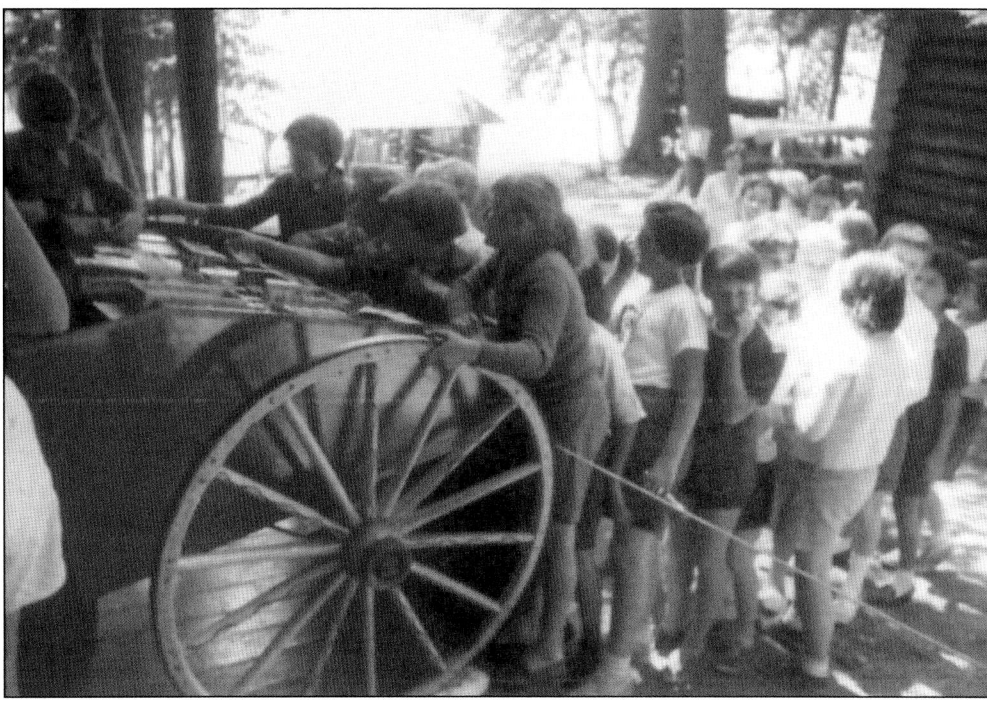

Everybody has a sweet tooth and money burning a hole in their pocket. Pictured are girls at Echo Camp lined up for their turn to choose their favorite candy.

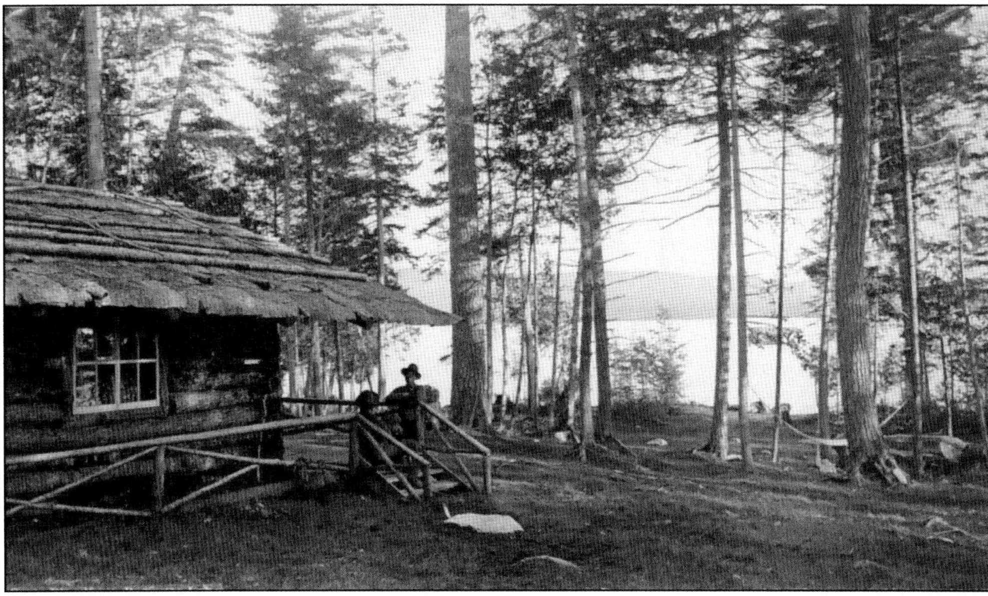

In 1877, William West Durant decided to build some cabins on Long Point. These single-story camps were of plain design. By 1879, however, Durant decided he wanted to build a great complex of buildings for his family and friends. This became Camp Pine Knot.

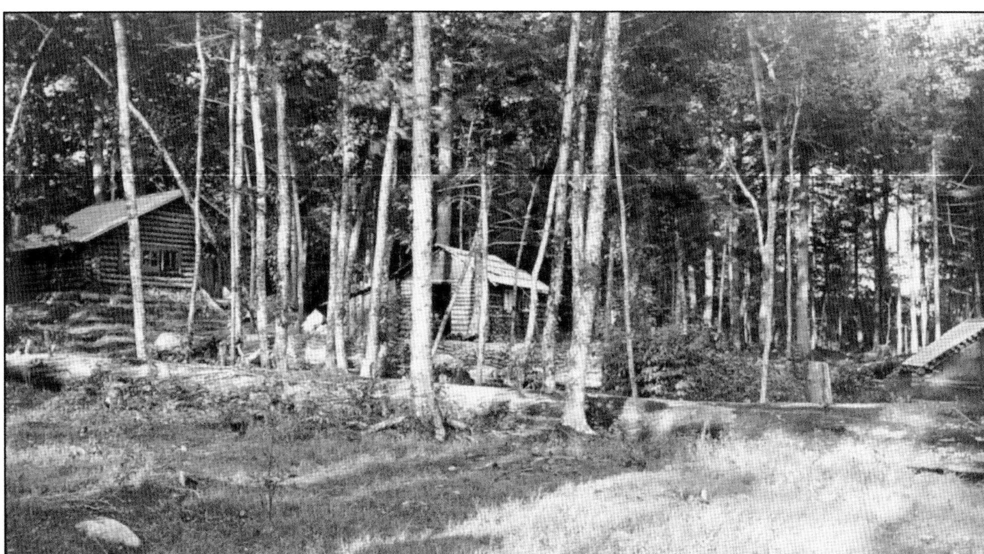

The buildings first erected were for Durant's own use and were hardly considered grand or great camps. The grounds at Camp Pine Knot were neither vast nor well kept.

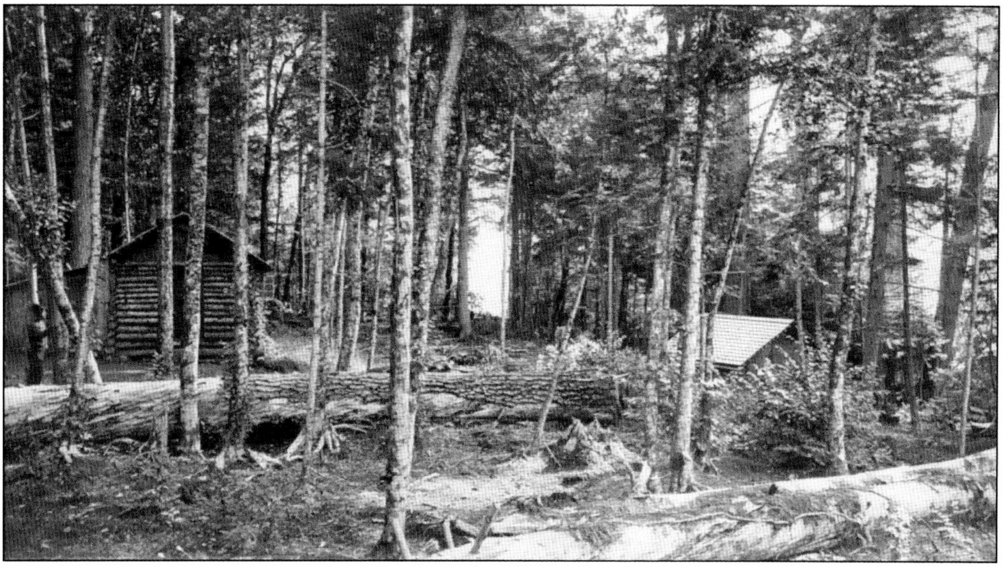

To create comfort for his family, William West Durant decided to tear down many of the plainer buildings, combine some of them to enlarge accommodations, and clean up the grounds.

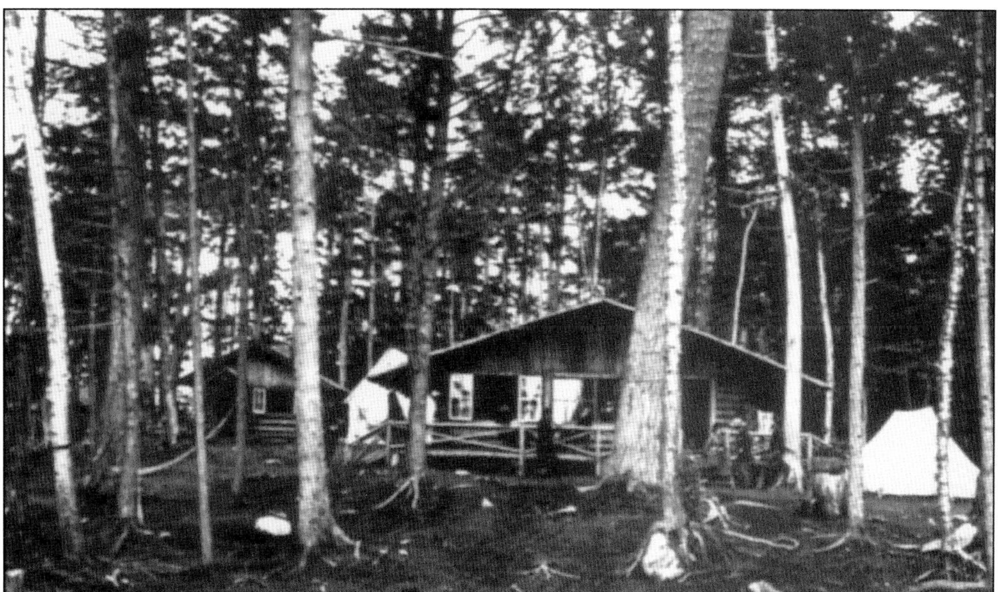

This early picture shows the chalet. The building is a single story, and the grounds are root and rock strewn. Well-kept lawns are not yet evident.

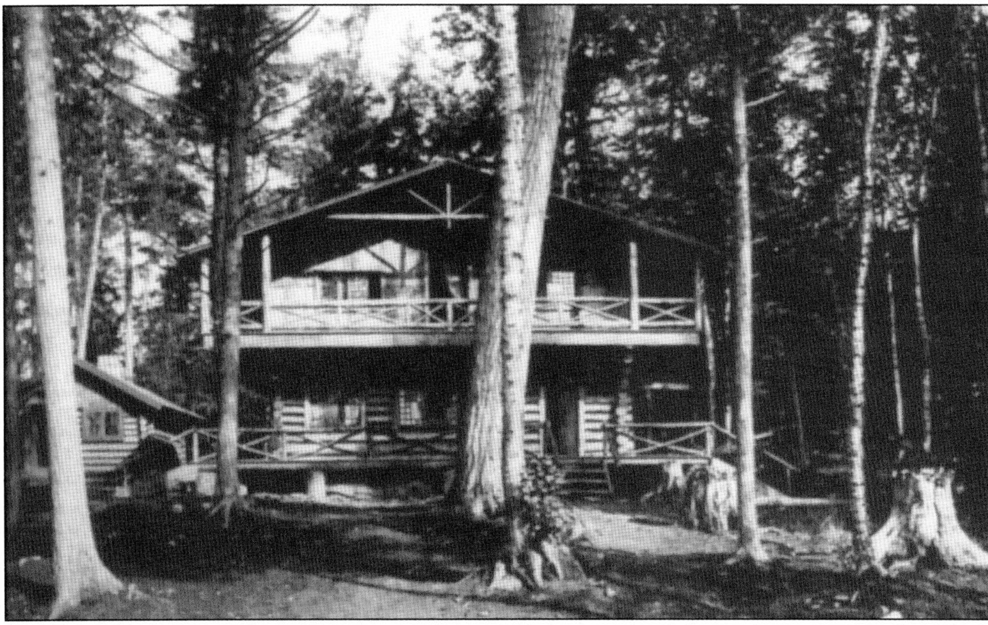

Soon the chalet grew to two stories, and the visibility to the lake and surrounding buildings broadened. Grounds were cleaned up, and paths to other buildings were more accessible.

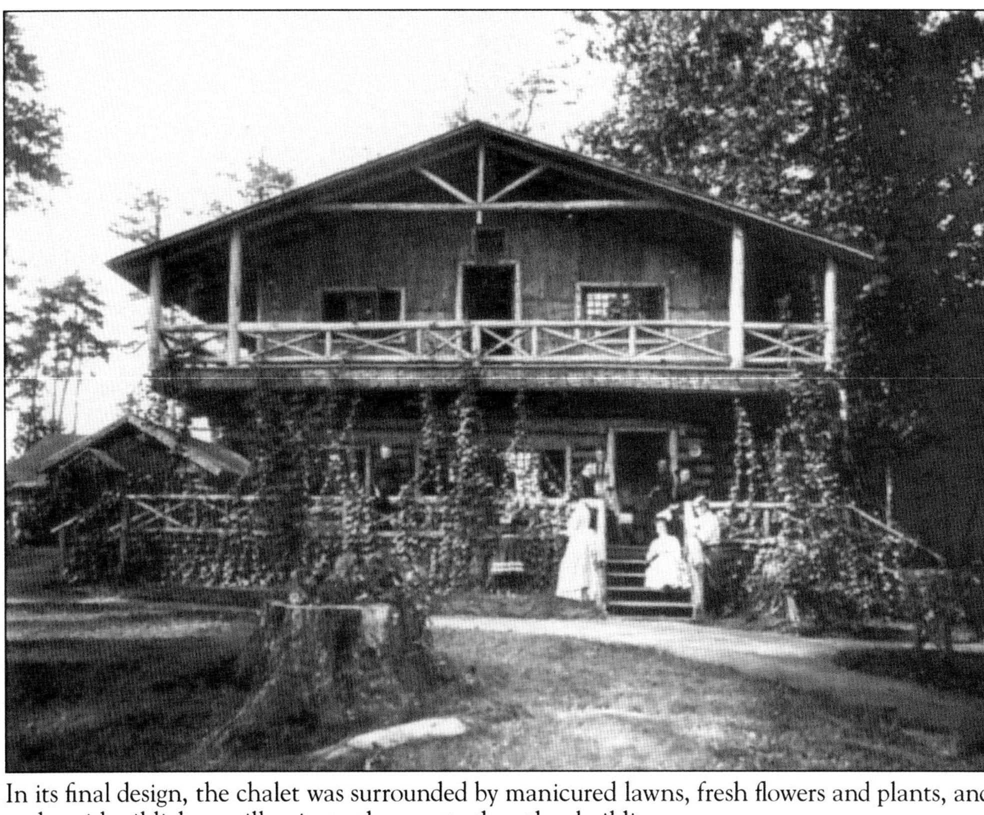

In its final design, the chalet was surrounded by manicured lawns, fresh flowers and plants, and paths with oil lights to illuminate the way to the other buildings.

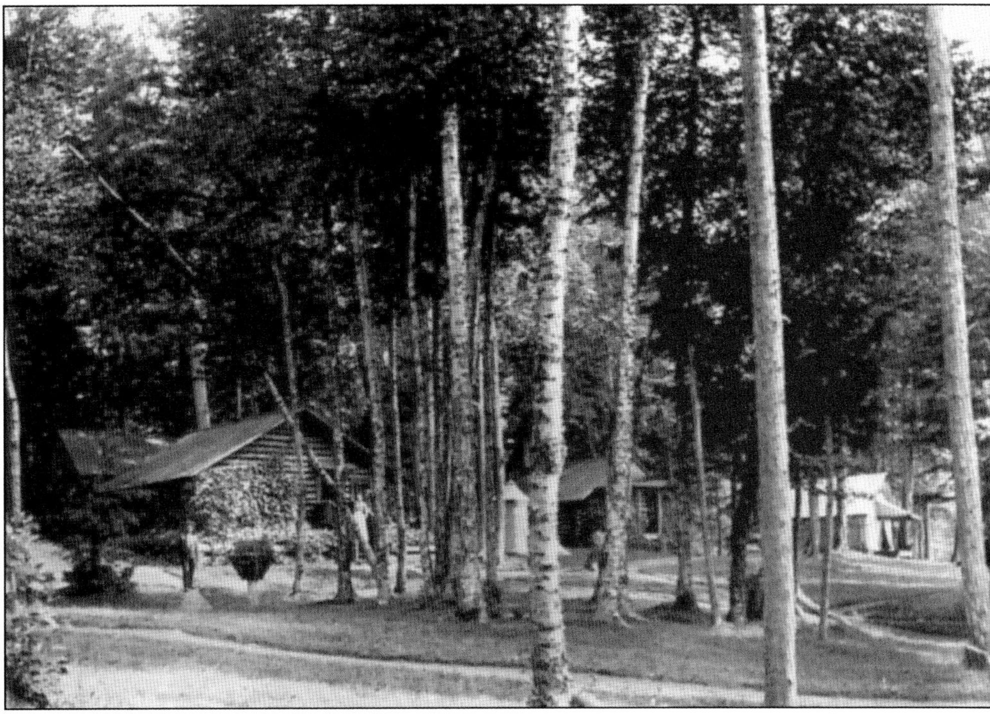

With the grounds cleaned up, guests could go from building to building on clear paths at all hours of the day.

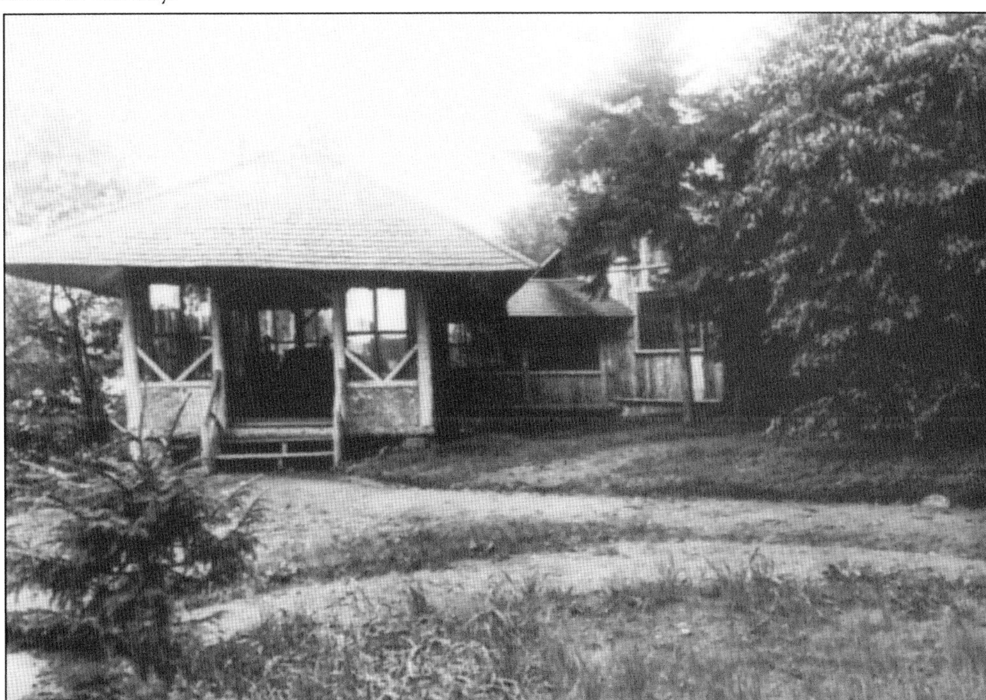

Guests could easily walk to the detached dining room. The glass walkway from the kitchen allowed the servants views of the lake as they brought out the meals.

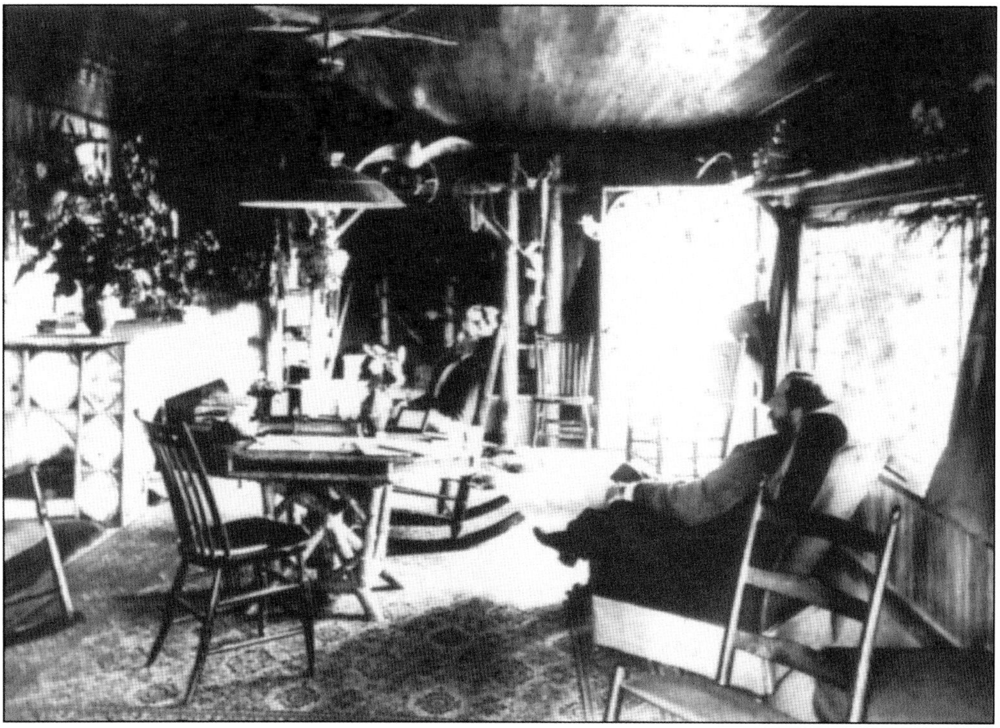

Interiors of the cabins were equally well done. Notice the patterned rug on the floor and the centrally hung oil lamp. Large windows insured the best view from inside the cottages.

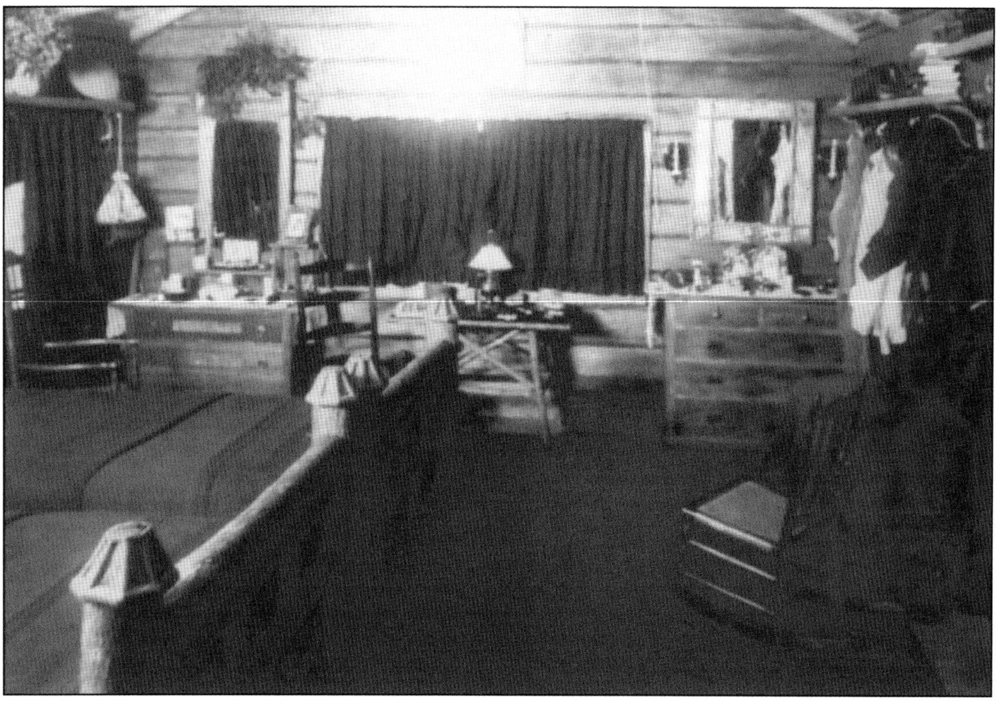

Bedrooms were spacious and bright. Notice the oil lamps on the wall and tables. The design of the beds is unique, along the lines of natural wood, and guests even had their own dressers.

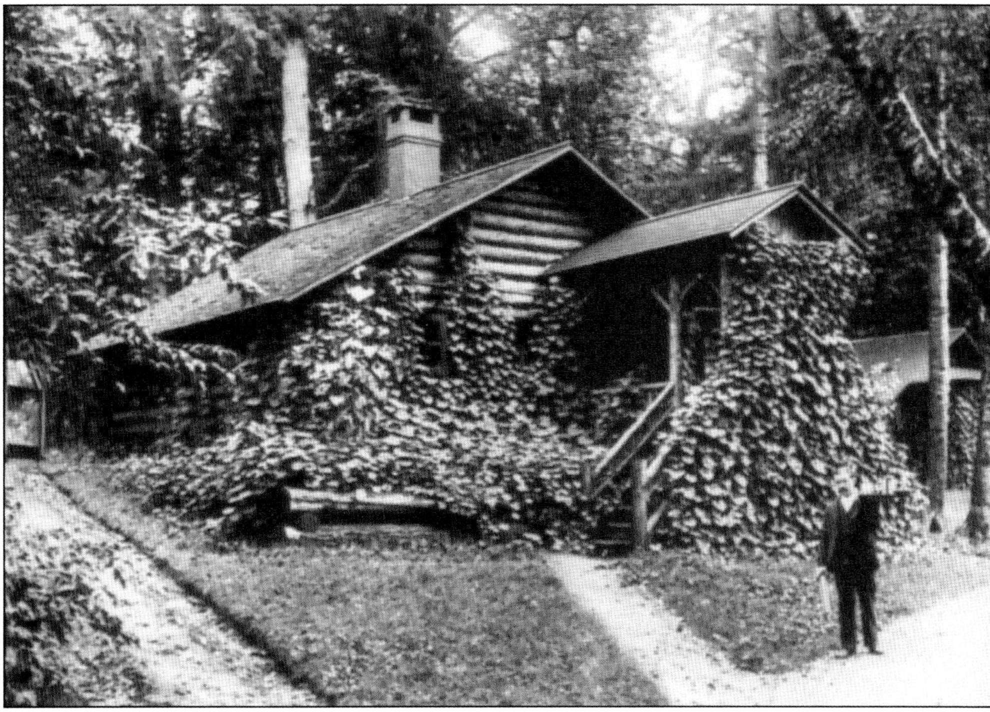

Camp Pine Knot guests were well pampered with many services. Notice the servant carrying a bottle-laden tray on his way to a guest cottage.

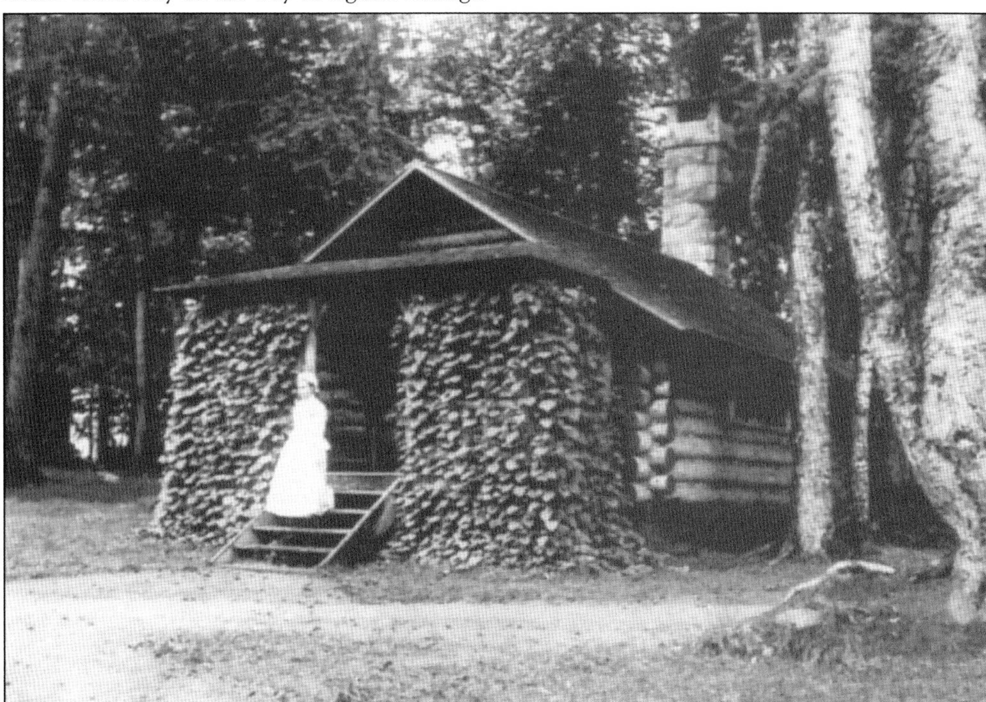

An on-duty nurse could attend to guests needing medical attention—perhaps for poison ivy or black fly bites.

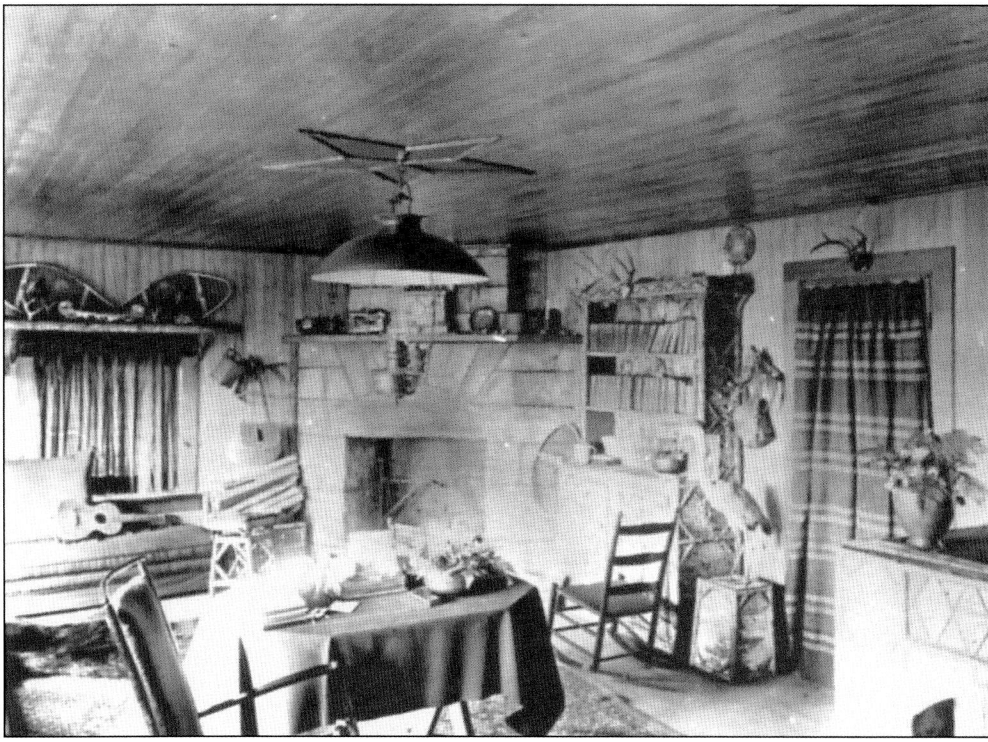

This interior shot shows central lighting, comfortable furniture, and a fireplace for cool, damp nights.

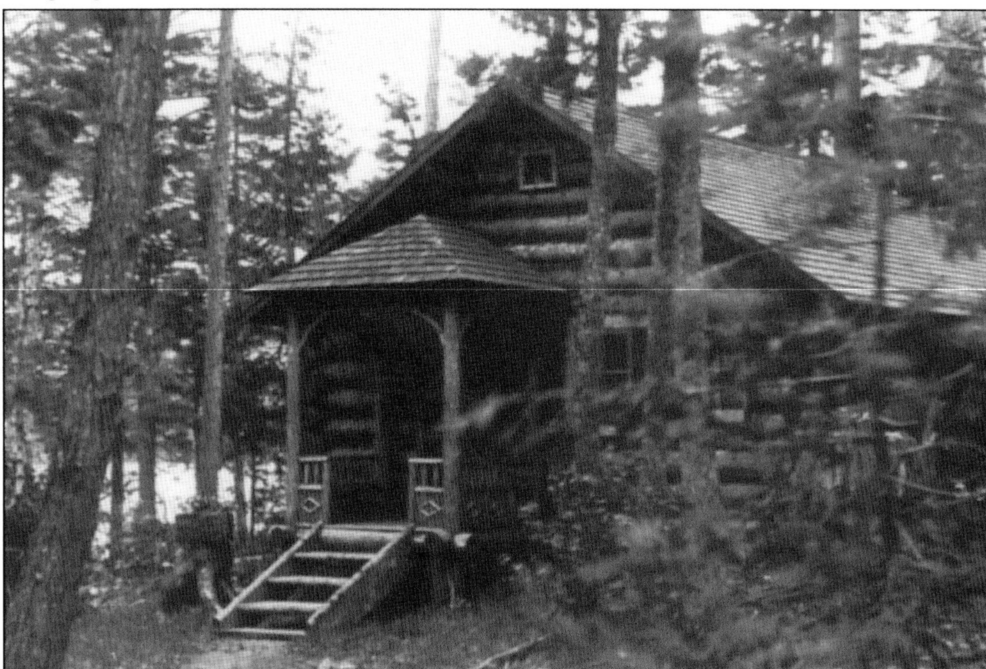

The days of simple cabin life in the darkness of the woods were gone. William West Durant had just begun a new way of cabin living.

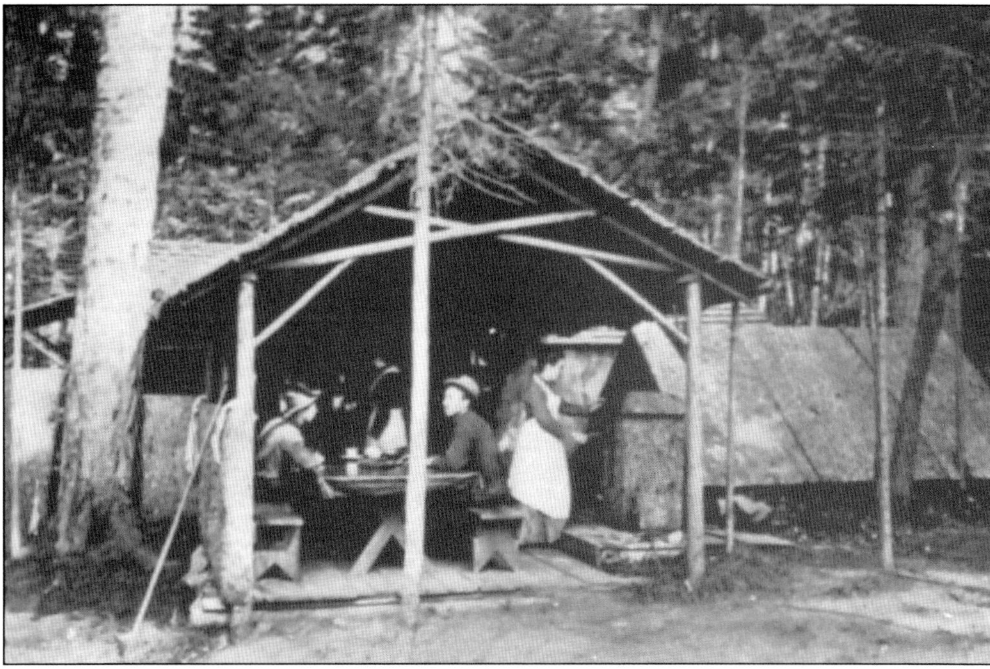

The staff members at Camp Pine Knot had their own cooking and dining area. Here some of them wait for their meal.

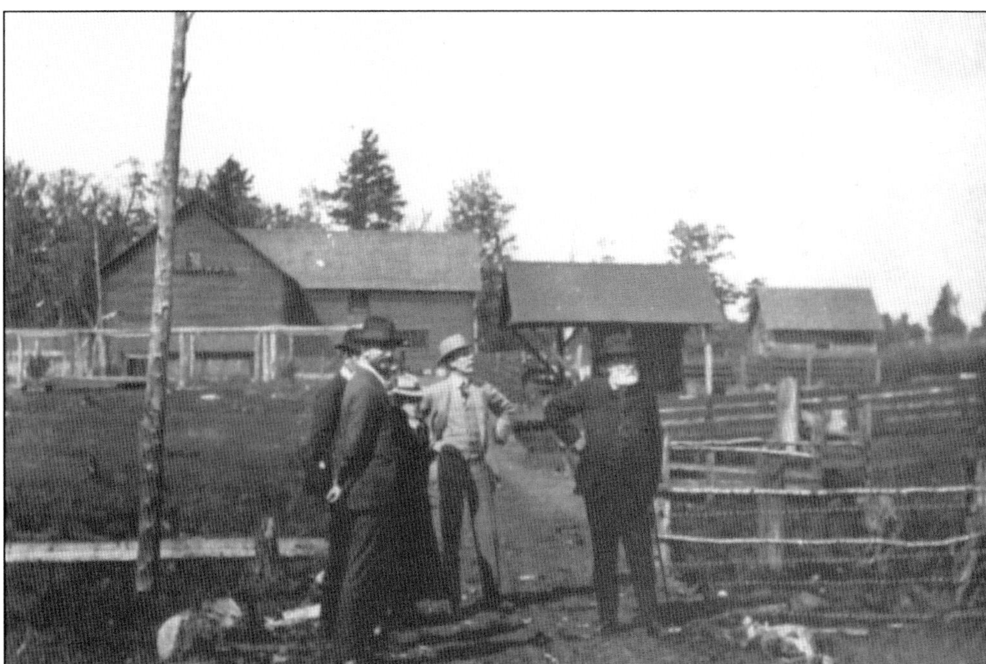

As with most great camps, fresh vegetables and meat sometimes came from an adjacent farm. Here William West Durant (in the light suit) and railroad executive Collis Potter Huntington view the Pine Knot farm. Huntington eventually bought the Pine Knot complex and resided here.

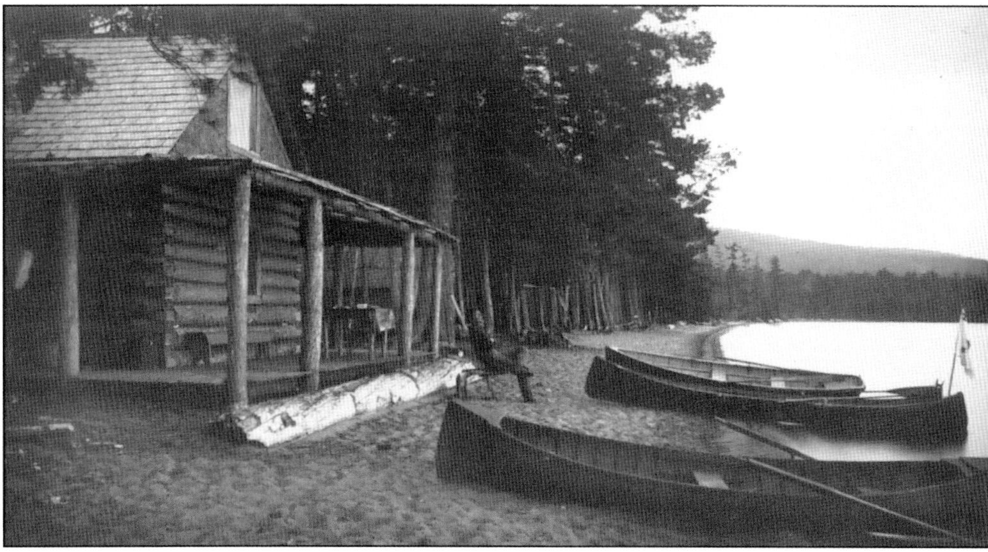

Going into South Bay a traveler was met by a beach with an expanse of golden sand, hence the name Golden Beach. Chauncey Hathorn (pictured), a guide at Raquette Lake, eventually set up camps for his guests and operated from here. In this early shot, not too many buildings are evident yet.

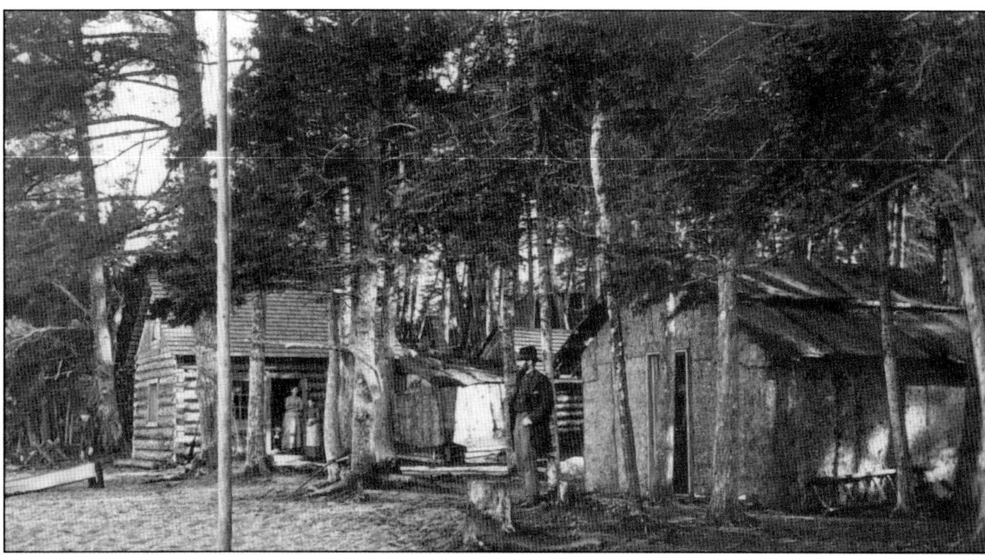

As time passed and more people were attracted to the area, Hathorn built more cabins, had more rooms, and employed a cook to prepare meals for the weary traveler.

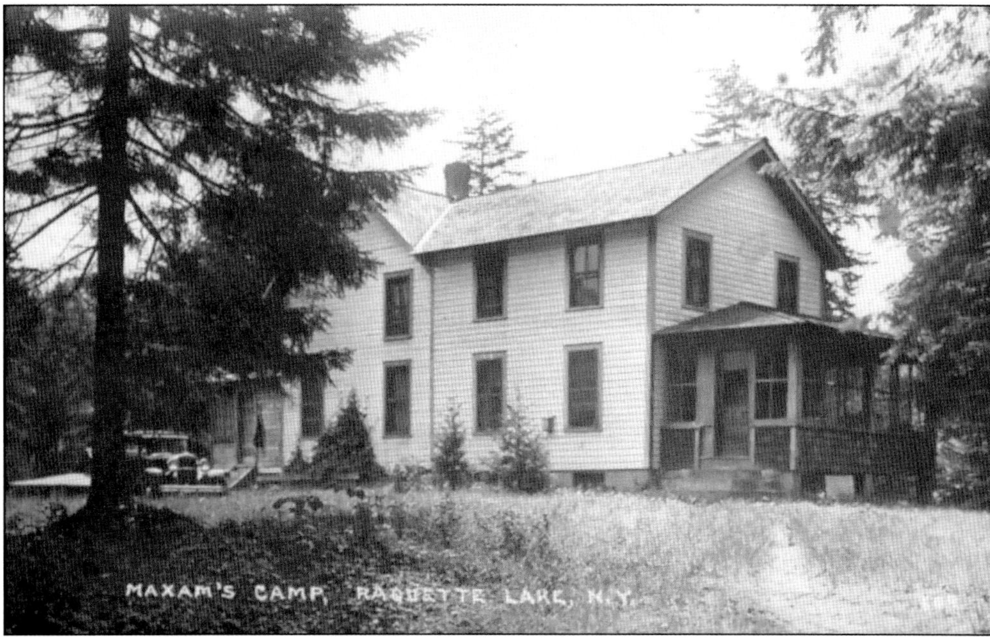

Fred "Mossy" Maxam was a guide at Raquette Lake. He often guided groups of guests for the Morgan, Vanderbilt, and Garvan great camps. He settled in South Bay, although he spent most of his time at the great camps. This postcard shows the Maxam camp shortly before 1930.

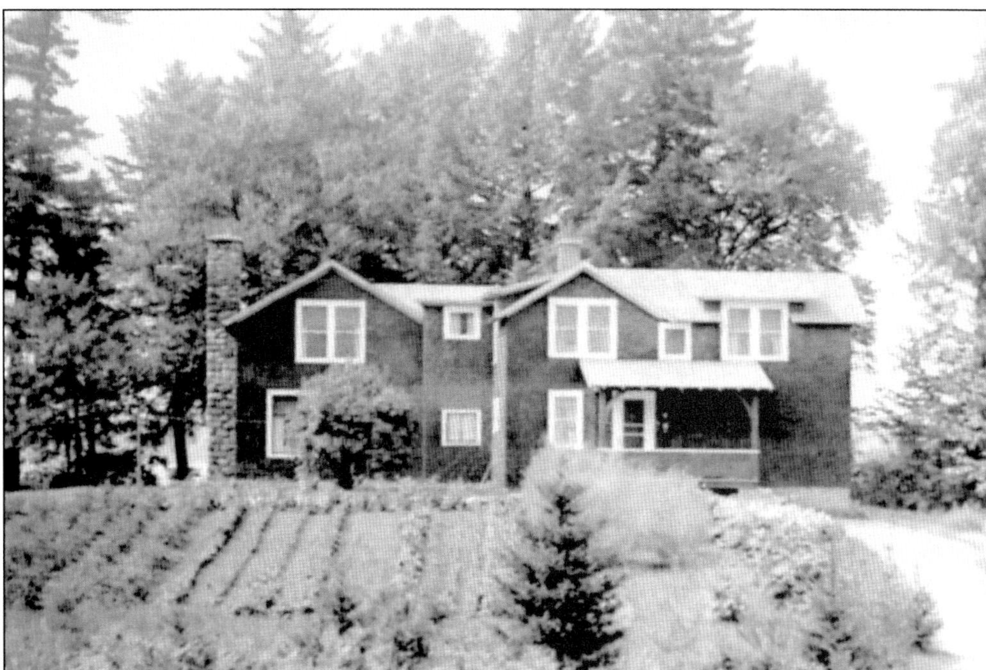

John Blanchard and his wife bought land in Raquette in 1908. The Blanchards lived in a house on the site. They constructed guide boats during the winter months as a family project. In the summer months, they ran tourist accommodations. Paul Blanchard inherited the property and ran it as a tourist site. The property still stands.

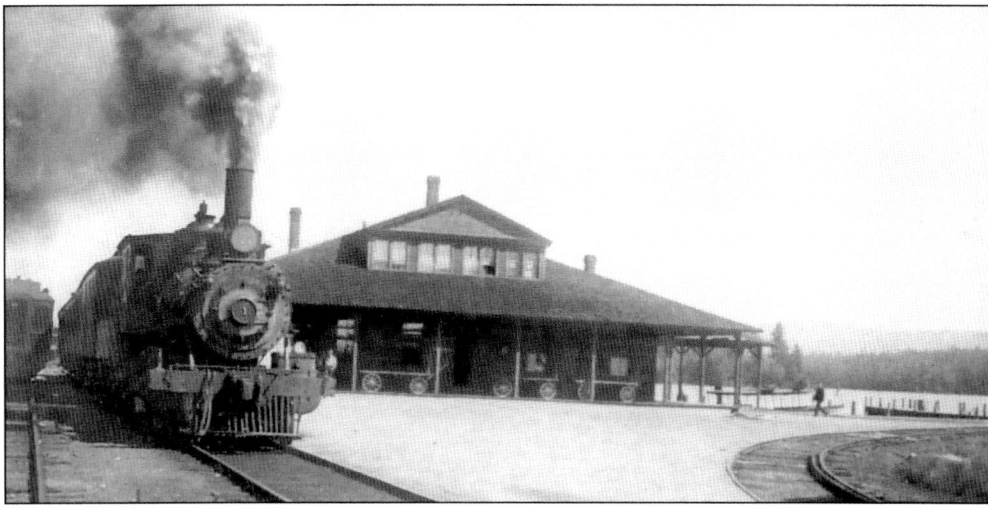

Around 1899, local guide Alvah Dunning had a camp situated at the mouth of the Brown's Tract Outlet. The Raquette Lake Railroad people came to him with the plan of buying his property. This area was the foundation for the current location of the Raquette Lake village. The railway station not only was to be the termination point for the Raquette Lake Railroad but also the start of the steamer service for Raquette Lake.

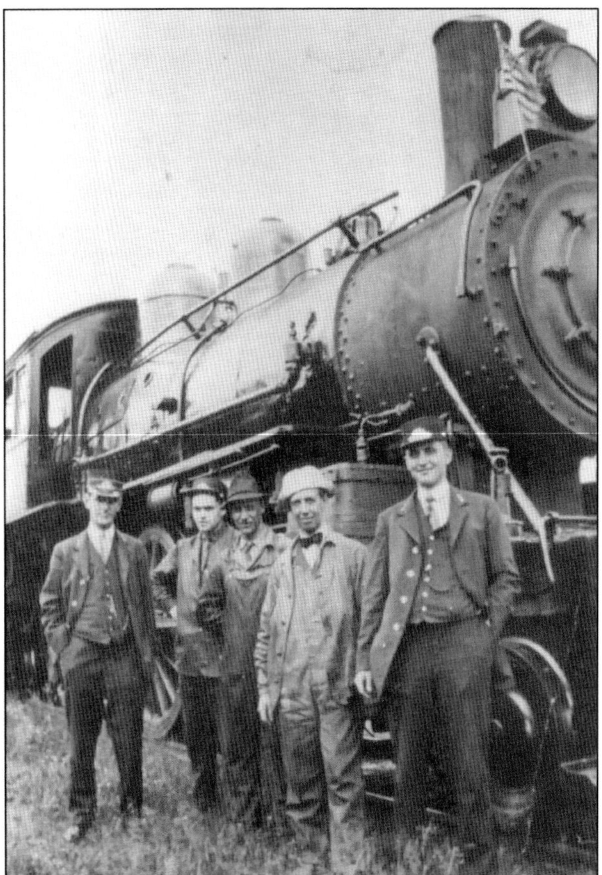

Conductors, firemen, engineers, and telegraph operators were all needed at once to ensure smooth operation of the railway and the steamer service and to run the station.

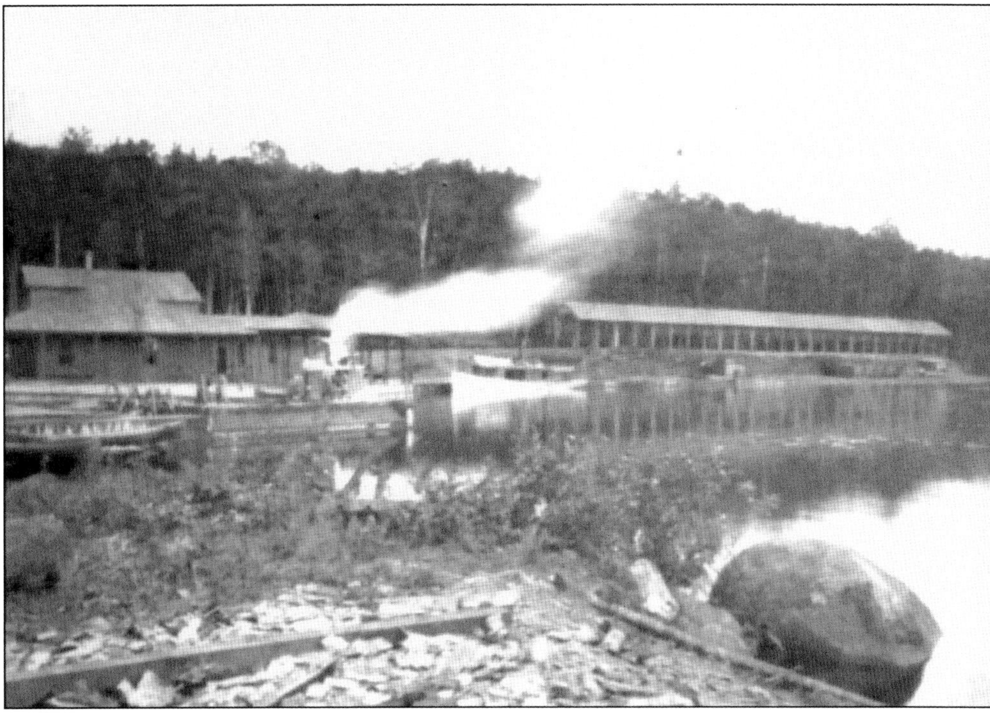

The Raquette Lake Railroad joined the regular rail line at Carter station and ended at Raquette Lake village. The initial investors in the line even had private carbarns where their personal Pullman coaches could be parked out of the weather.

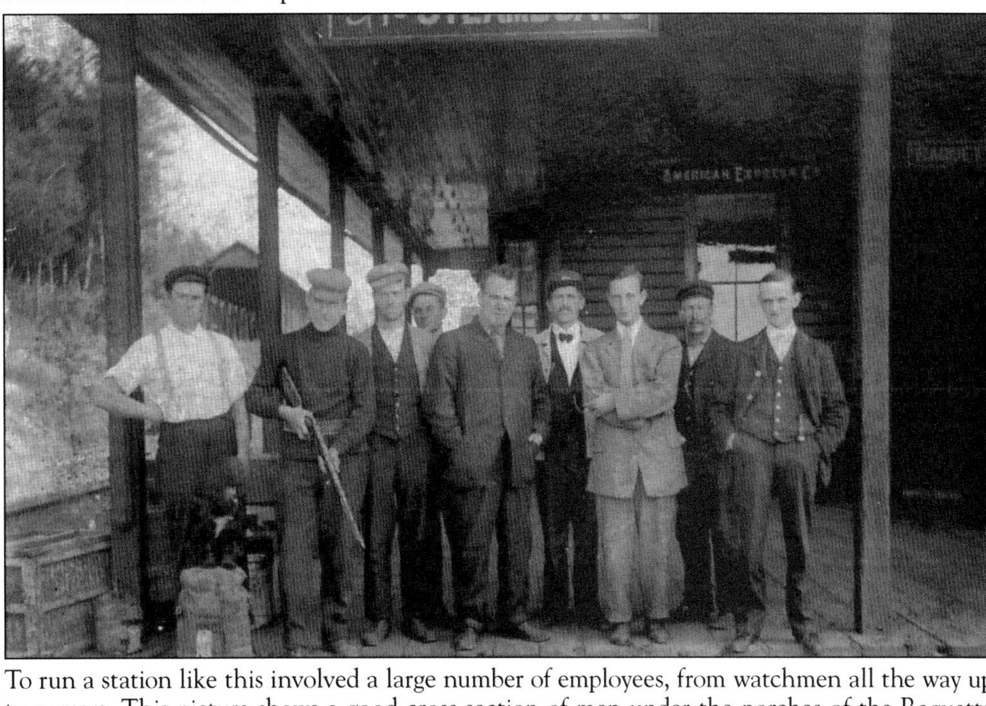

To run a station like this involved a large number of employees, from watchmen all the way up to pursers. This picture shows a good cross-section of men under the porches of the Raquette Lake Railroad station around 1918.

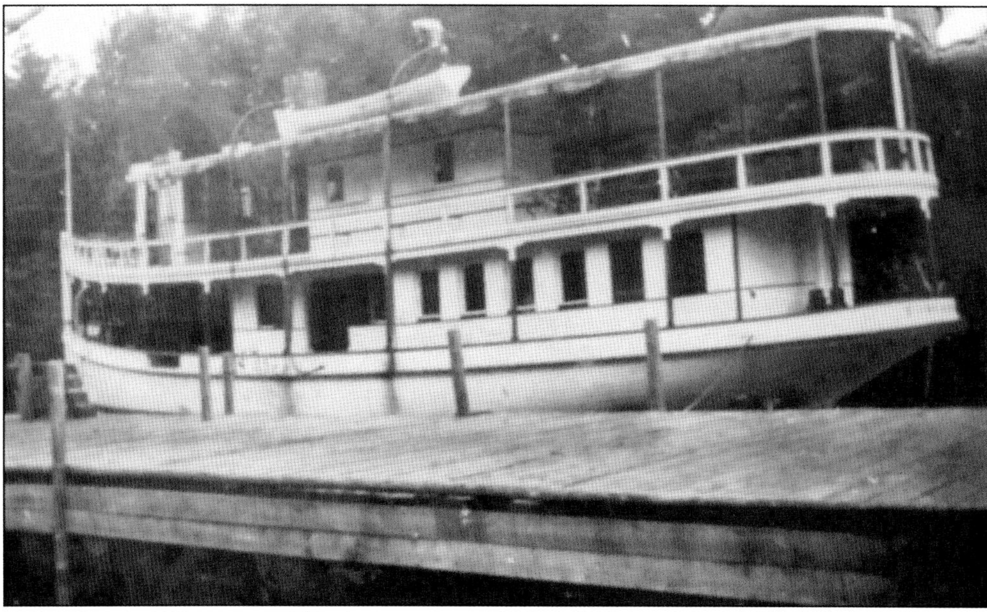

Before Route 28 was completed, passengers departed the rails to take a steamer to their destination. The double-decker *Lillian* is shown at the town dock waiting for people to board.

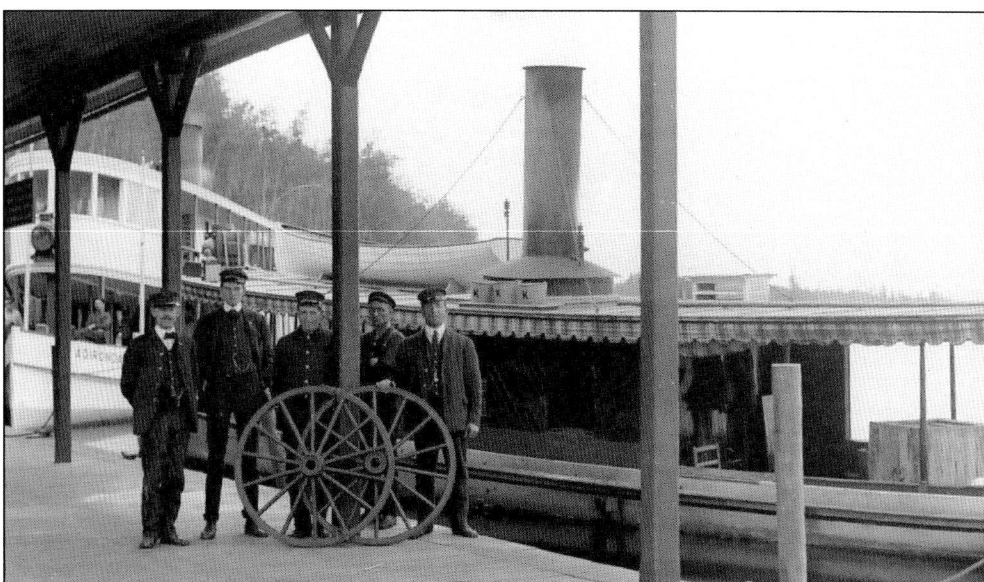

As with the railway, qualified help was needed to run the steamers. In this view, men are shown waiting for riders next to the station. Beside them, at the dock, is the *Killoquah*, and to the rear is the double-decker *Adirondack*.

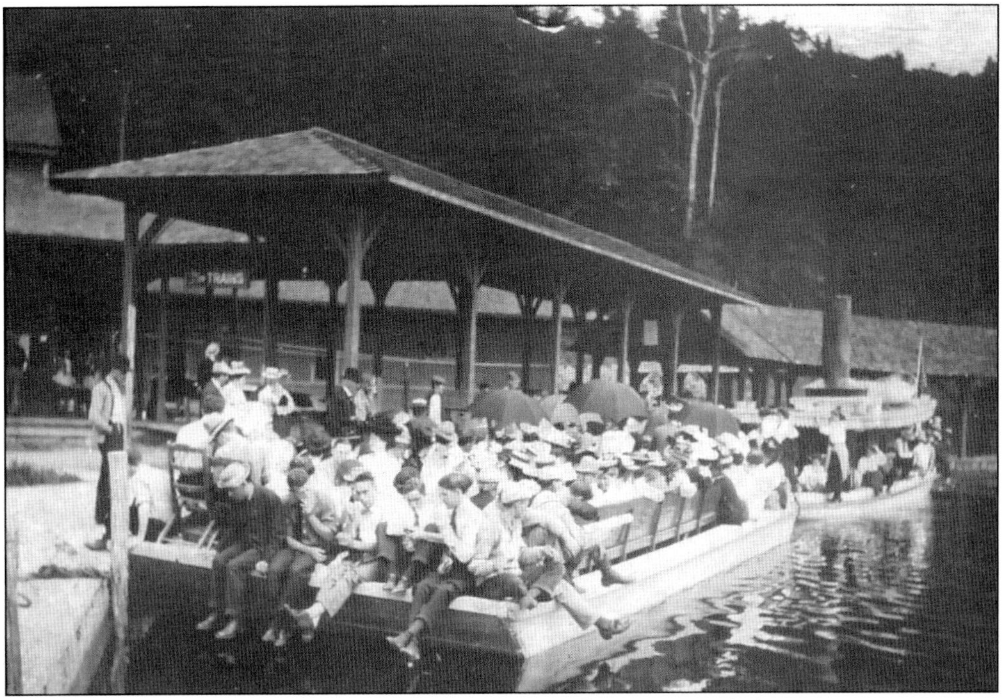

It was always good business to keep the employees and the townspeople happy. Here everyone is jammed onto a barge and steamer for free ride day. The year is 1912. Either the day was hot or rain was about to fall. Note the raised parasols.

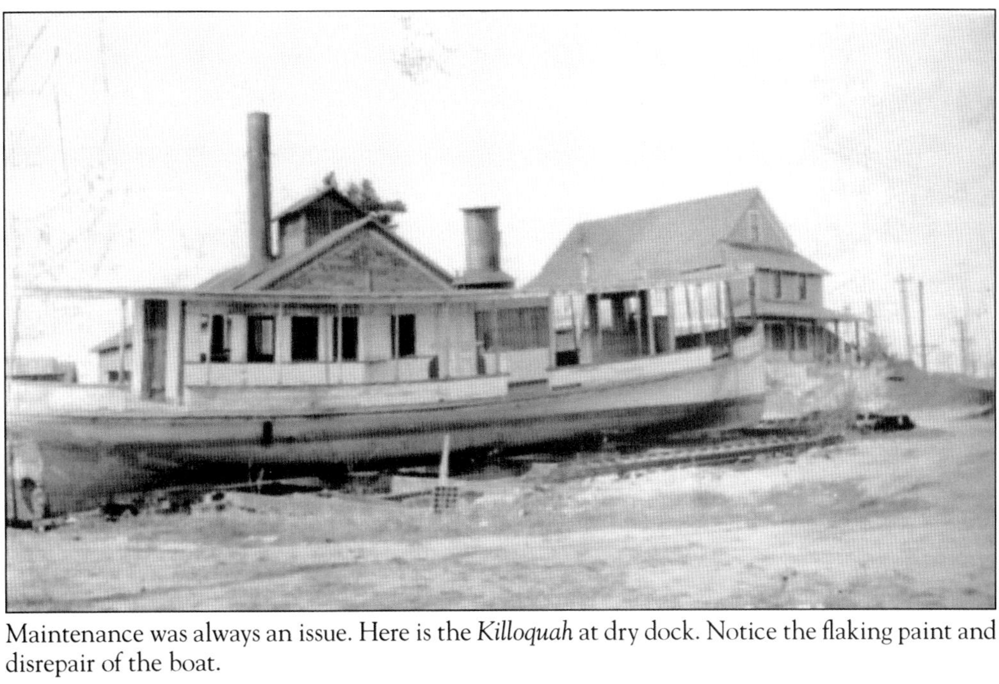

Maintenance was always an issue. Here is the *Killoquah* at dry dock. Notice the flaking paint and disrepair of the boat.

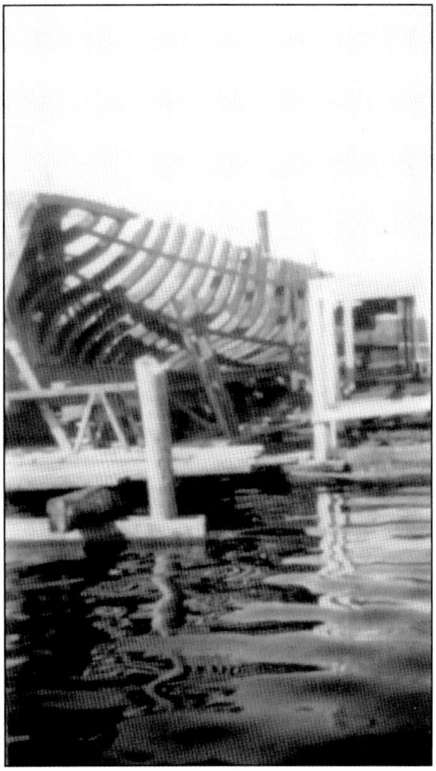

Because of the need for service boats, boatbuilding went on at several locations at Raquette. This shot, next to the Raquette Lake General Store, shows men at work.

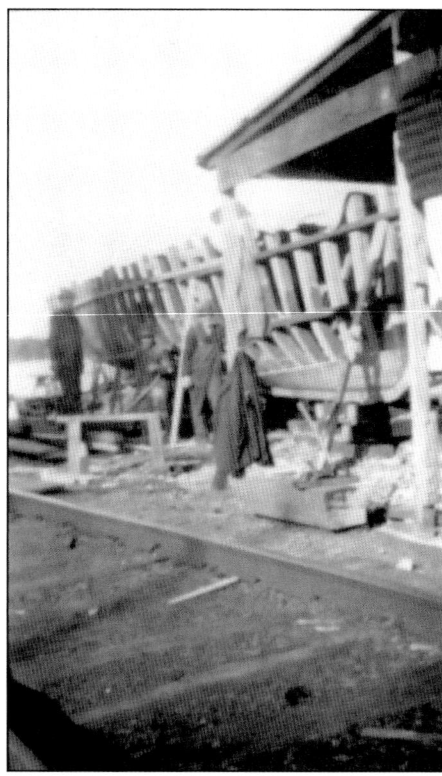

In a second location onshore near the store, keels laid and ribs attached are next to a rail ready to launch them into the water.

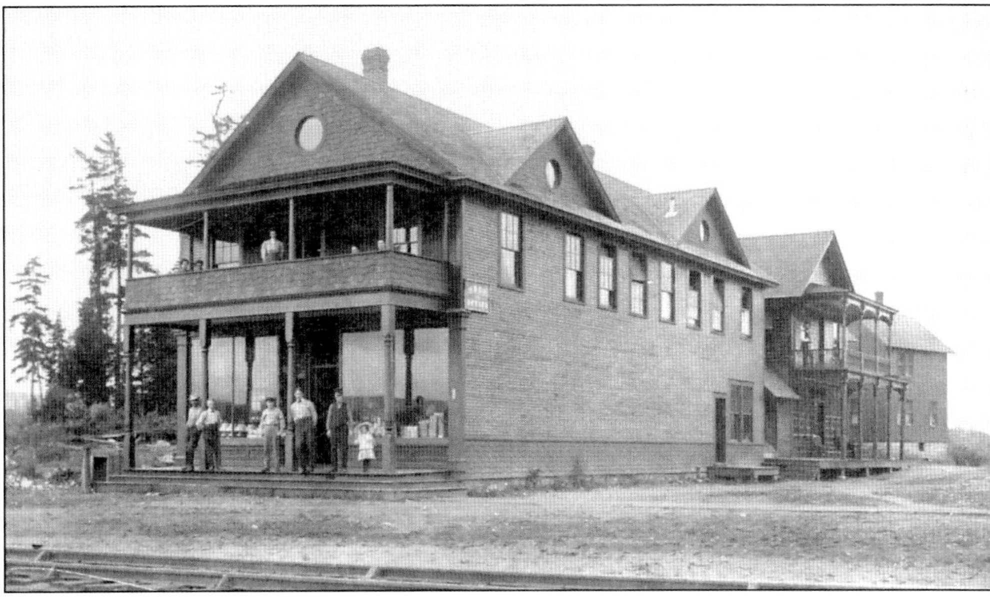

Along with prosperity came the need for more services. This picture shows customers in front of the new Raquette Lake Supply Company. A patron could buy a pair of shoelaces, get some groceries, and even buy a pair of boots to put the laces in.

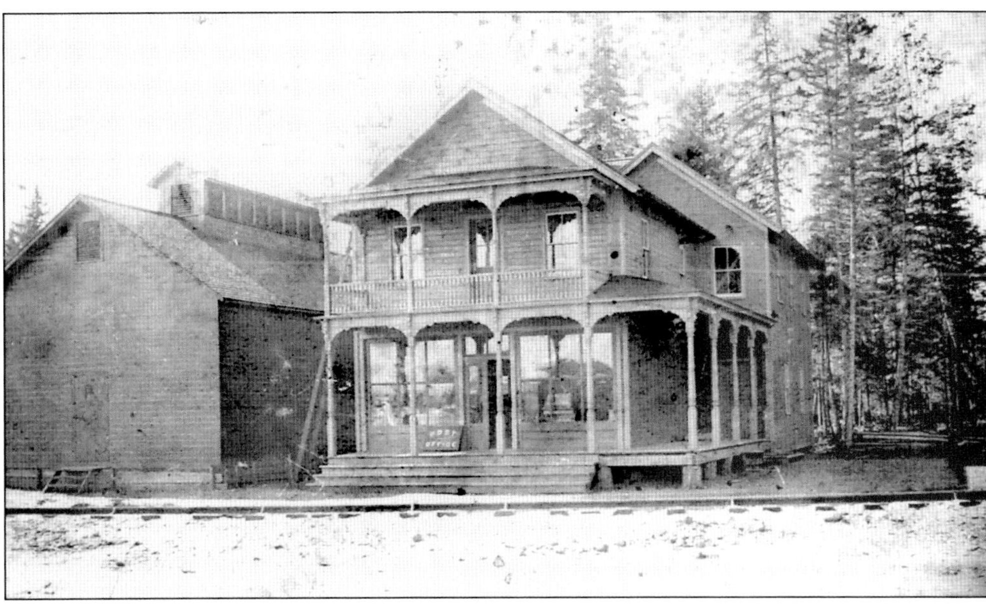

Additional buildings housed lumber, coal, and ice, and one building was used for a new post office.

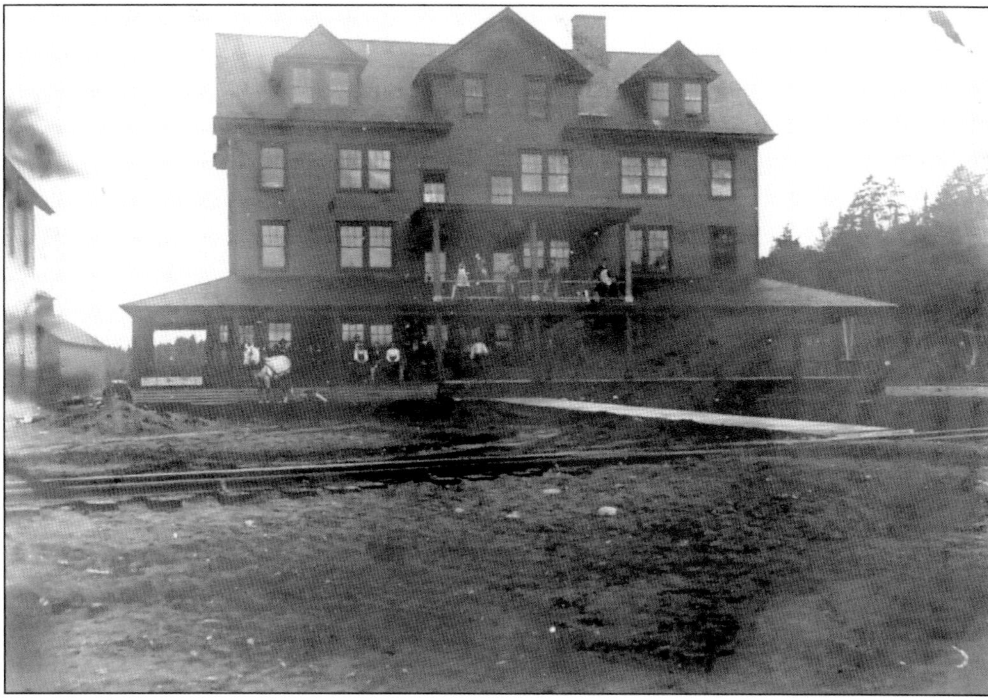

Next to the Raquette Lake Supply Company was the multistory Raquette Lake House. The hotel offered good meals and overnight accommodations, and it stood within walking distance of the railway station. Note the railway turnaround, or loop, in front of the hotel.

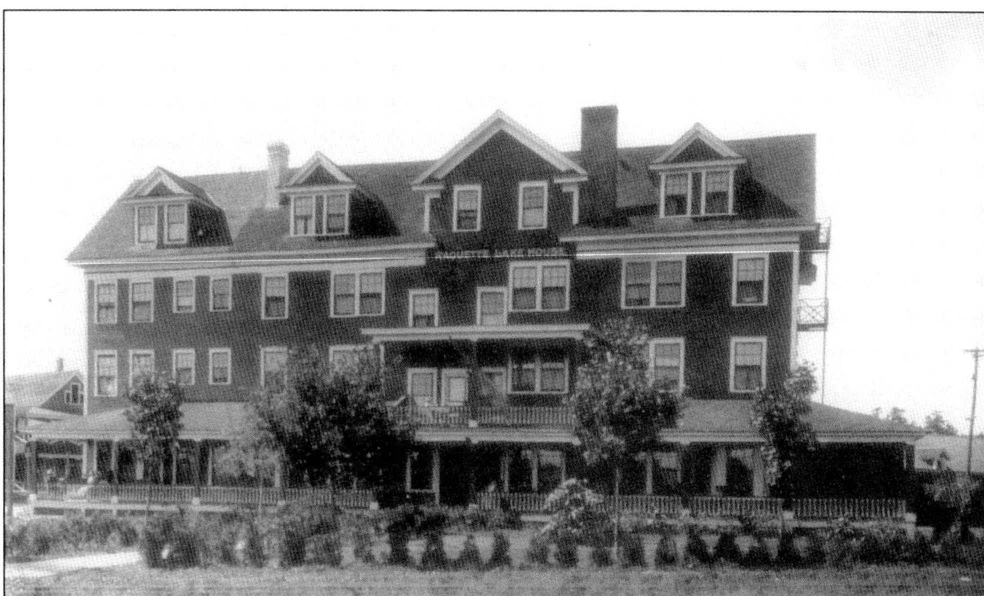

As train passengers increased, the Raquette Lake House expanded. The addition of more rooms is evident by the change in the shade of the roof shingles. This was the Raquette Lake House at its grandest and final appearance.

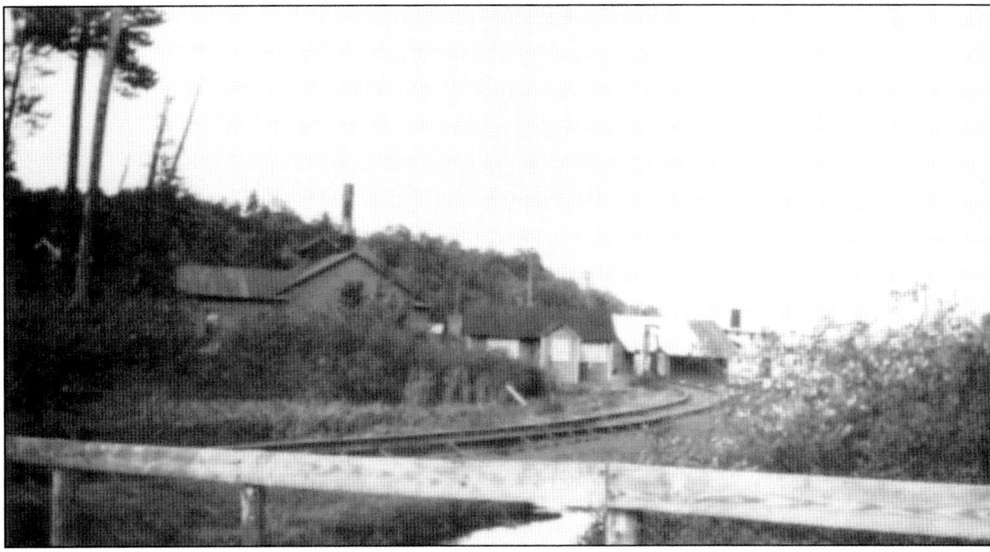

Taking the loop around the hotel and store brought one past the powerhouse, which is the building with the stack. Raquette Lake village did not see power by wire until several years later.

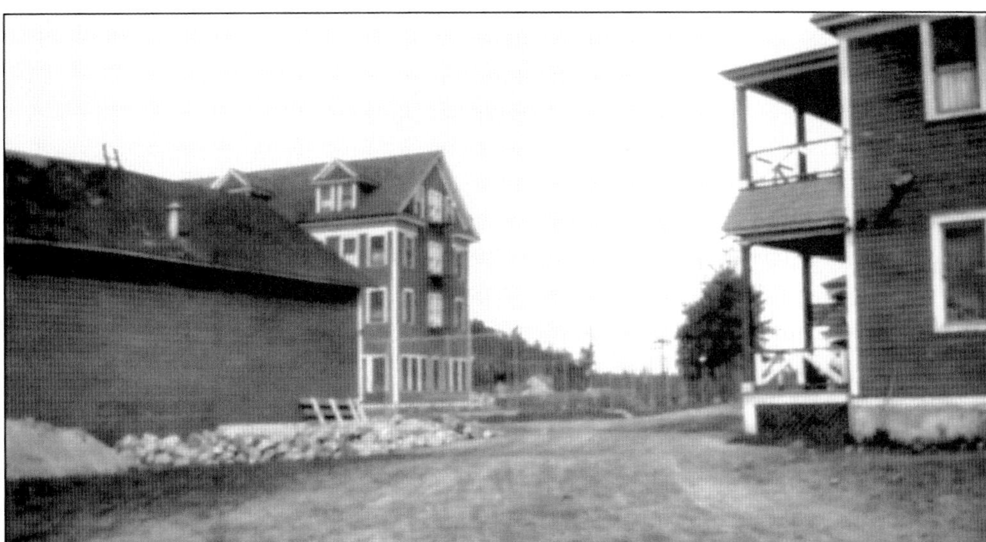

The turnaround came out behind the Raquette Lake House and service buildings. Note the fire escapes on the hotel.

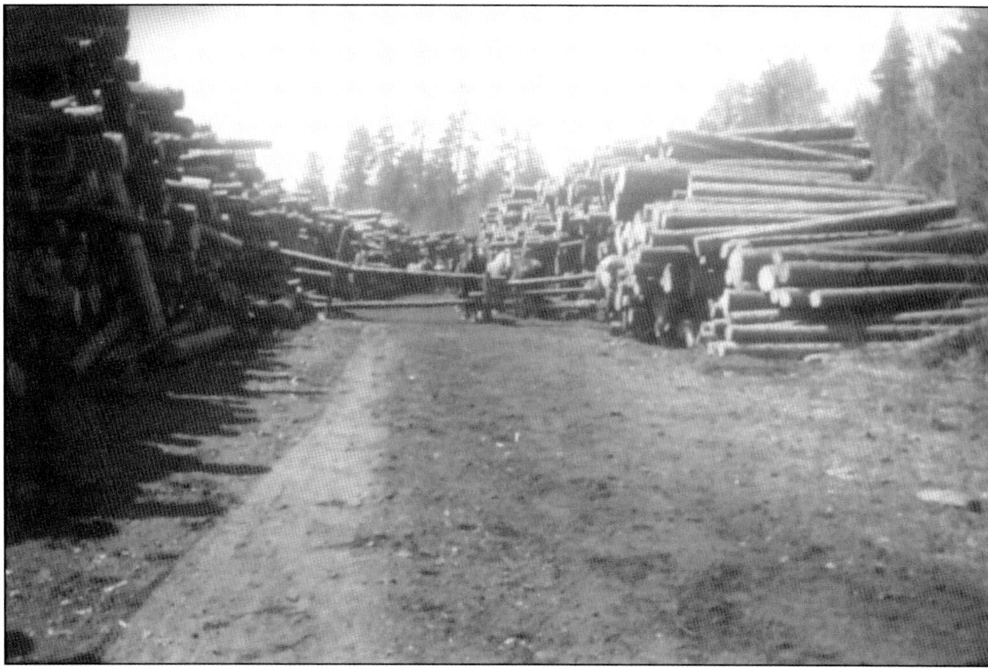

Behind the store and hotel were the collecting yards for logs for the sawmill. This facility was constructed of many of the components from the Marion River Sawmill.

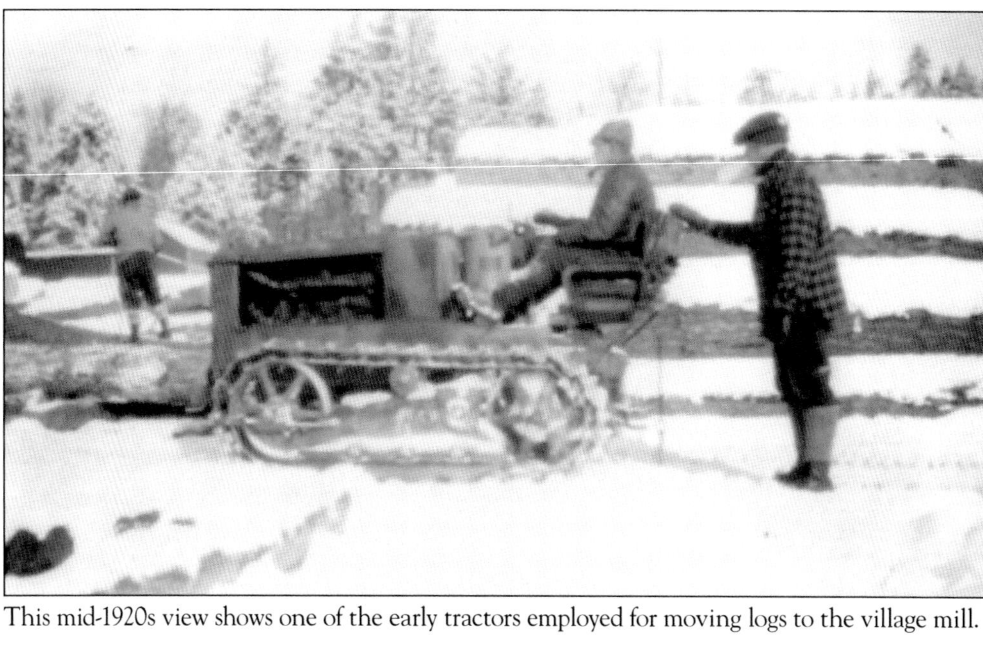

This mid-1920s view shows one of the early tractors employed for moving logs to the village mill.

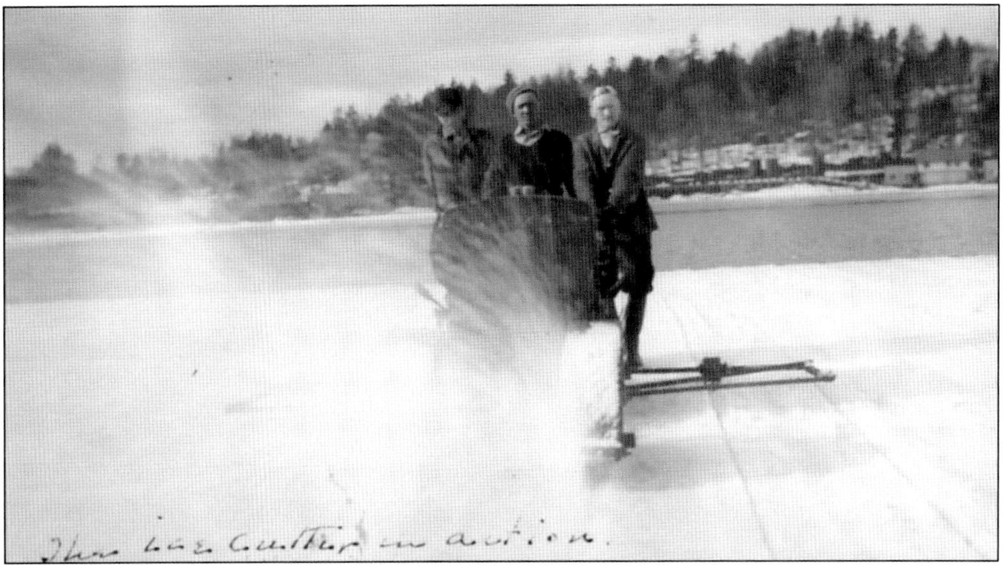

One of Raquette Lake's large businesses was the shipping of ice by New York Central railcar down to New York City and beyond. With a vast space already behind them, three men cut ice in the village bay.

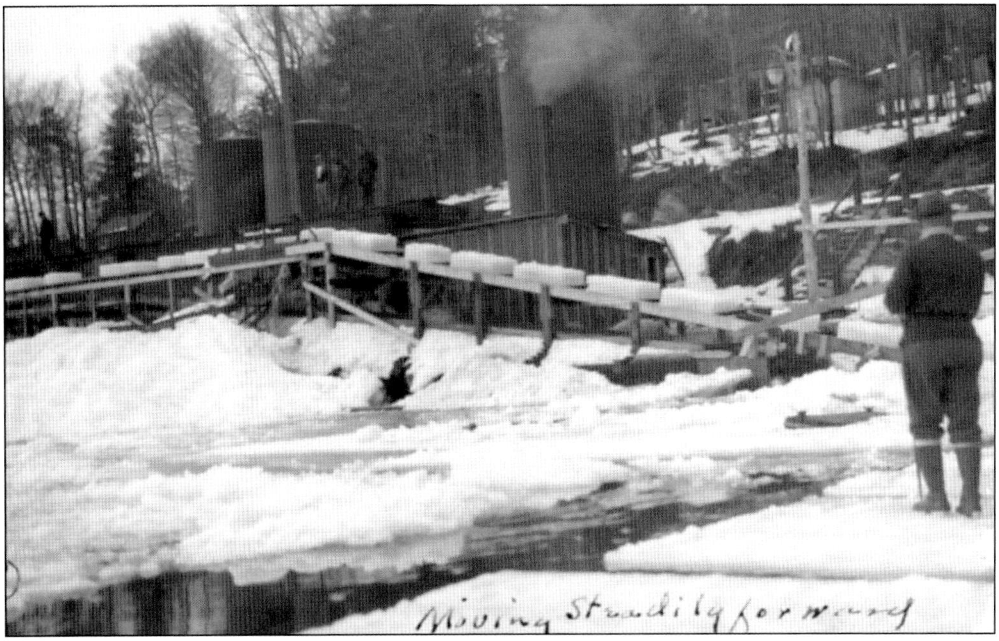

After ice was cut in a central location, it had to be poled down troughs to the edge of the shore.

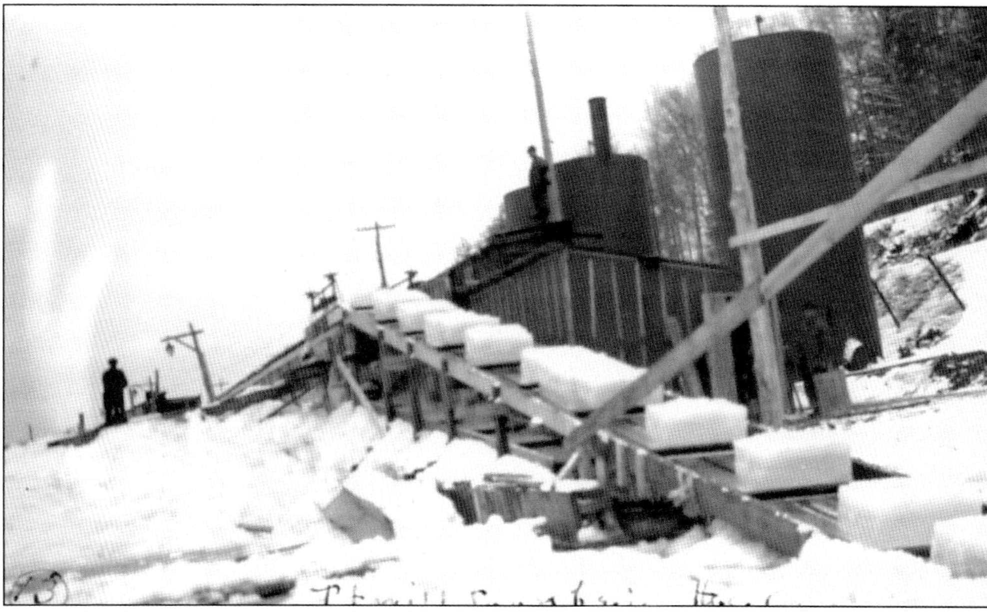

As blocks of ice were taken from the lake, they were deposited onto a special conveyor that took them down the shoreline to waiting railcars near the old station.

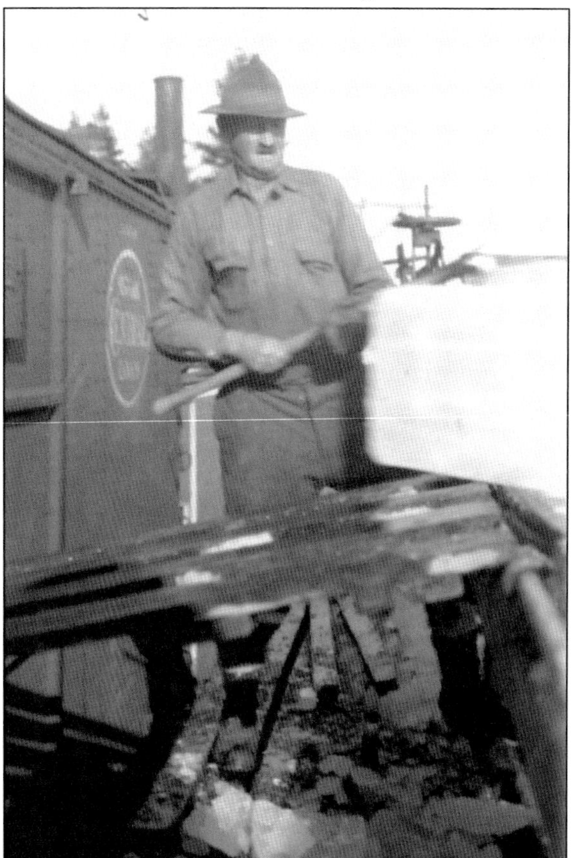

Here the blocks of ice were loaded into New York Central boxcars for shipment. This was a two-man job, with one man inside the car stacking the blocks.

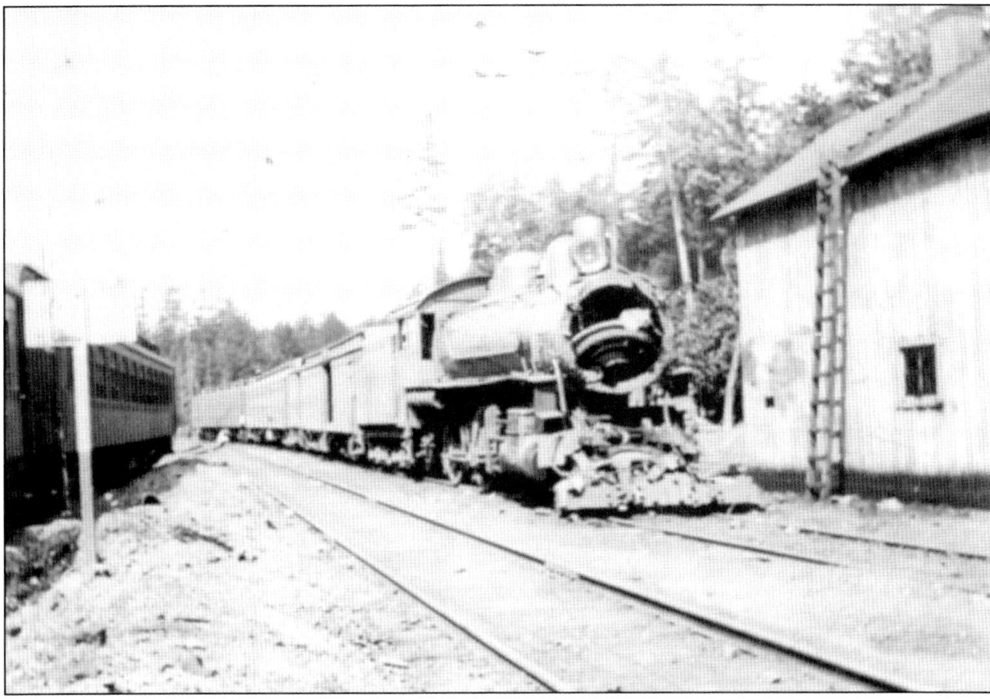

Accidents could happen in the heat of fast business. This locomotive was going too fast as it entered Raquette Lake village and could not stop in time.

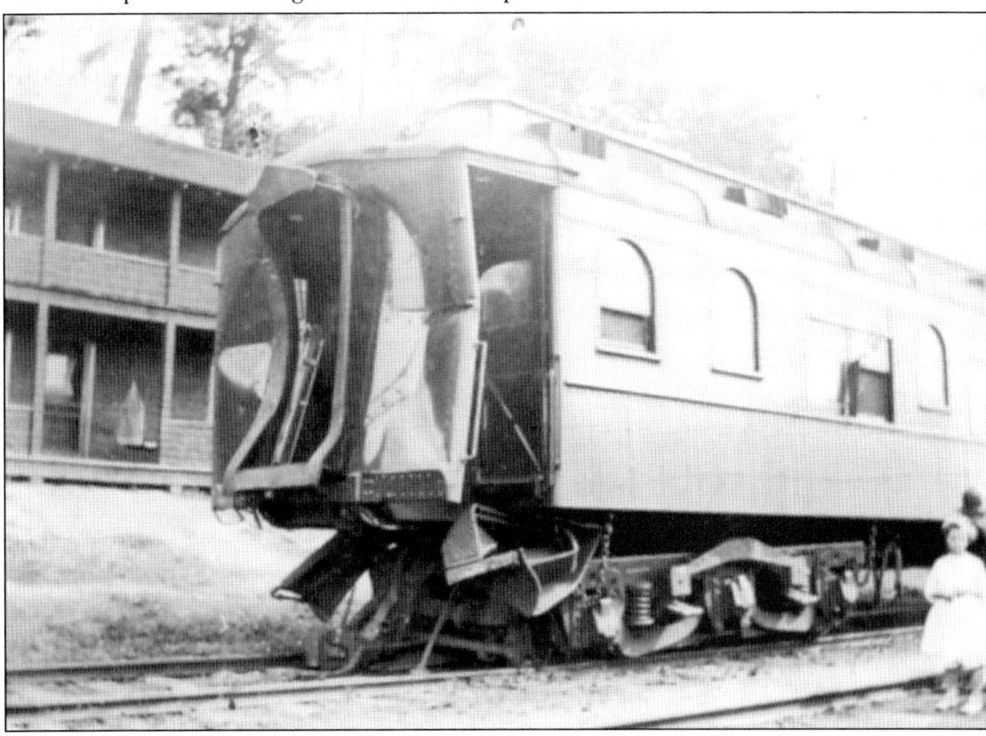

Not being able to stop, the locomotive plowed into the back of a Pullman car, severely damaging the rear of the coach and shoving it up the rail line.

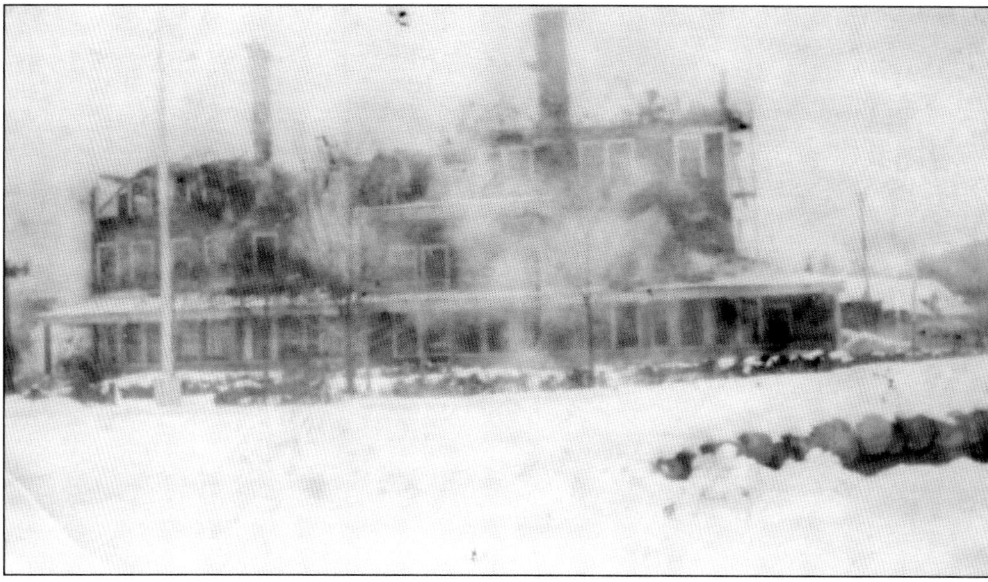

The appearance of Raquette Lake village changed dramatically on February 20, 1927. The sight of smoke coming out of an upper window of the Raquette Lake House soon became a fire that spread through the town.

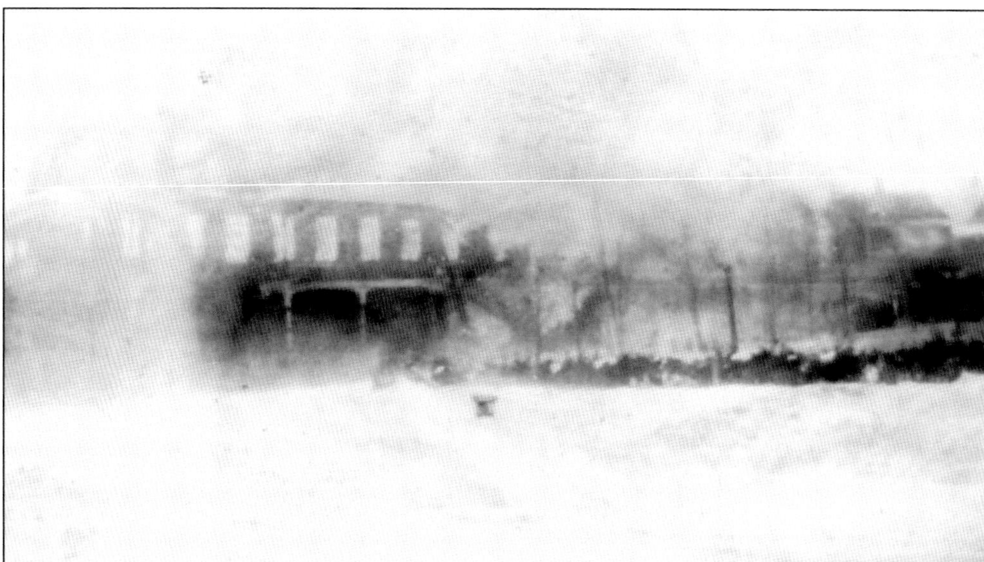

Fed by a strong wind, the sparks soon leapt to the neighboring Raquette Lake Supply Company building and involved some smaller outbuildings.

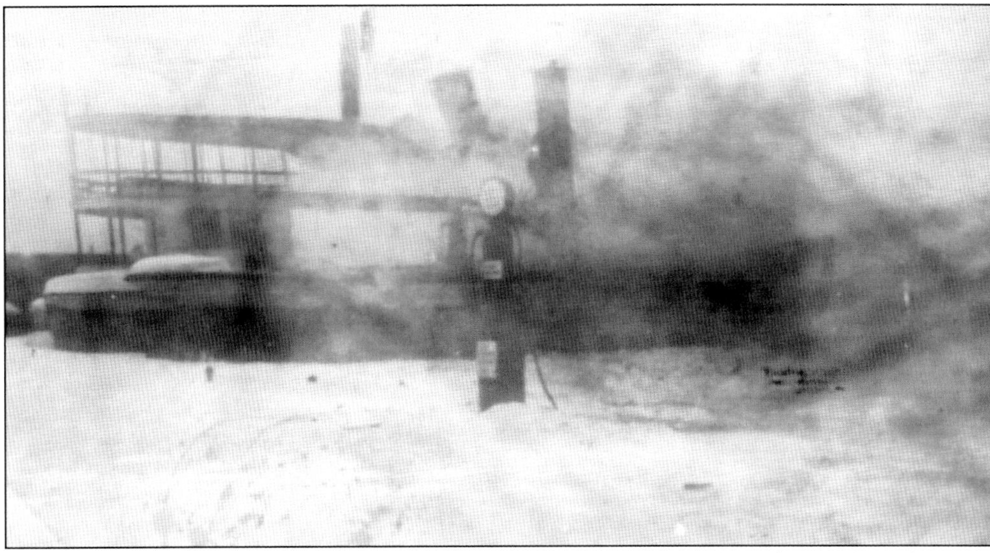

Flames jumped from the Raquette Lake Supply Company building to the *Adirondack*, in dry-dock, and fully involved the majestic double-decker steamer.

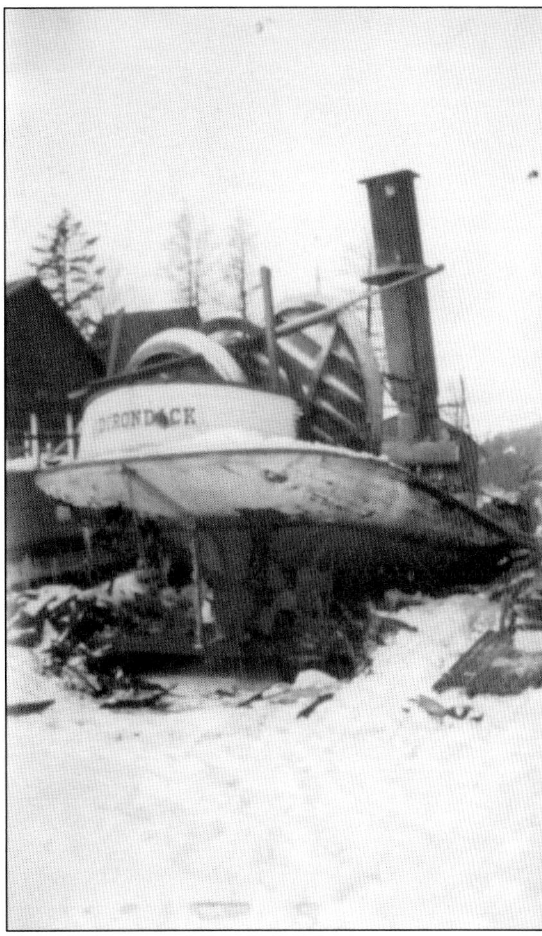

By daybreak, the town was the scene of vast devastation. The steamer *Adirondack* was a total loss.

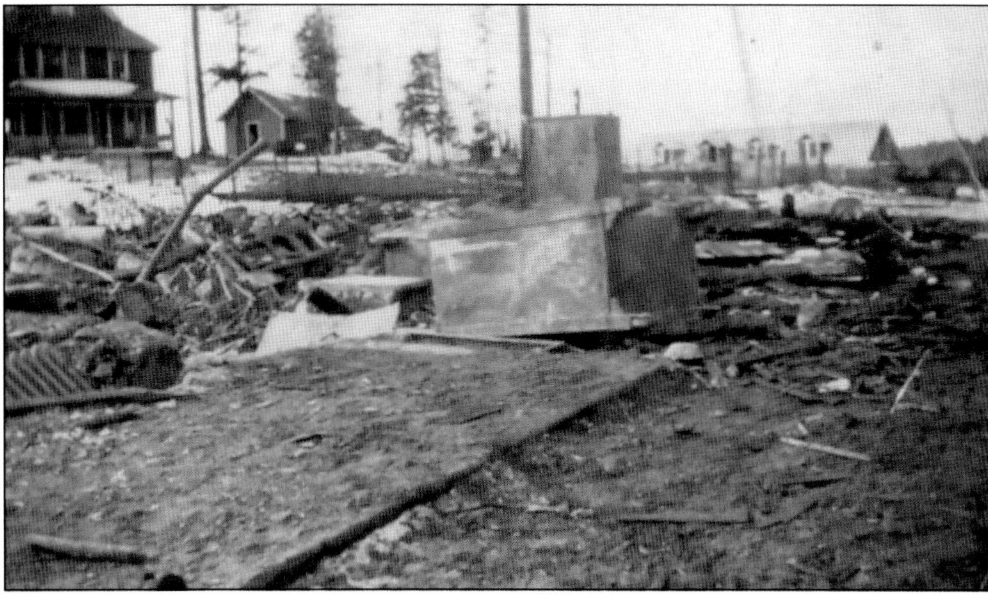

The former Raquette Lake House was just a hole in the ground. The flames had consumed everything but metal. The hotel safes lie on their sides on the ground after the fire.

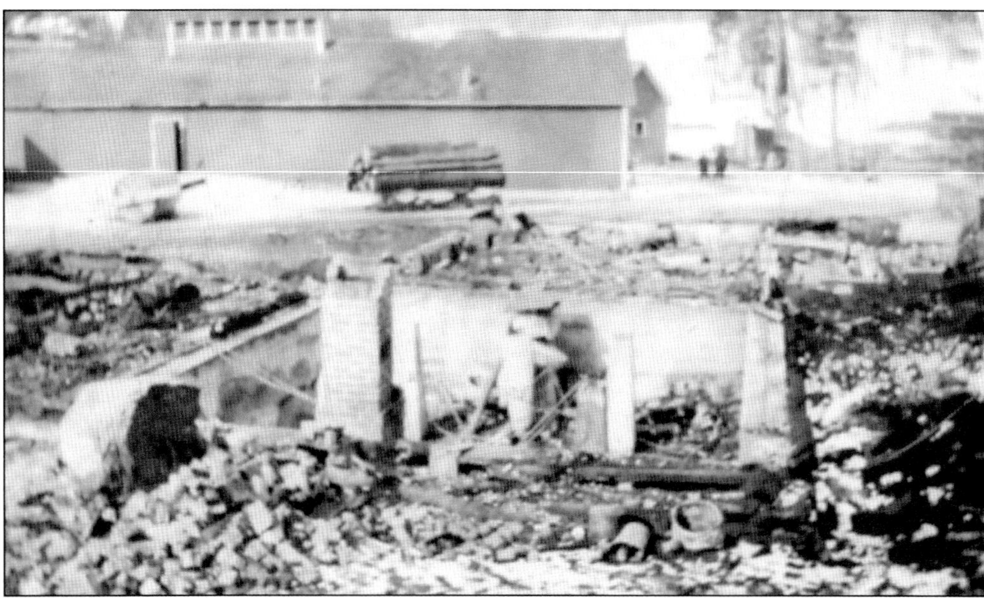

The Raquette Lake Supply Company building was a complete loss, burned down to the basement.

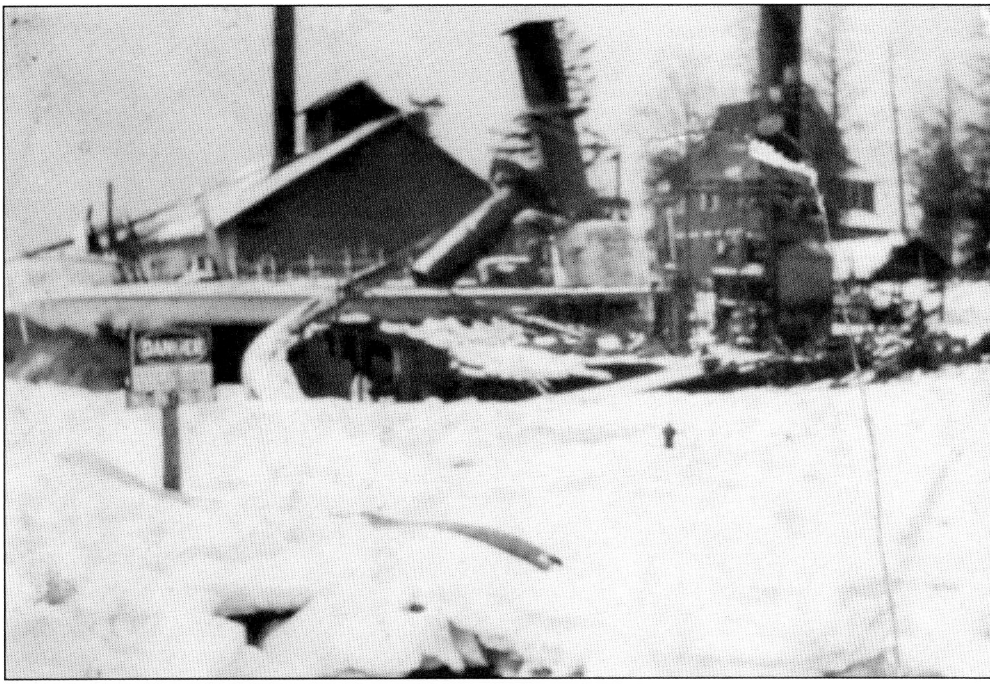

Fortunately the powerhouse, located right next to the steamer *Adirondack*, survived.

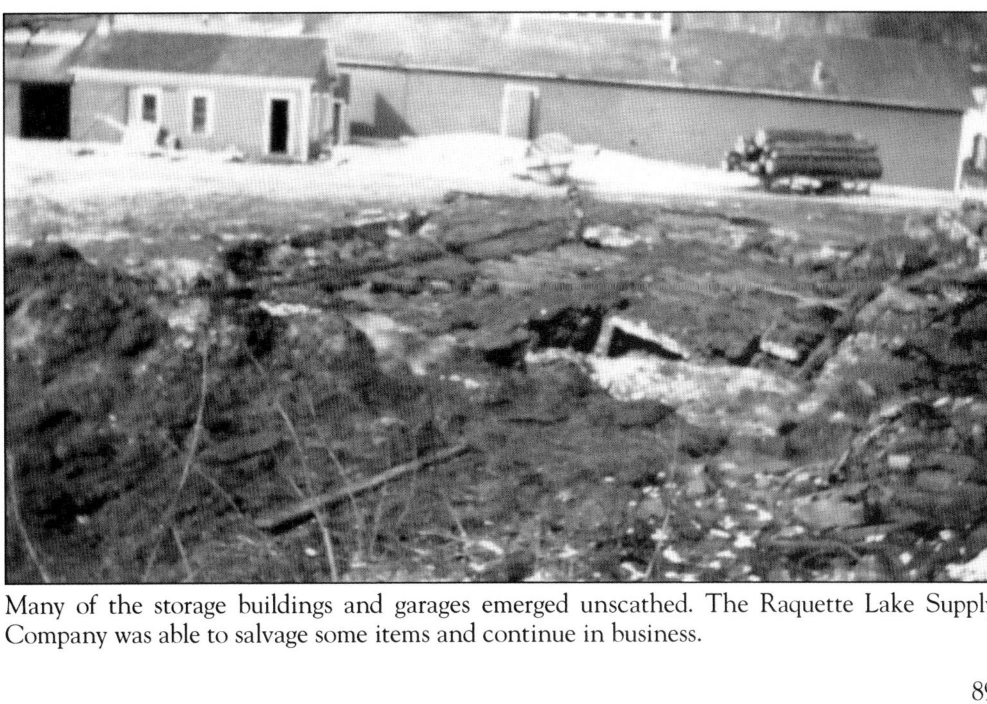

Many of the storage buildings and garages emerged unscathed. The Raquette Lake Supply Company was able to salvage some items and continue in business.

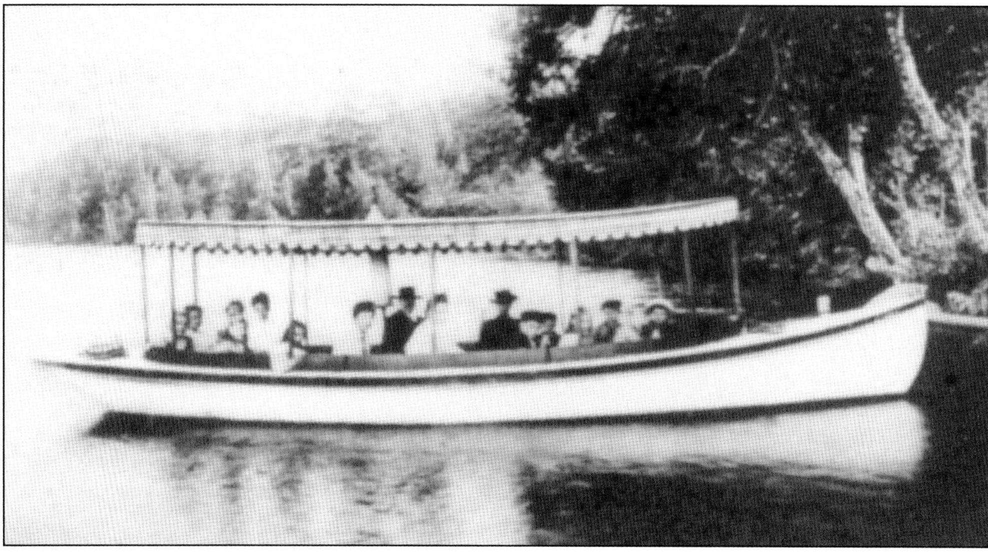

The first school in Raquette Lake was located in the original village on Long Point. When water was open, a rowboat made its rounds to collect the children. Around 1905, the rowboat was replaced by a steam launch.

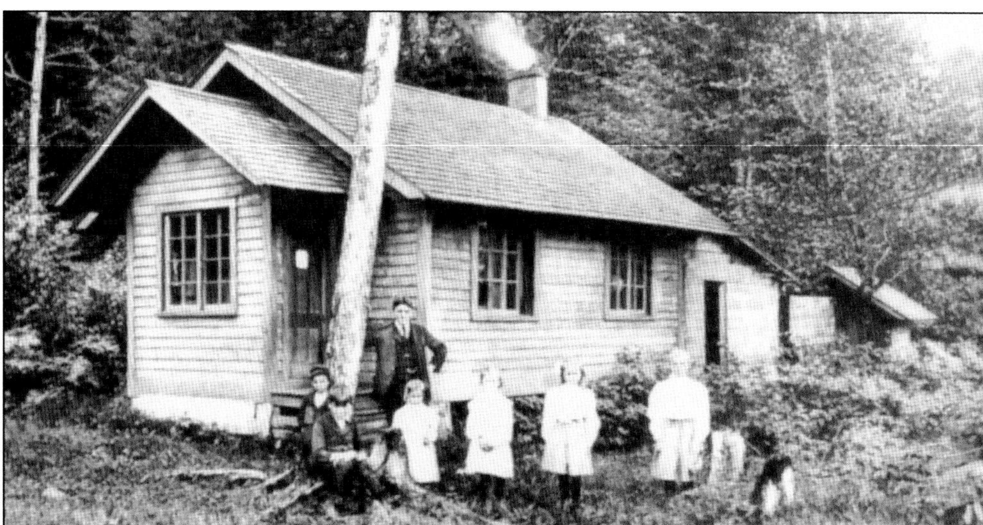

The one-room schoolhouse on Long Point was heated by wood and had an outhouse in back. Usually one student was chosen to make sure the school was always warm with a good fire.

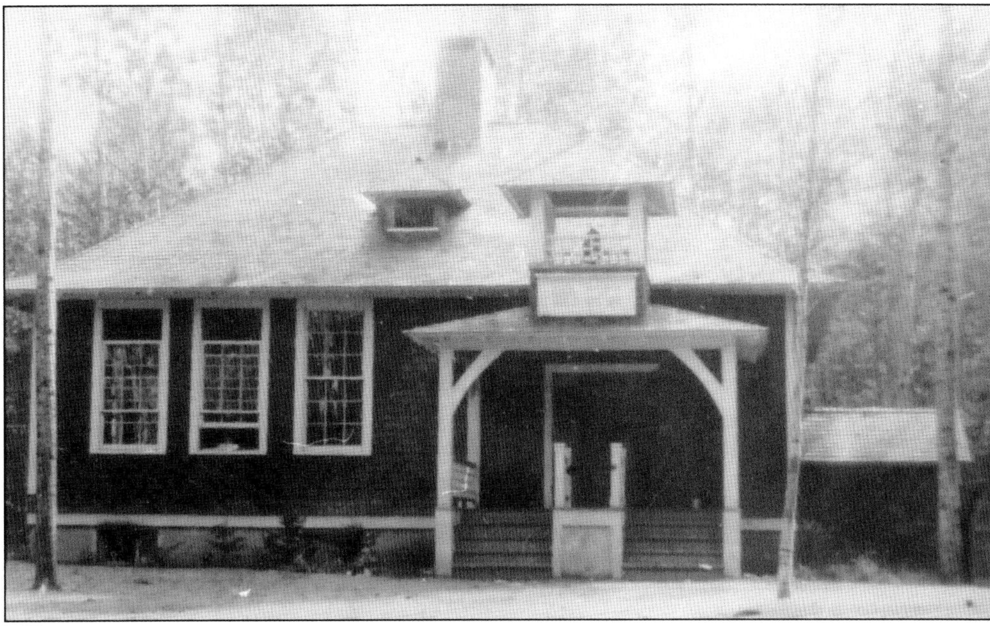

The second school was built at its current location in 1911. It was necessary for the schoolchildren to walk from the village across a wooden bridge to school. This bridge was also used as a connection to Great Camps Sagamore, Uncas, and Kill Kare.

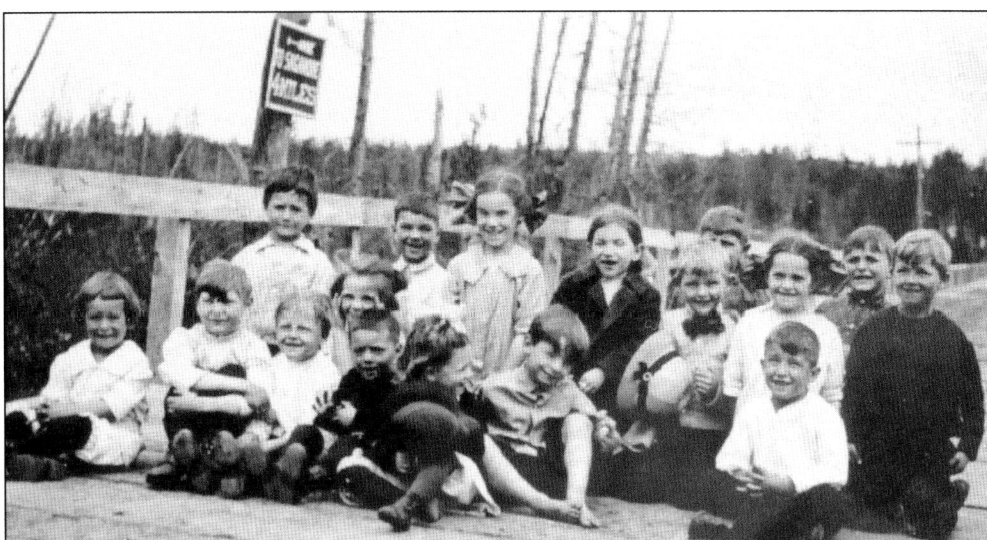

The sizes of school classes depended on the number of workers employed around the area, as well as the year-round people. There was no dress code. Mode of dress depended on what families could afford. The youngsters on the bridge are near the school and only four miles from Great Camp Sagamore (note the sign).

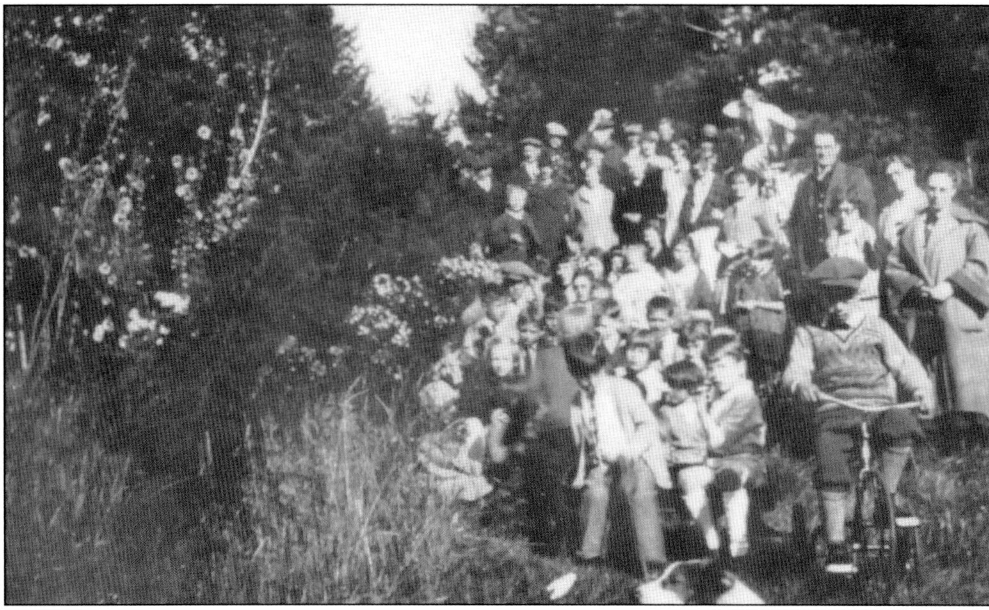

As the size of families grew, so did the need for increasing the size of the school. This grouping shows students, teachers, and some parents on an outing away from the school.

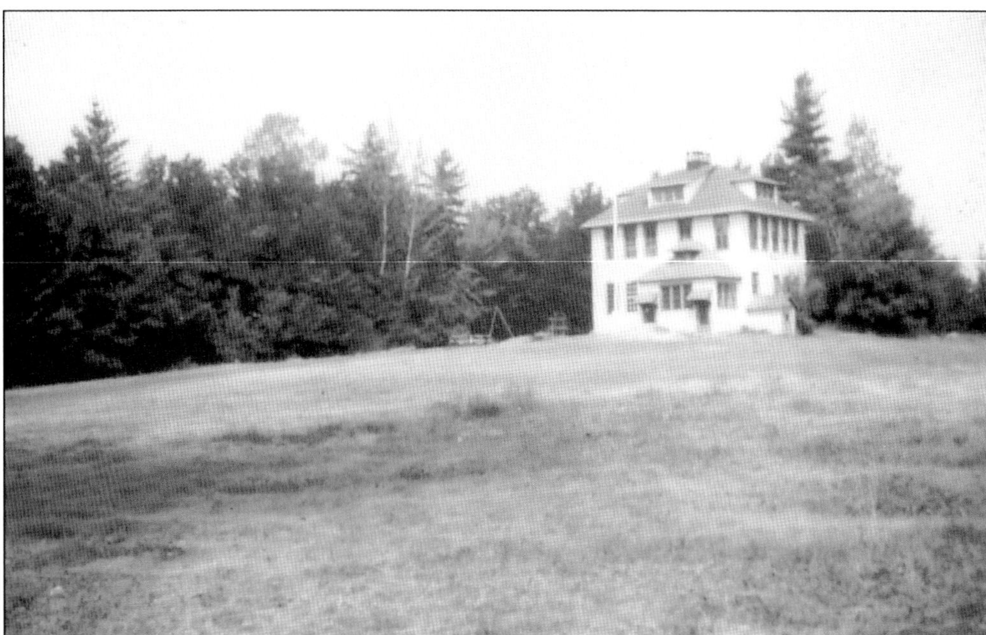

In 1915, the school was expanded with a second story. The school had a playground on the left and a sports field in the foreground. It remained in this form until it was rebuilt in 1973.

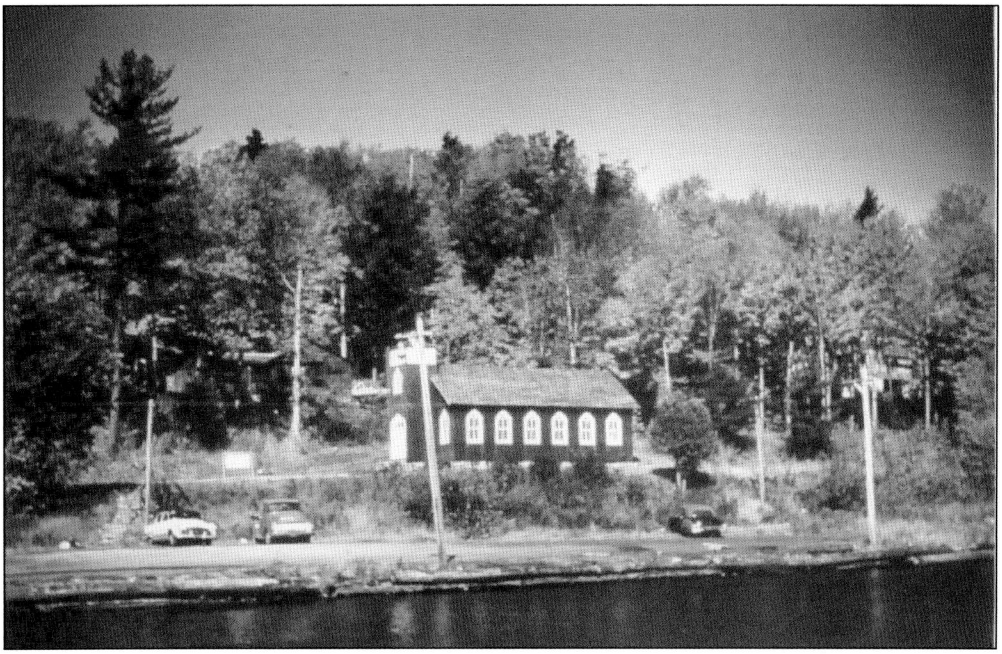

When the village moved from Long Point to its current location, there was a need to establish a place for Protestant worship. Some parents even went so far as to send their children to Catholic church on Sundays because of the convenience of having a new St. Williams at the new village. With a contribution of property from the Huntington family and funding from Dr. Samuel Evans of Tioga, a Protestant chapel was built and dedicated by 1927 on the site of the old railway siding.

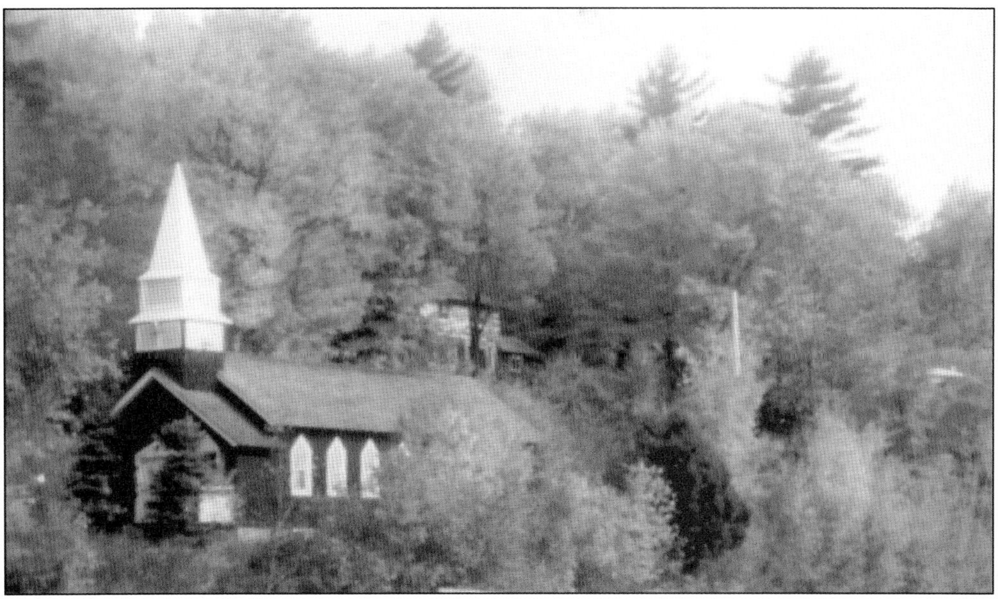

Over the years, many improvements have been made to the little church. The building was remodeled around 1959. Wiring was updated. Chandeliers from the Antlers dining hall were installed to light the center aisle. Around 1967, the chapel was again enlarged, and a steeple was added in 1968.

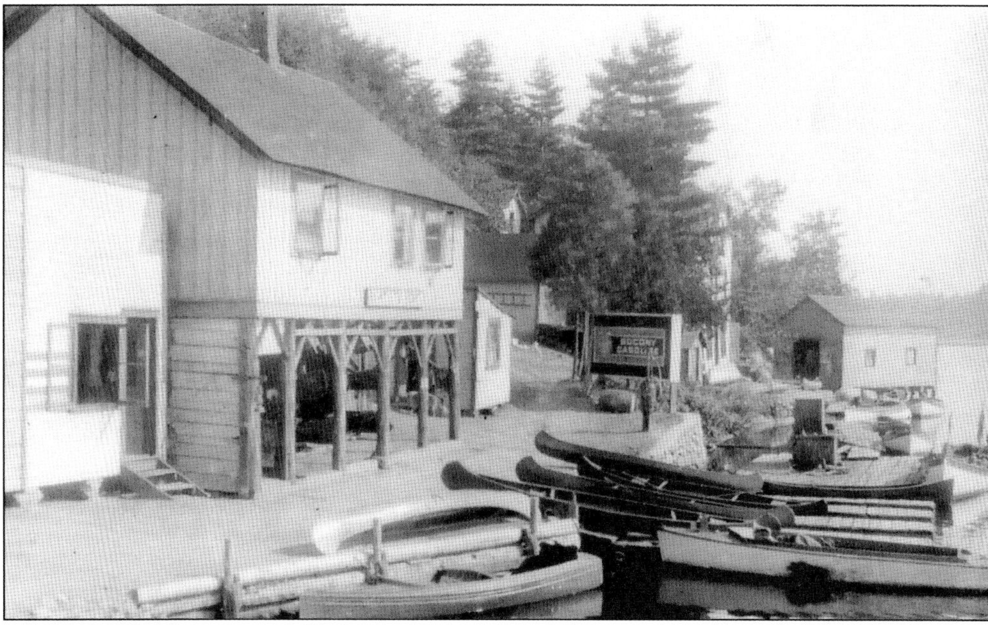

Finishing off the corner of the bay in town was Carlin's Boat Livery. In 1900, Frank Carlin established a boat transportation business in the village. Here he erected a large building that was to double as a repair outlet and living quarters. Later other buildings were added, as boats were propelled by other means but still required service and fuel.

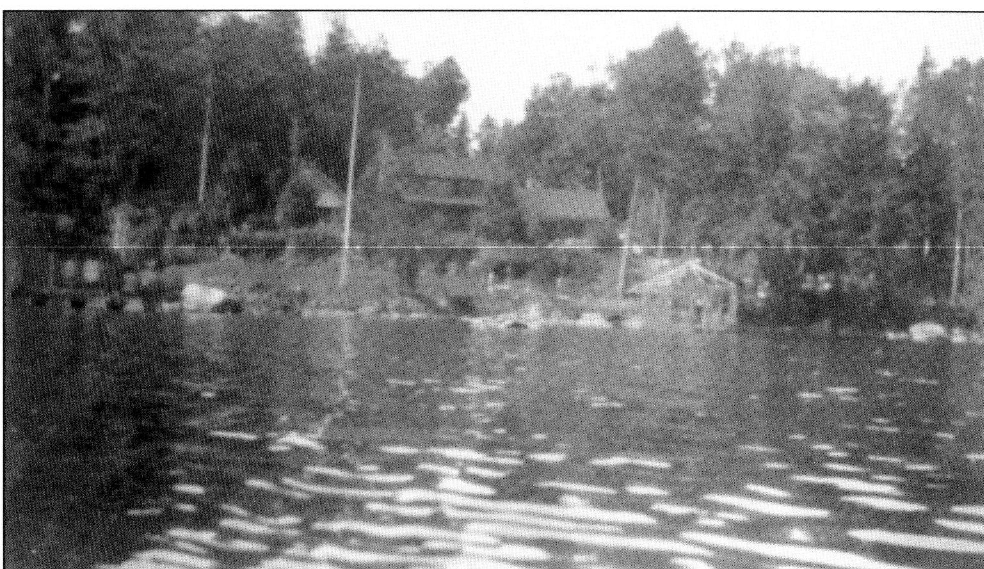

Up the shore from Carlin's is a plot of land originally bought by John Golding, a real estate man who built his camp here. Upon Golding's death, George Whelan bought the property. The Whelans established a summer home here and occasionally entertained friends such as the William Randolph Hearst family of newspaper fame.

Four

The Great Camps

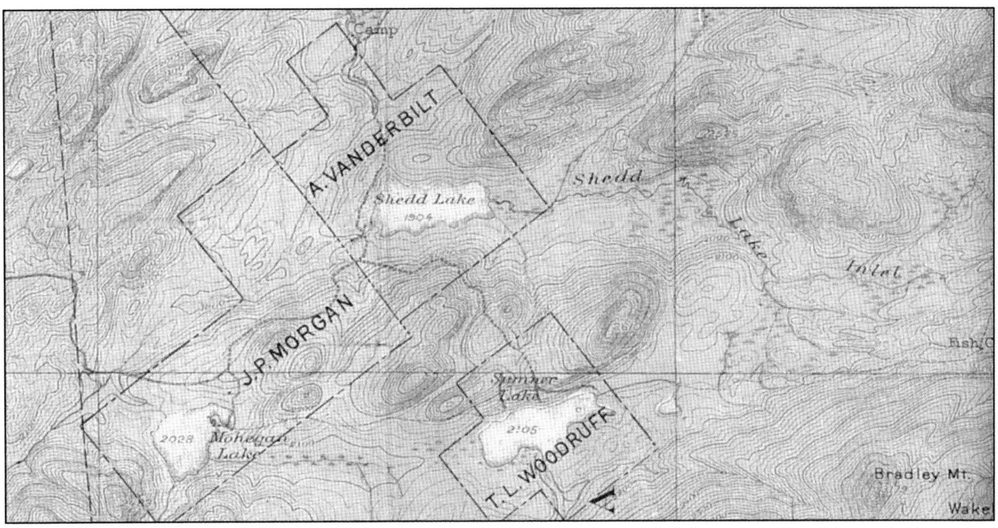

This map shows the lakes just to the south of Raquette—Mohegan, Shedd, and Stamner Lakes—where some of the great camps were built.

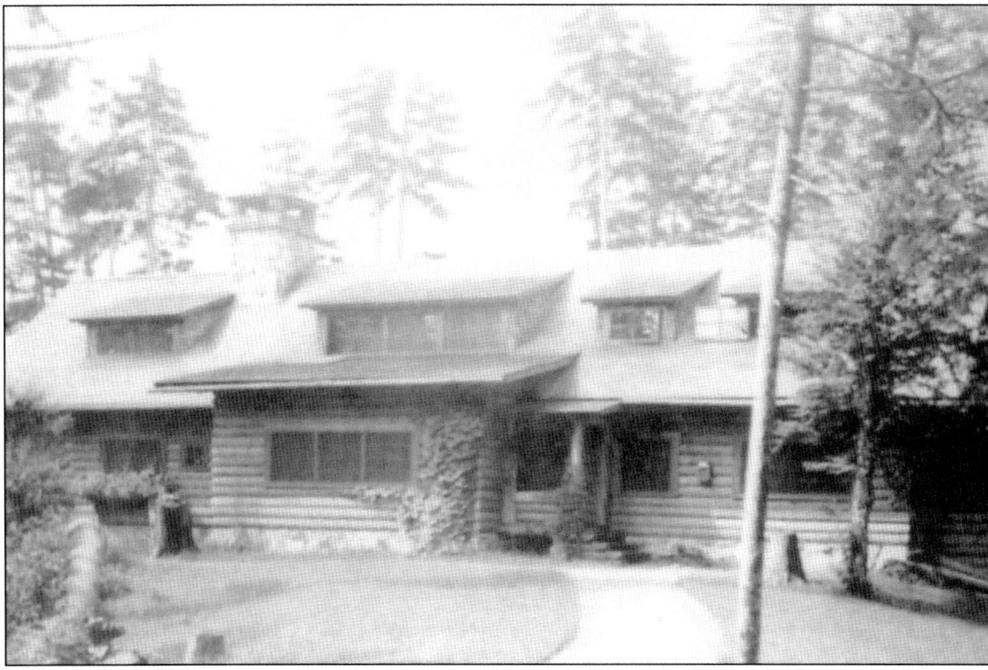

Among the properties owned by William West Durant was land south of Raquette Lake up in the woods. Between 1890 and 1892, he started to build a fabulous camp on the shore of Mohegan Lake. Here Great Camp Uncas was formed. Again the structures were of log design. Pictured is the main house.

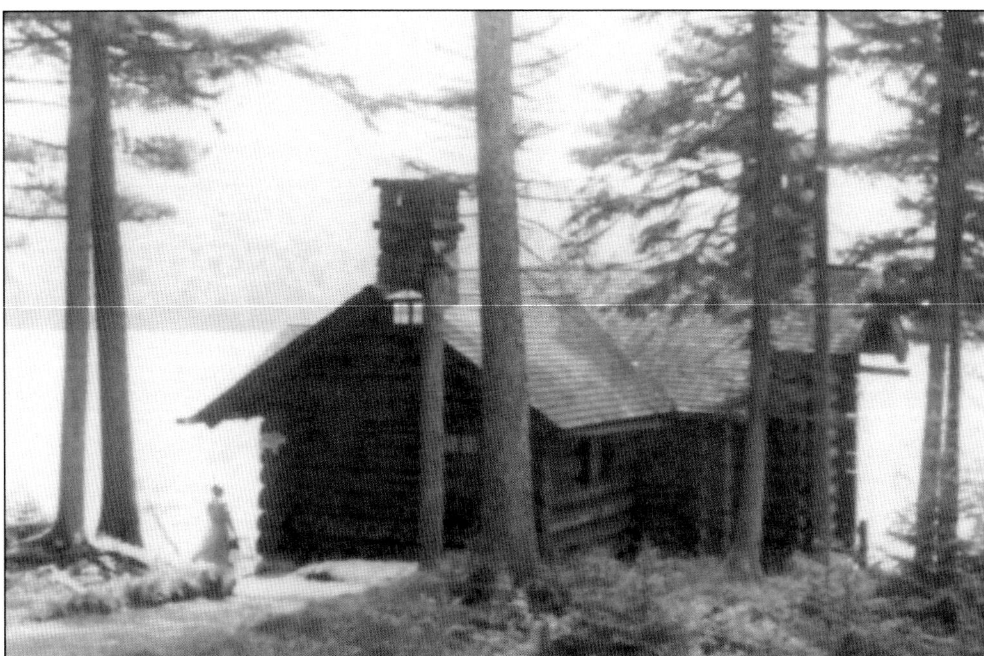

Durant's guests could choose from staying in the main house or in one of the outbuildings, also located along the shoreline. This picturesque cottage on the shore near the main house was called Chingachgook.

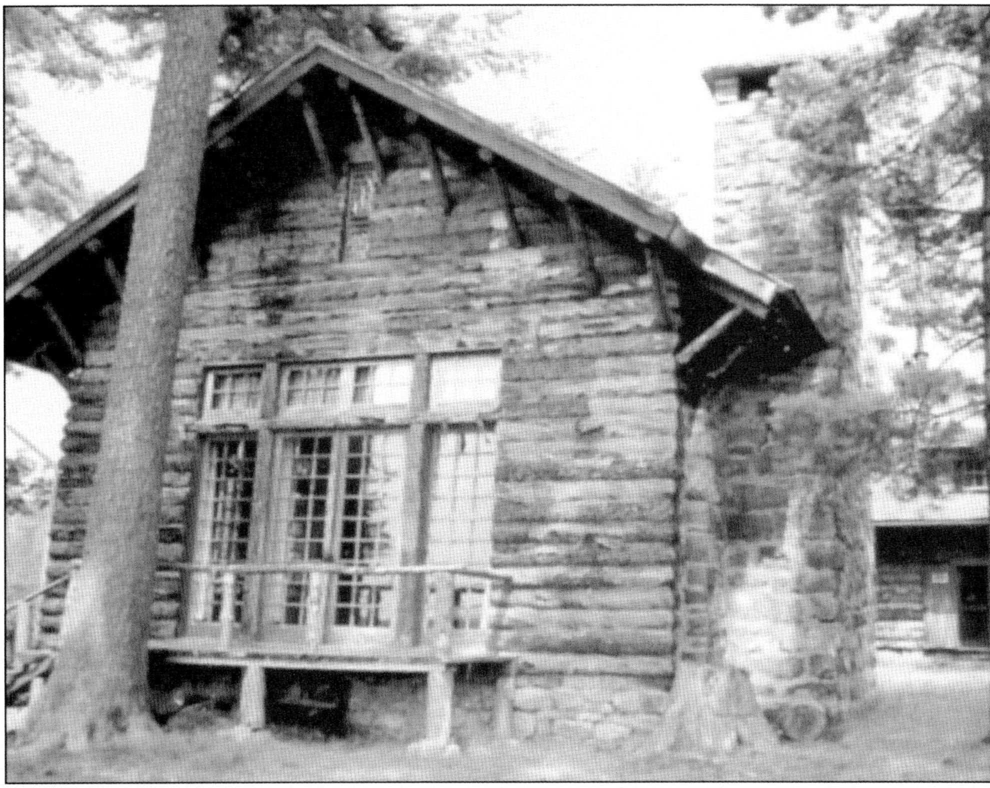

A separate dining hall overlooked Mohegan Lake. Modified French doors afforded a spectacular view of the lake.

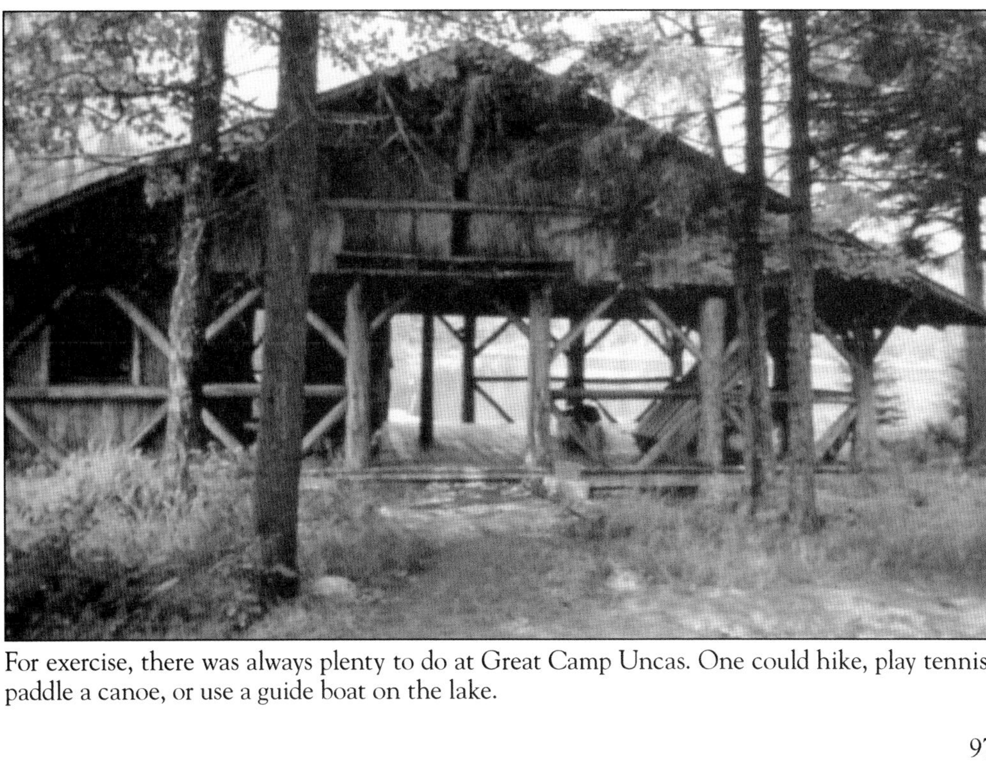

For exercise, there was always plenty to do at Great Camp Uncas. One could hike, play tennis, paddle a canoe, or use a guide boat on the lake.

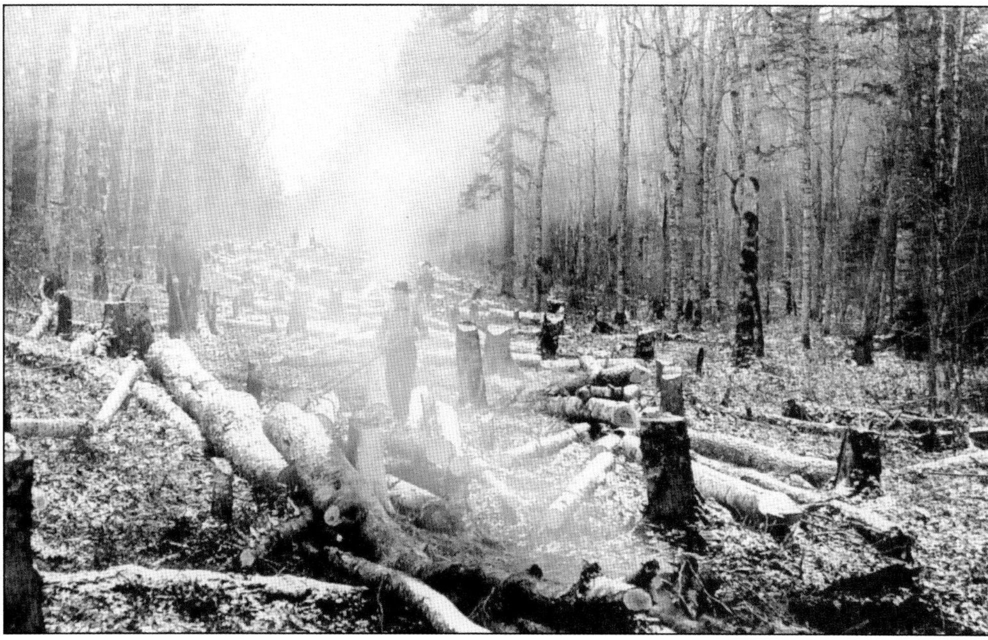

Because Route 28 was not yet built, William West Durant had Mohegan Road built to his Mohegan Lake. Today the average worker probably could not imagine attempting a task like this. The first step was to cut down the trees and burn the brush.

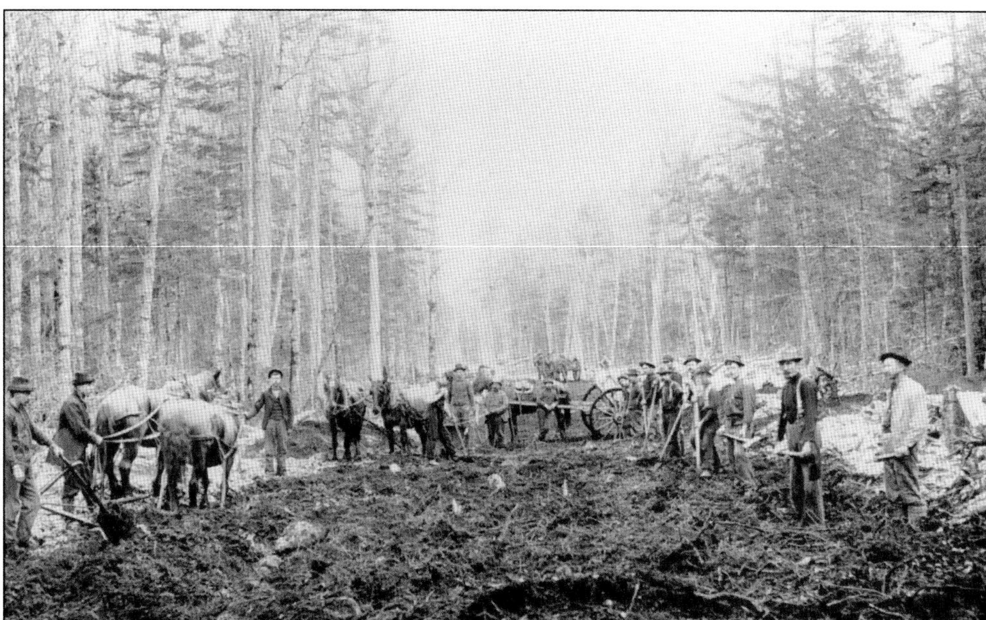

Once the trees and brush were out of the way, the roadway had to be cleared of roots and rocks before it could be smoothed.

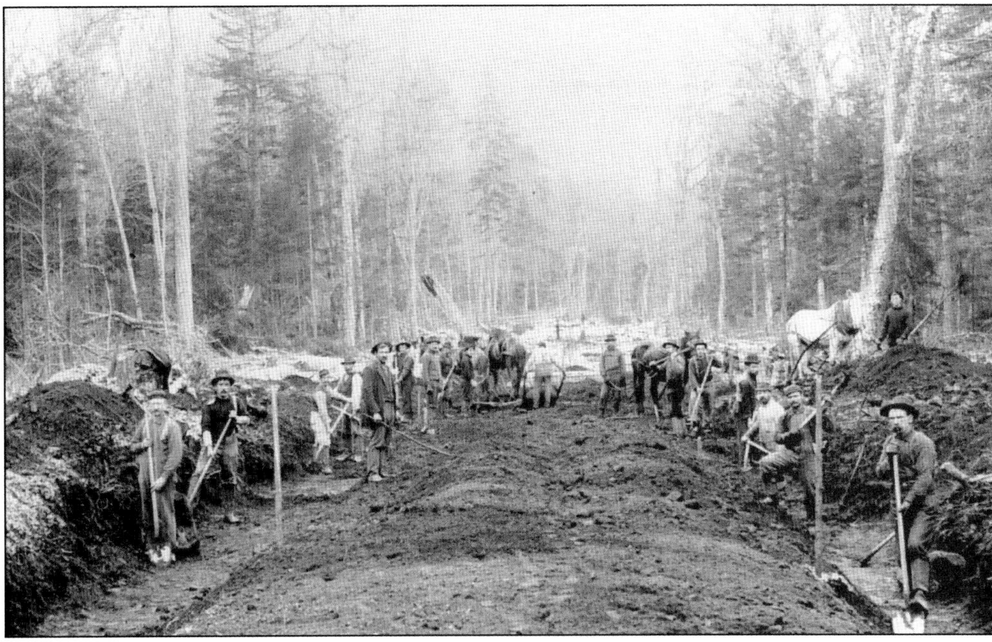

The roadway was then cleared and crowned, and drainage was dug along each side.

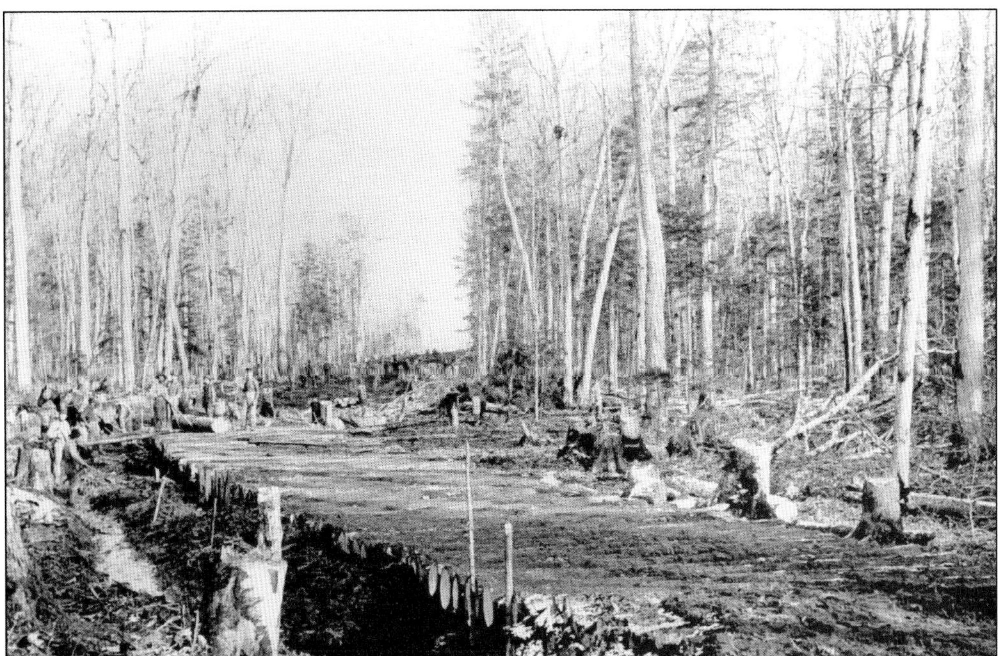

In poor soil areas, the trees that were cut down to make the road were used as a log base structure for the new road.

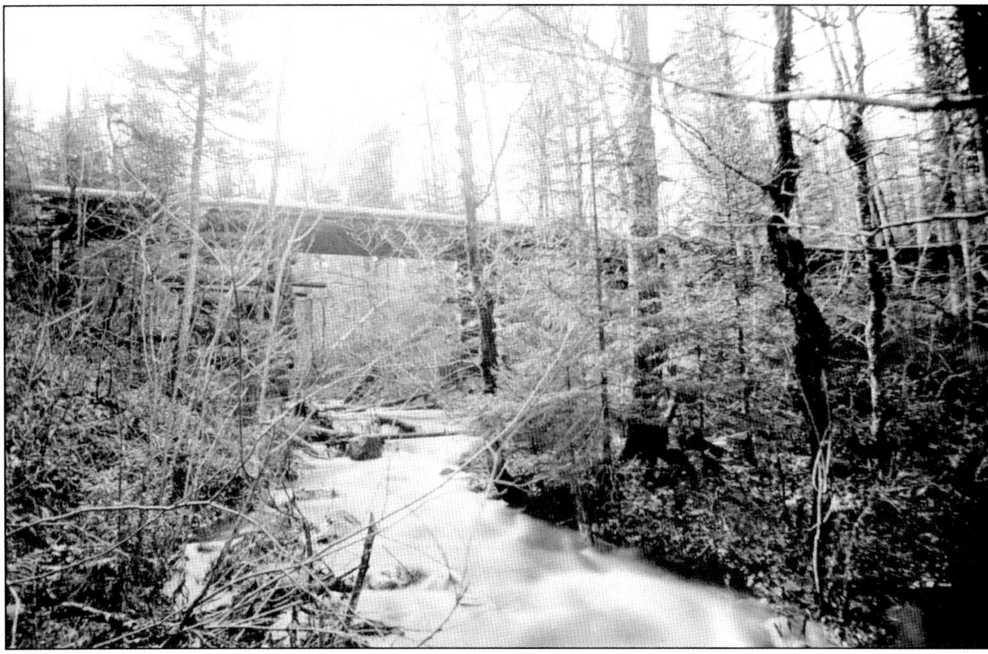

Where water was involved, bridges had to be built to go over streams.

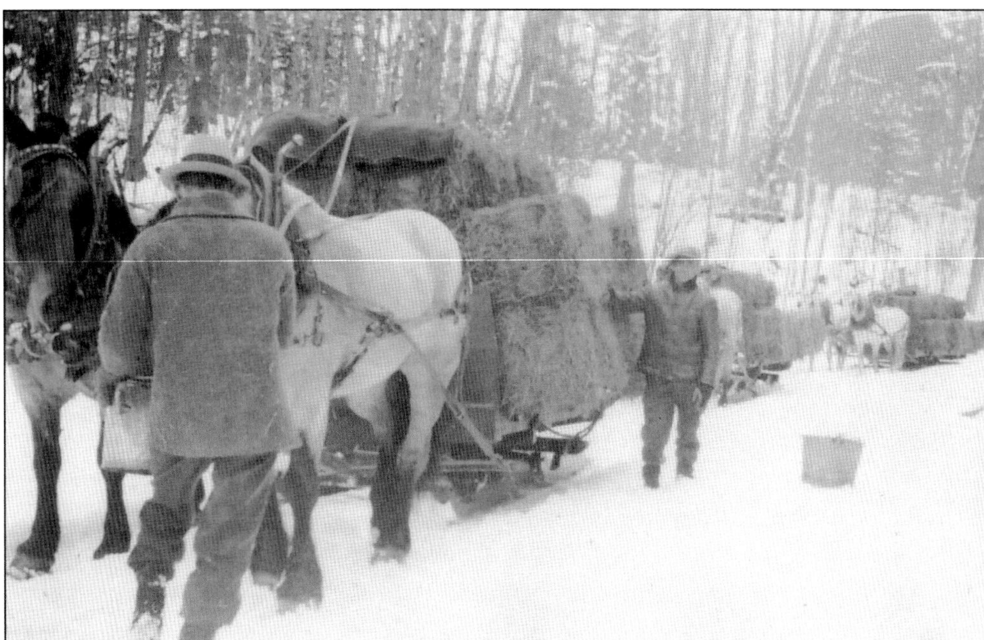

During this time, work supplies and food had to be refilled, not only for the men but for their teams of horses too.

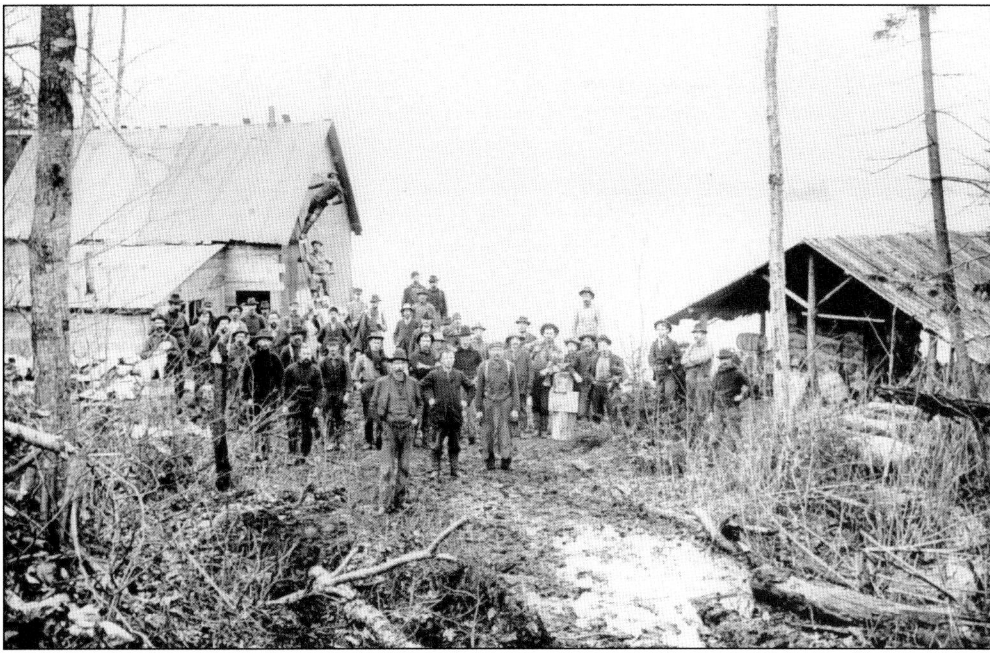

In several locations of the project, work teams had to live on site to make sure progress was ongoing.

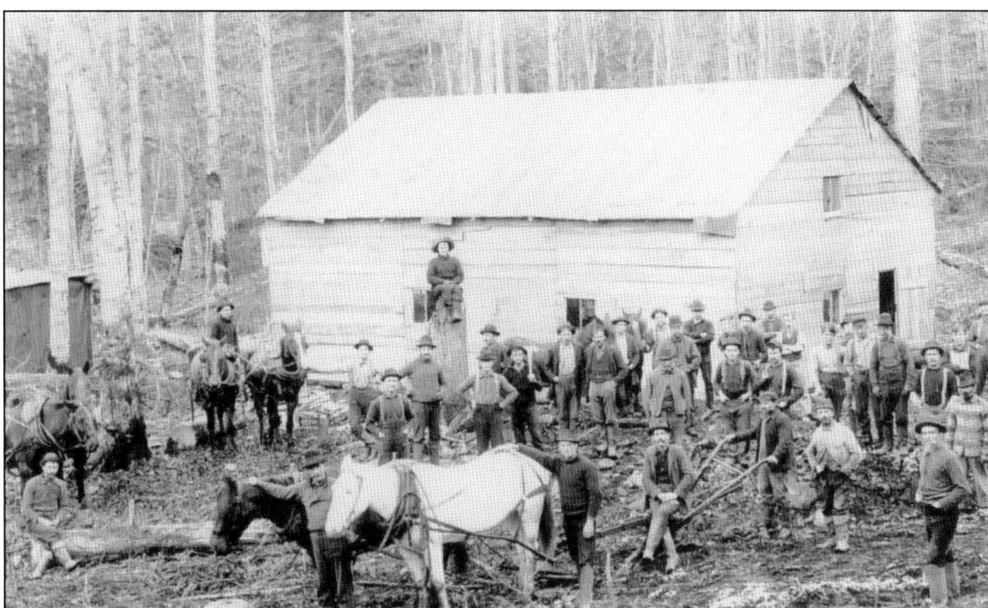

As the work teams moved closer to Great Camp Uncas, work shacks were left behind as rest stops for the upcoming travelers.

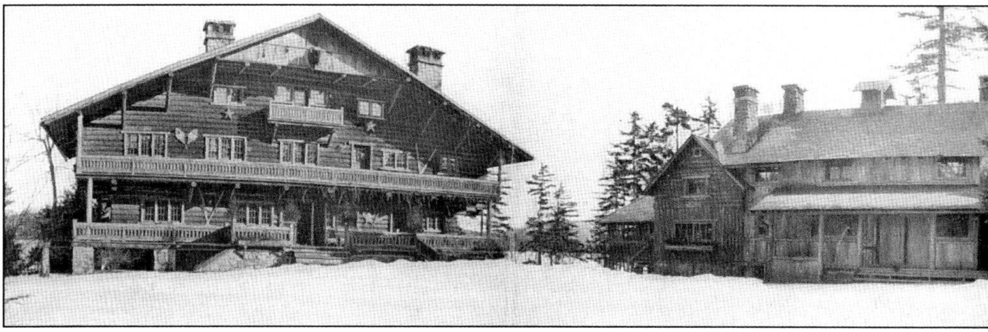

In 1897, William West Durant sold Great Camp Uncas to financier J. P. Morgan and moved to Shedd Lake, where he was building Great Camp Sagamore. This panoramic shot shows the main house and dining hall.

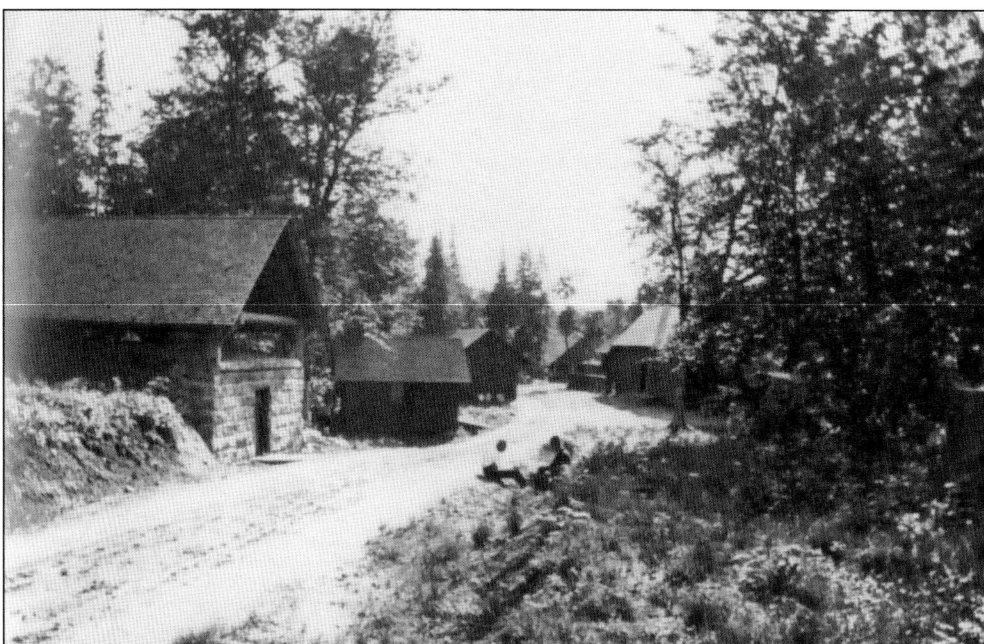

Typical of Durant's great camps, Great Camp Sagamore had many faces. It had a main house, kitchen, dining room, laundry, and game room to mention a few. This shot shows service buildings, which compromise a root cellar, blacksmith shop, and caretaker's house.

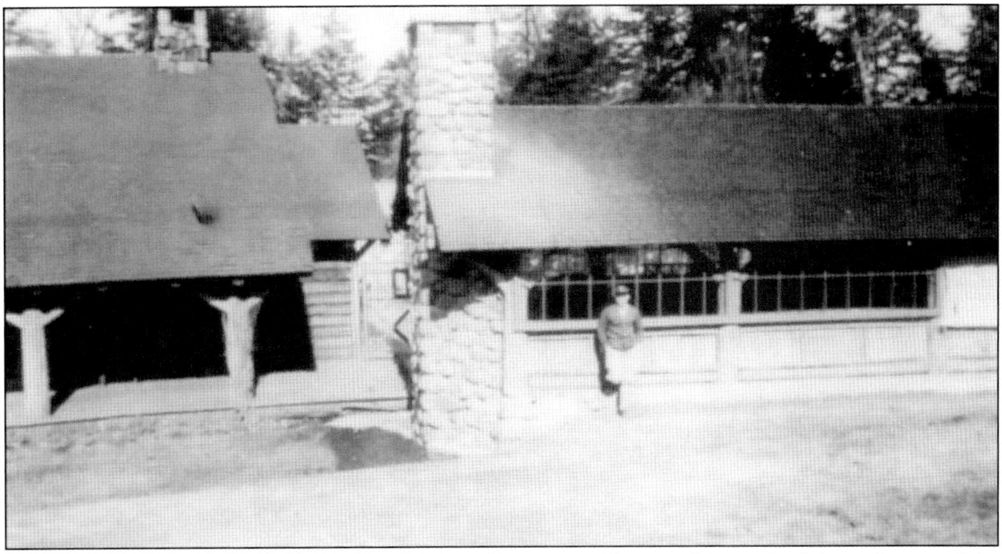

Many pastimes were available at Great Camp Sagamore. One could use the lake to boat or fish, take a hike around the lake, or pass the time away in the game room.

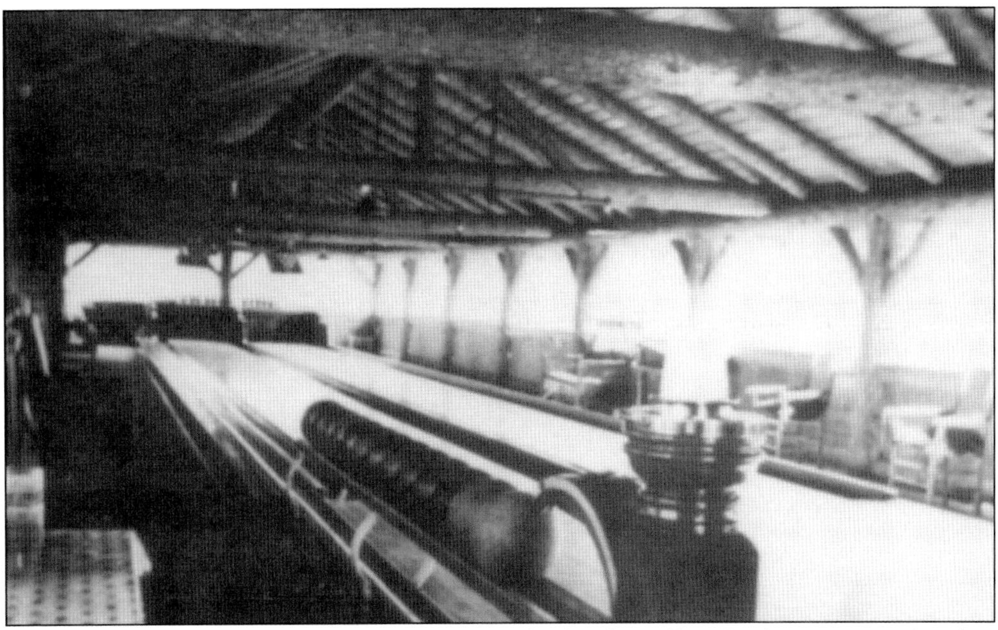

The most noted activity in the game room was the bowling alley. Workers were employed to reset the pins for the bowling guests.

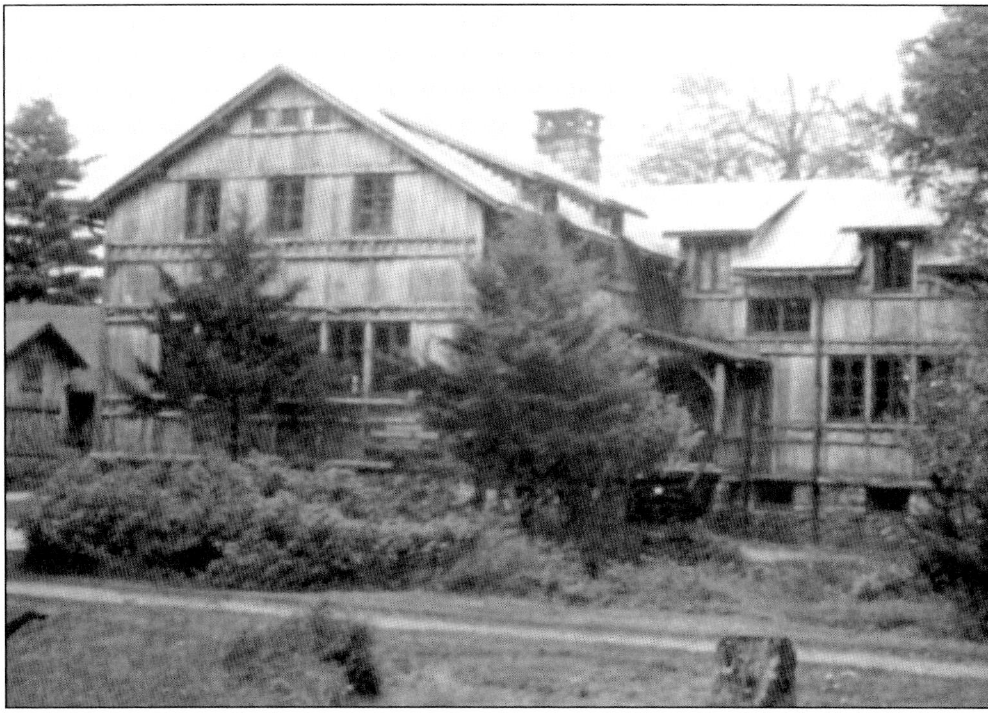

While at Great Camp Sagamore, guests did not have to wash their own clothes. A new laundry took care of washing and drying the visitors' clothes.

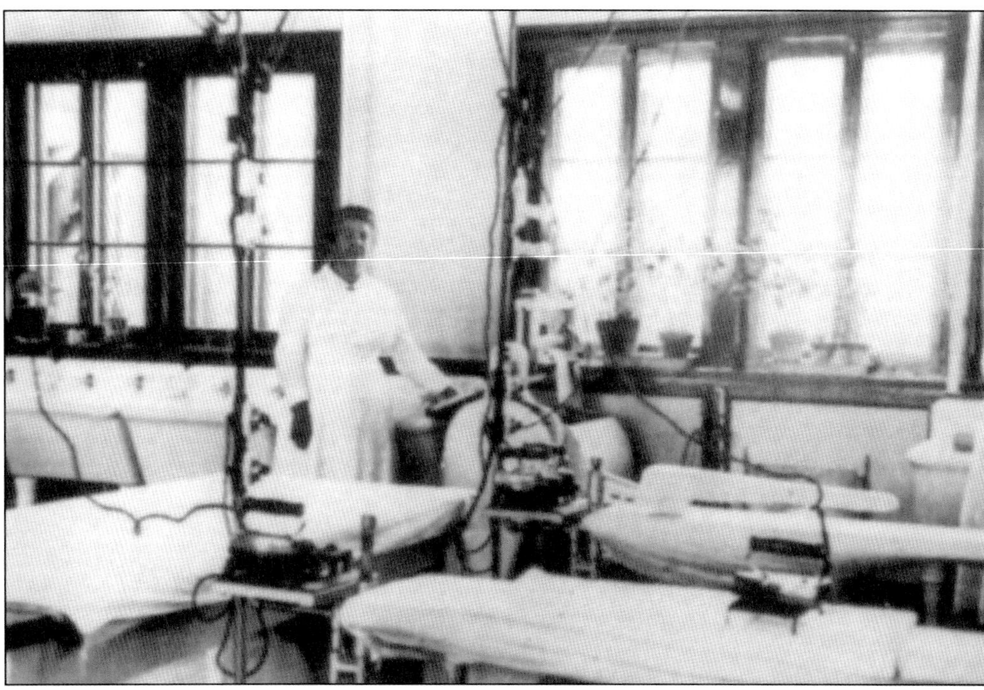

There was even a staff member to take care of the finishing touches like ironing.

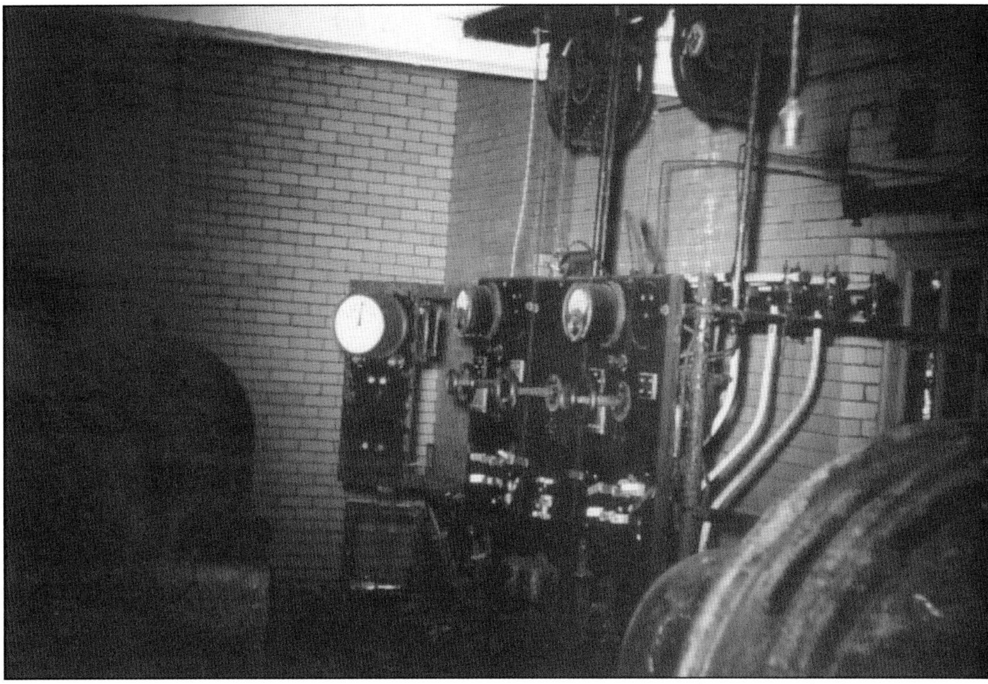

To handle the electrical needs of Great Camp Sagamore, a powerhouse was built on the south inlet of Raquette Lake.

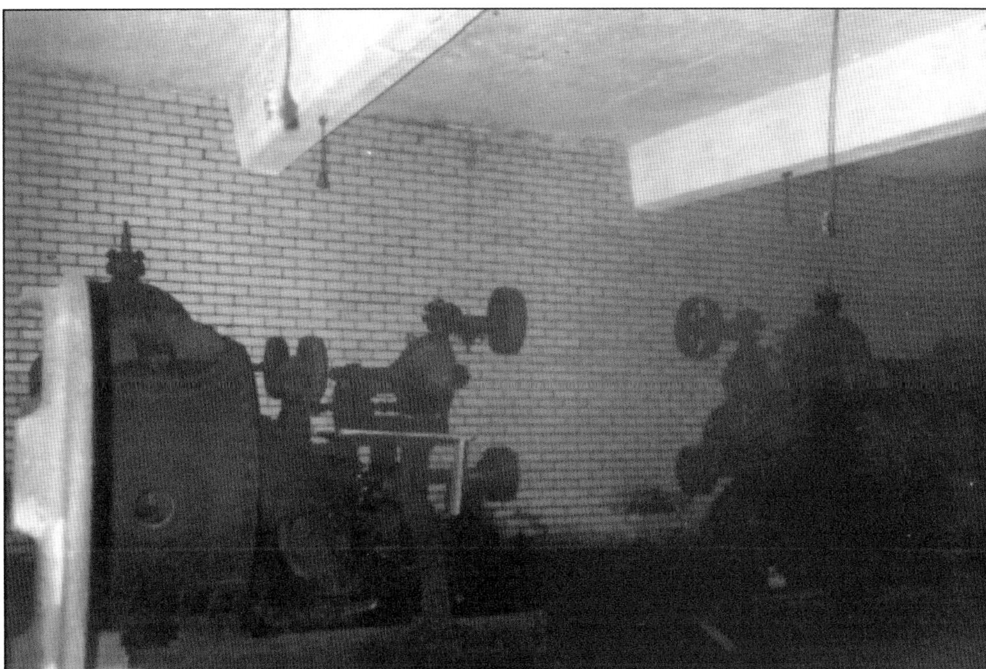

This direct-current powerhouse handled the entire needs of Great Camp Sagamore until it was replaced by a powerhouse closer to the estate.

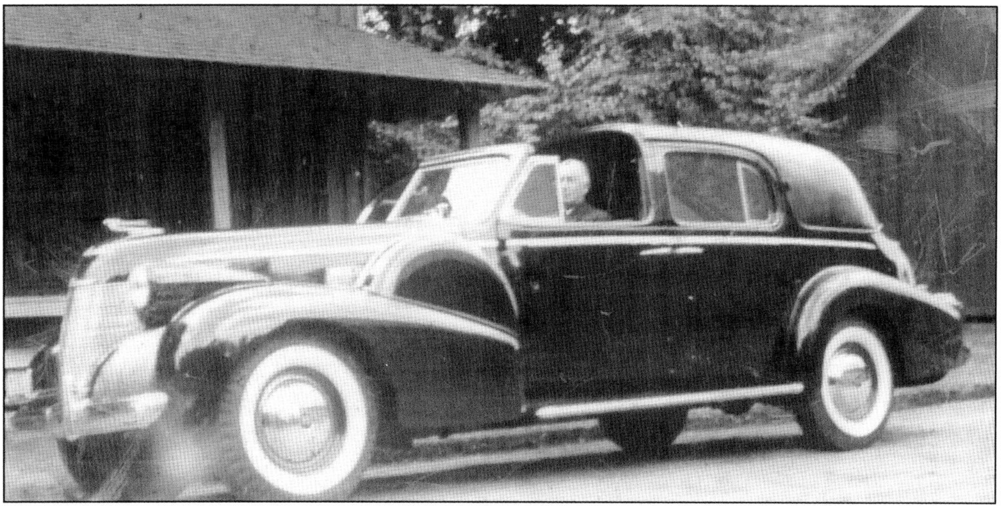

While building the great camps, William West Durant did not always sustain a profit. The expense of building Great Camp Sagamore finally made him move on in 1901 by selling it to sportsman Alfred Vanderbilt of the renowned Vanderbilt family. Vanderbilt and his wife frequently used Great Camp Sagamore for themselves and their guests.

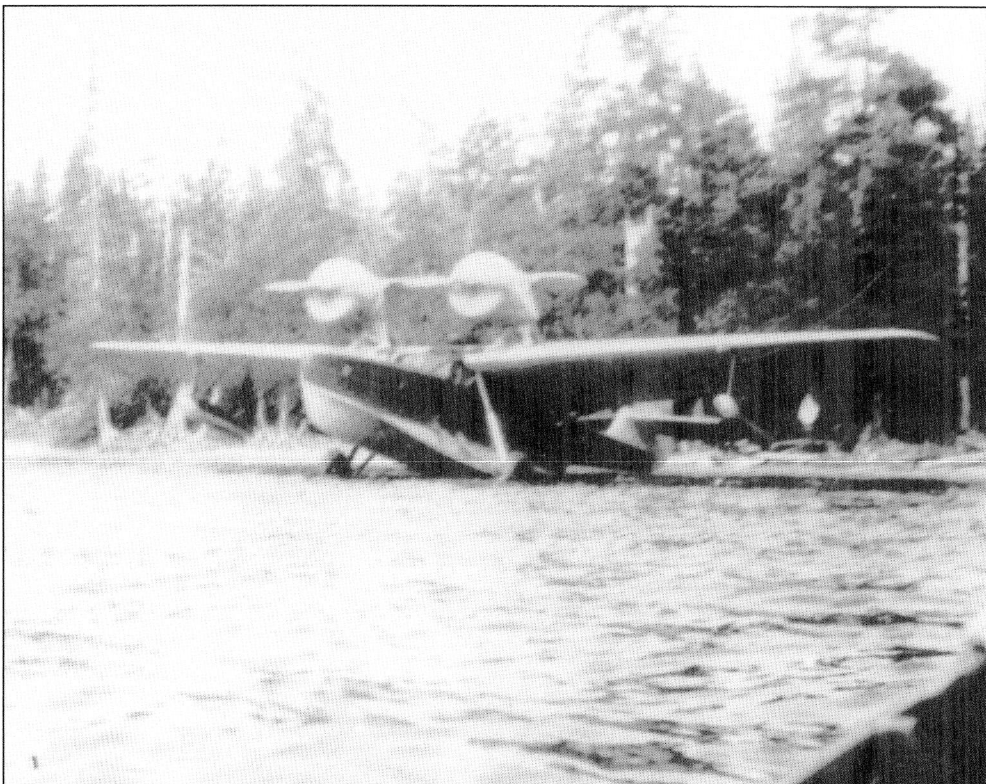

The Vanderbilt lifestyle was one of luxury, and Alfred Vanderbilt loved technology. The advent of airplanes and fancy automobiles became evident. Vanderbilt died aboard the *Lusitania* after it was torpedoed in May 1915. His widow, Margaret Emerson, continued to retain Great Camp Sagamore for year-round use.

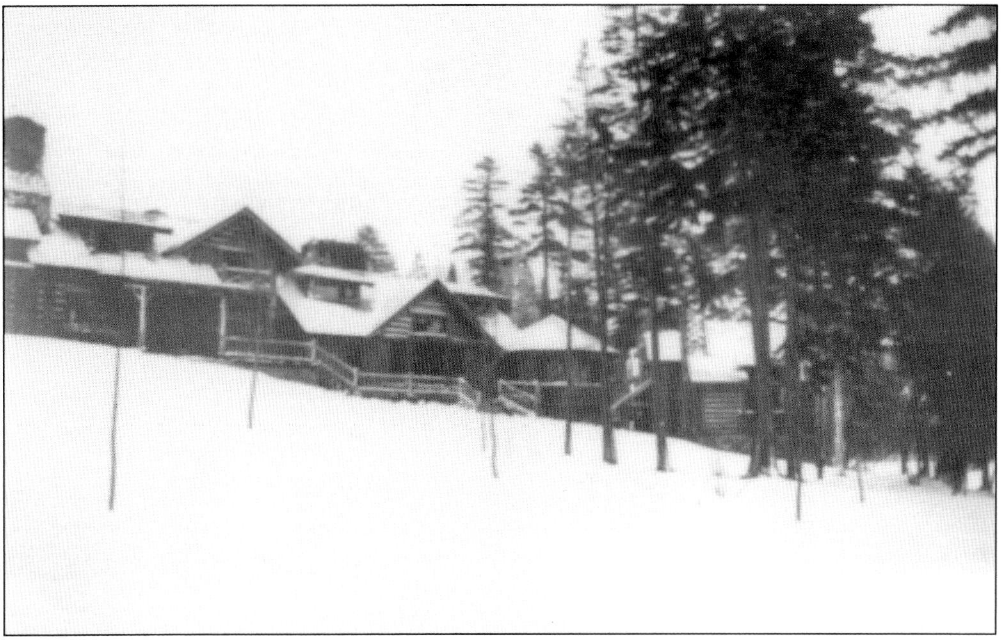

William West Durant had owned the property around Sumner Lake, but in 1898, to add to his cash flow, he sold the area to Lt. Gov. Timothy Woodruff, who erected Great Camp Kill Kare. The great camp theme was followed again, with log construction, stone fireplaces, and large porches. This winter view shows the main house complex.

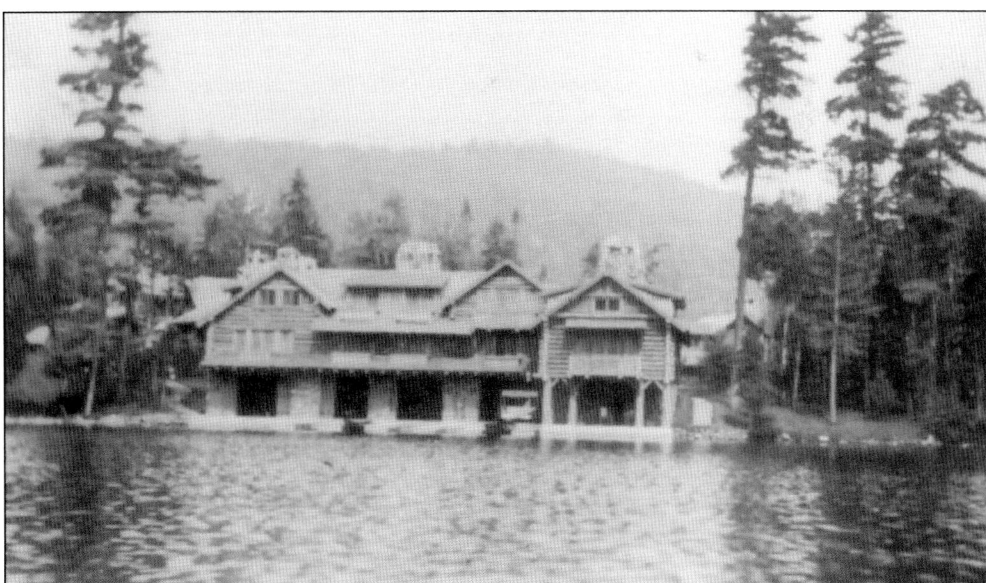

Down at the edge of the lake was a beautiful log boathouse. Lakeside were canoes and guide boats to use, and upstairs were more living quarters.

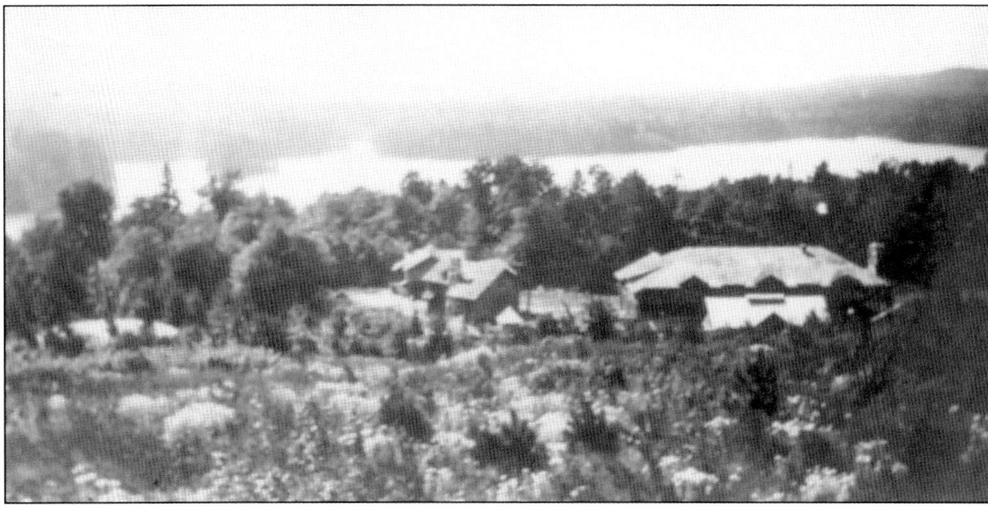

As with the other great camps, Great Camp Kill Kare had a farm complex. The most noted building was the barn, which had an elaborate tile floor. This view taken from a side hill shows the farm complex.

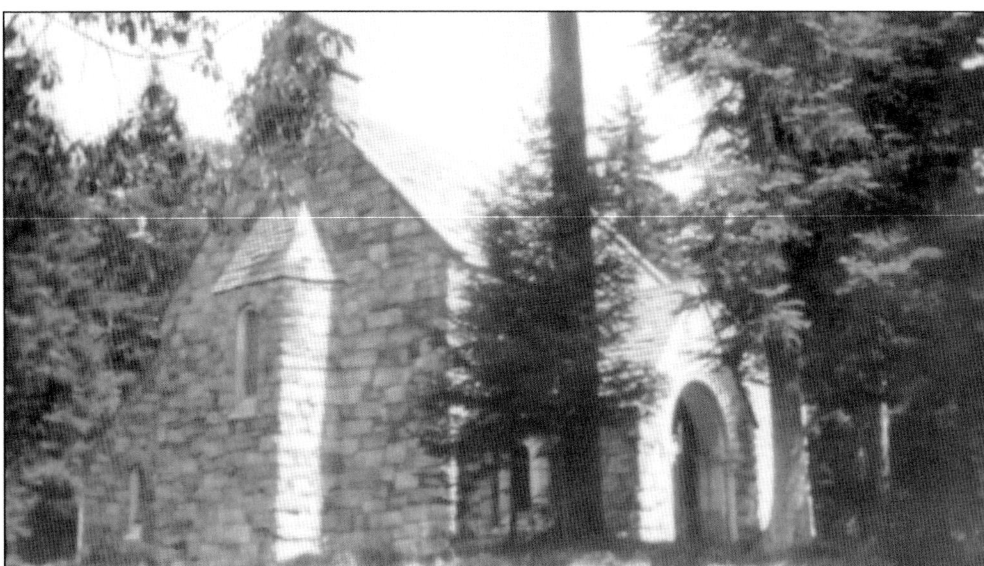

The Vanderbilts bought Great Camp Kill Kare in 1913 and in turn sold it to Francis P. Garvin. When the main camp was lost to fire, it was replaced by a structure of similar design. This photograph shows the stone chapel in which Mrs. Garvin received private mass.

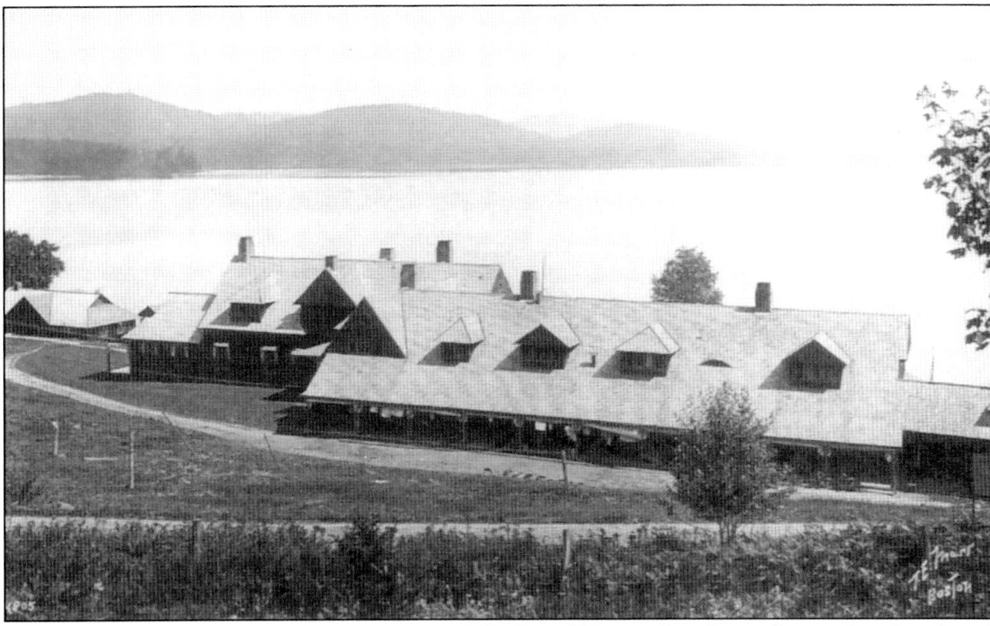

William Seward Webb was born in New York City. Educated to be a doctor, he abandoned his initial career, dabbled in Wall Street, and soon thereafter became president of the Wagner Palace Car Company. He remained at its helm until 1899, when it became part of the Pullman Car Company. By 1891, Webb had built a railway on his own property. He did not trespass on other lands and kept himself a plot of 40,000 acres. This was called Nehasane Park. His beautiful home, called Forest Lodge, was built on Lake Lila in 1893.

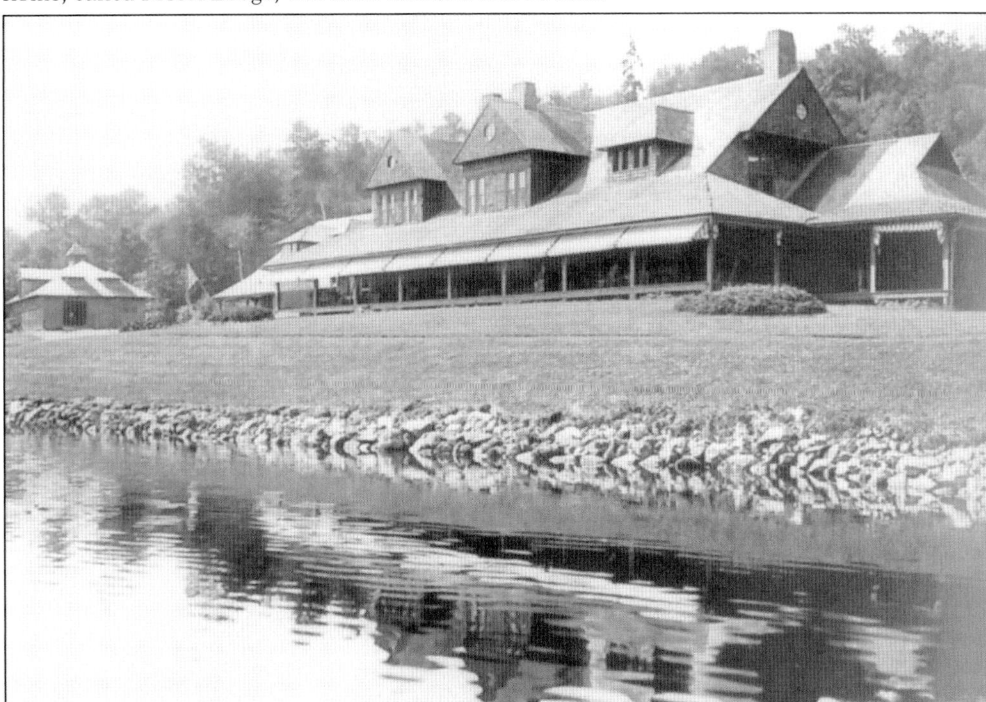

This was not just a home but a group of buildings along the shore with the complement of a staff.

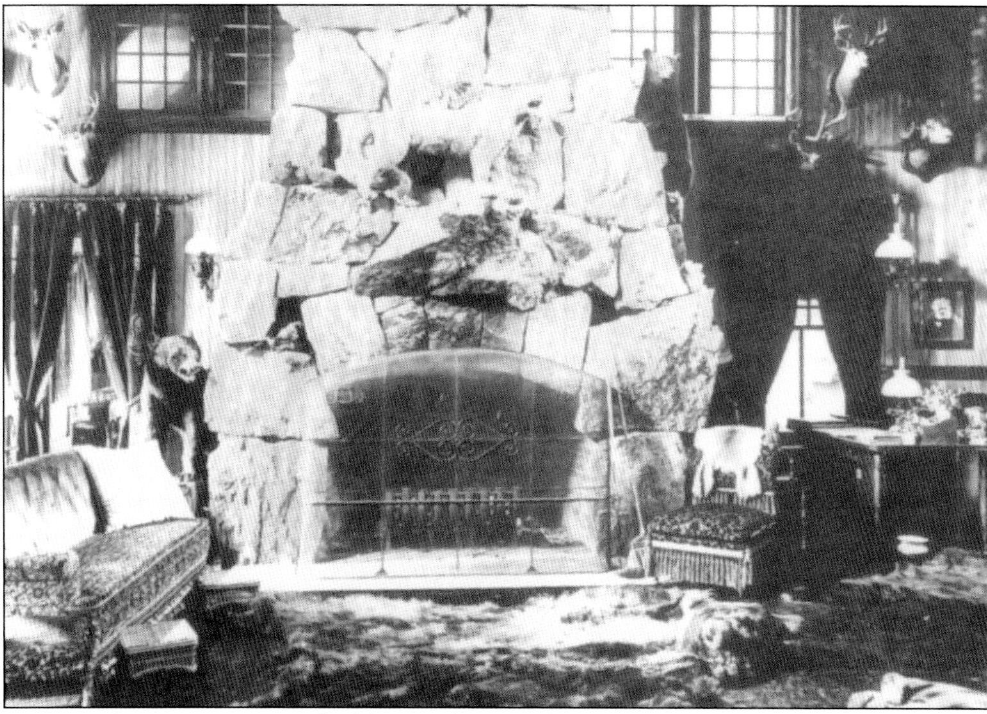

Forest Lodge was a majestic building with natural woods and stone fireplaces inside. The furniture, however, was not of the Adirondack style.

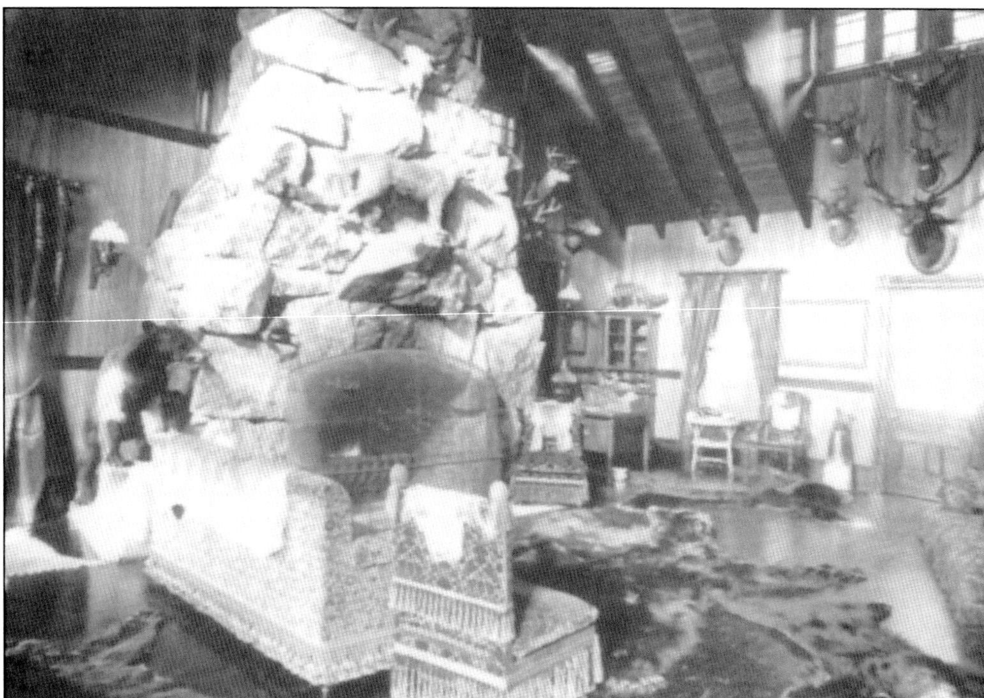

Numerous trophies were displayed around the house. A partial display is shown here around the fireplace.

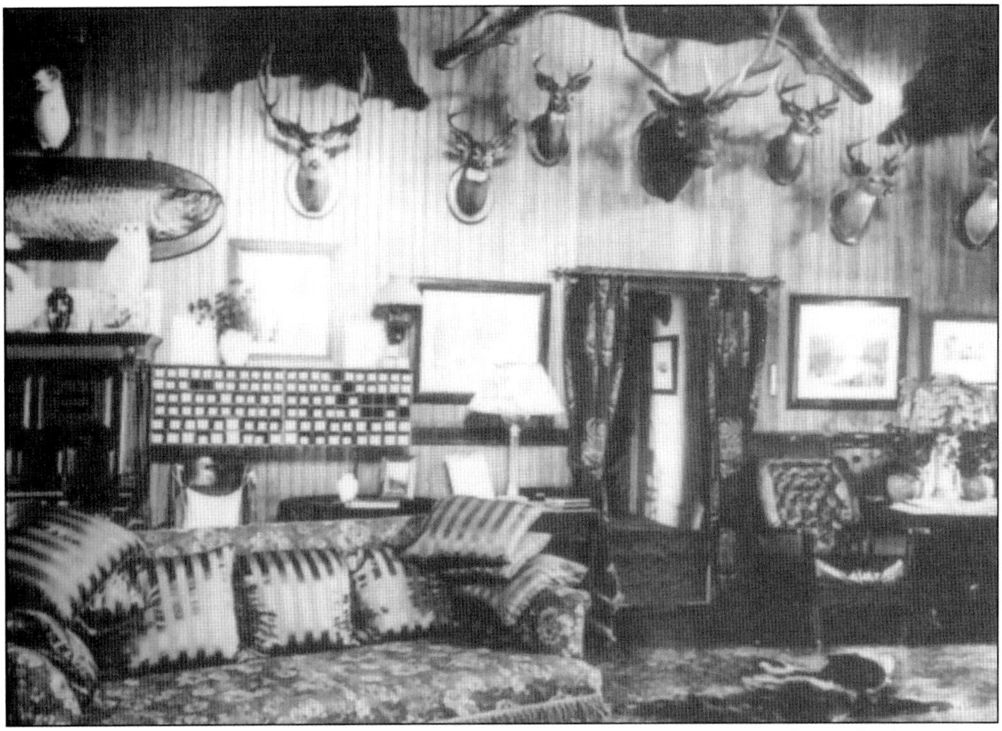

Besides the carpeting over hardwood floors, there were also bear rugs. On the walls throughout the home, a collection of local art and mounted fish hung.

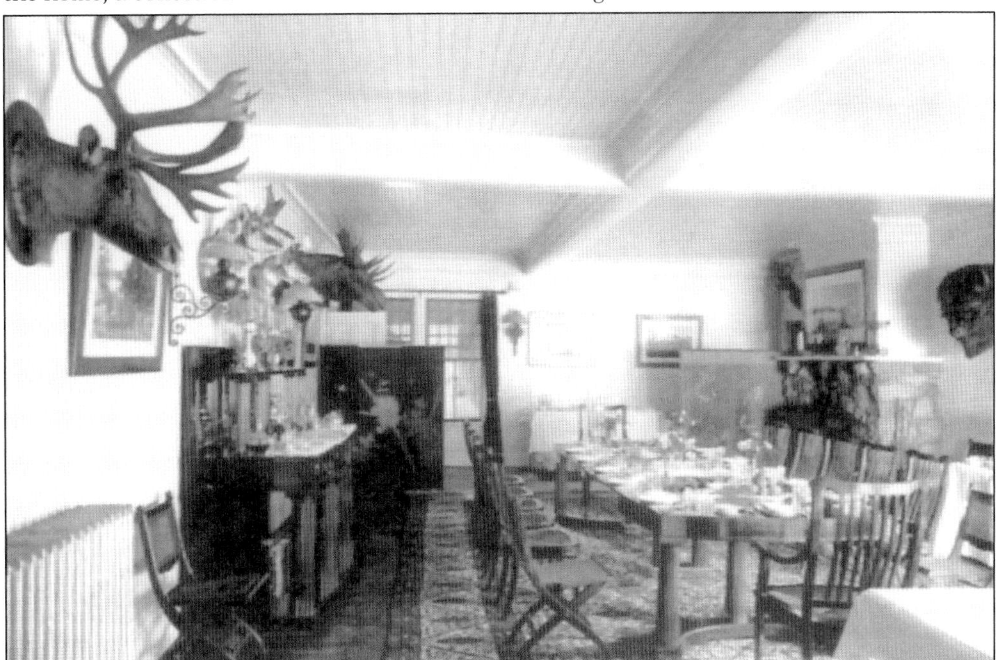

Because of the constant array of guests, the dining room could normally seat 14 people. The staff not only cooked and cleaned but also did laundry. In the basement were steam drying rooms that dried laundry.

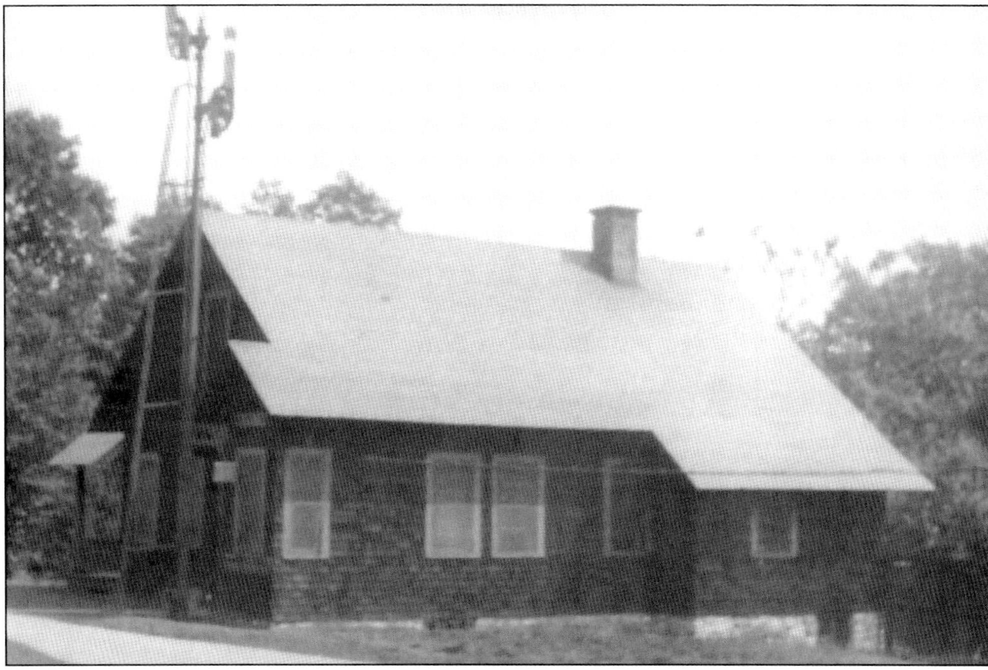

At first the railway station at Nehasane Park served William Seward Webb's lumber business and was a stopover for people coming and going.

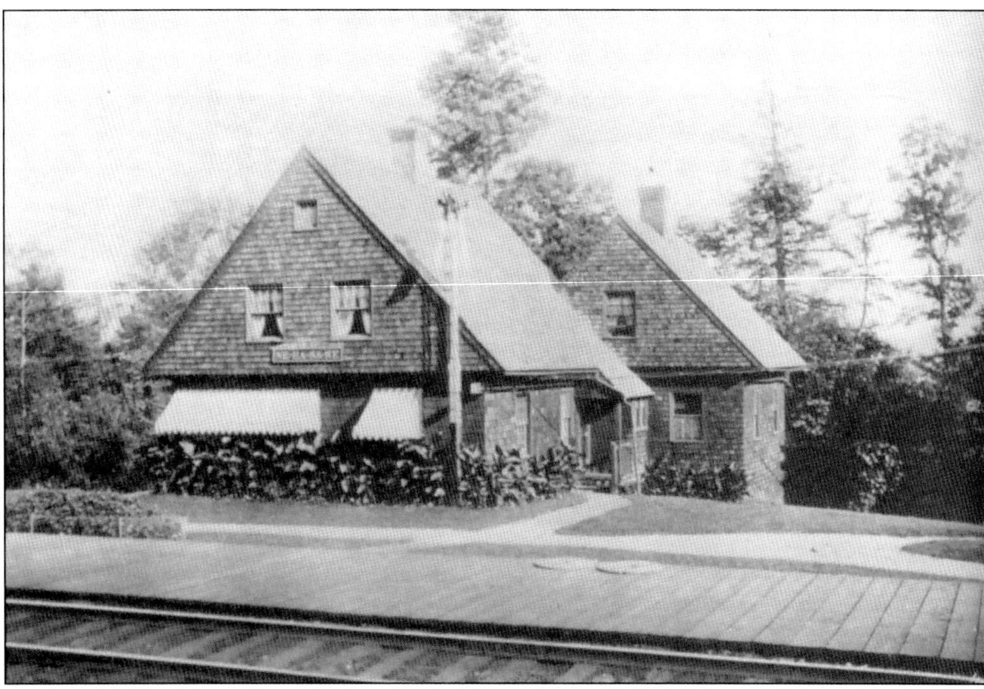

Soon, however, the grandeur of the main house spread its decor to the depot. People arriving at Forest Lodge truly knew they had arrived.

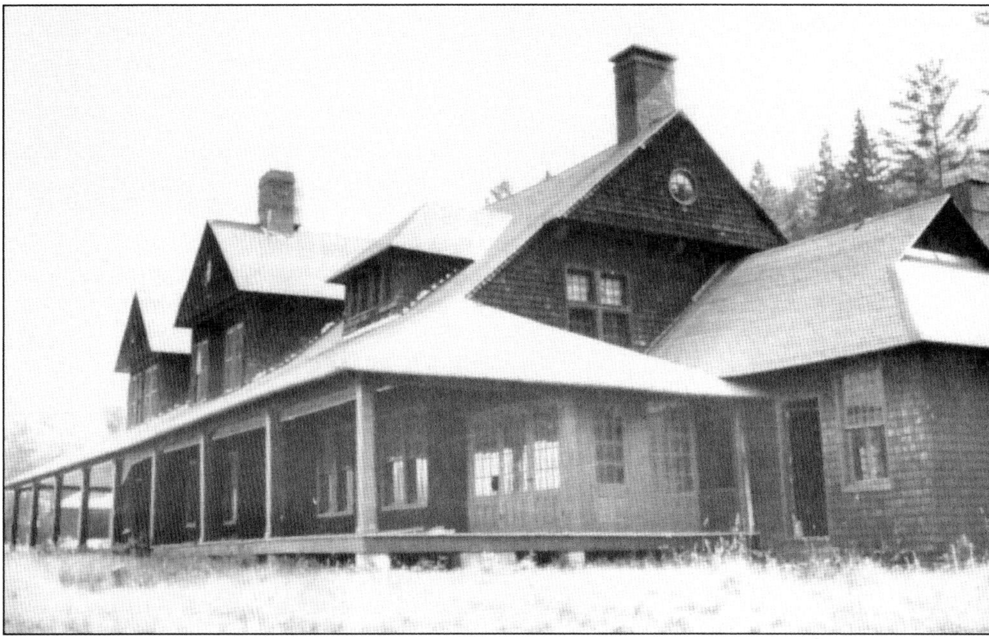

Unfortunately Forest Lodge was torn down around 1979. This picture shows the lodge on its day of destruction.

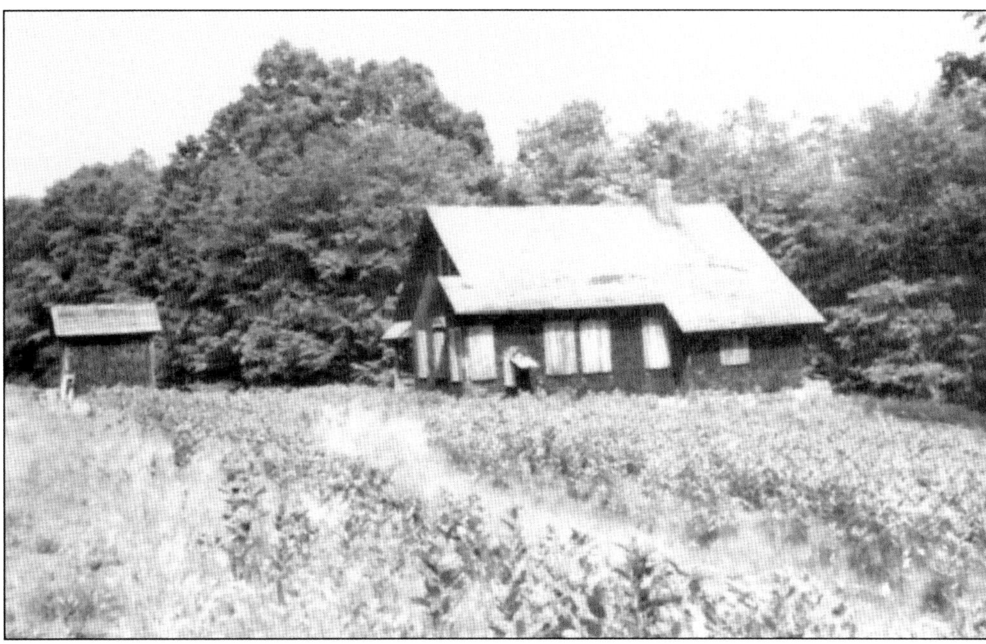

The railway station did not survive either. This picture shows it on its last day.

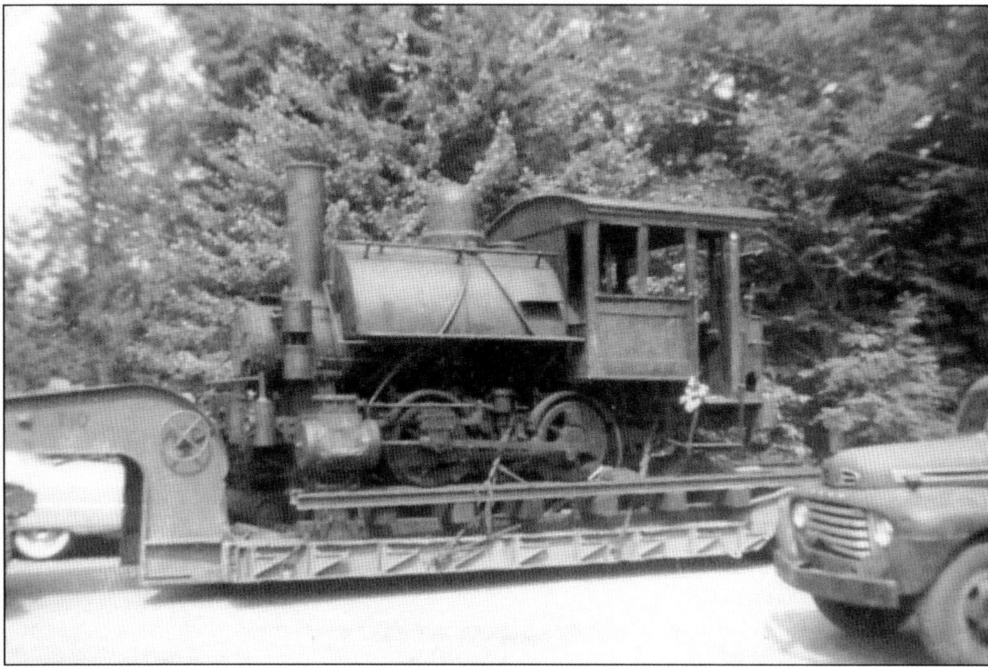

Some pieces of history have survived. This picture shows the moving of the Marion River Carry Railroad engine on a flatbed to its display at the Adirondack Museum in Blue Mountain Lake.

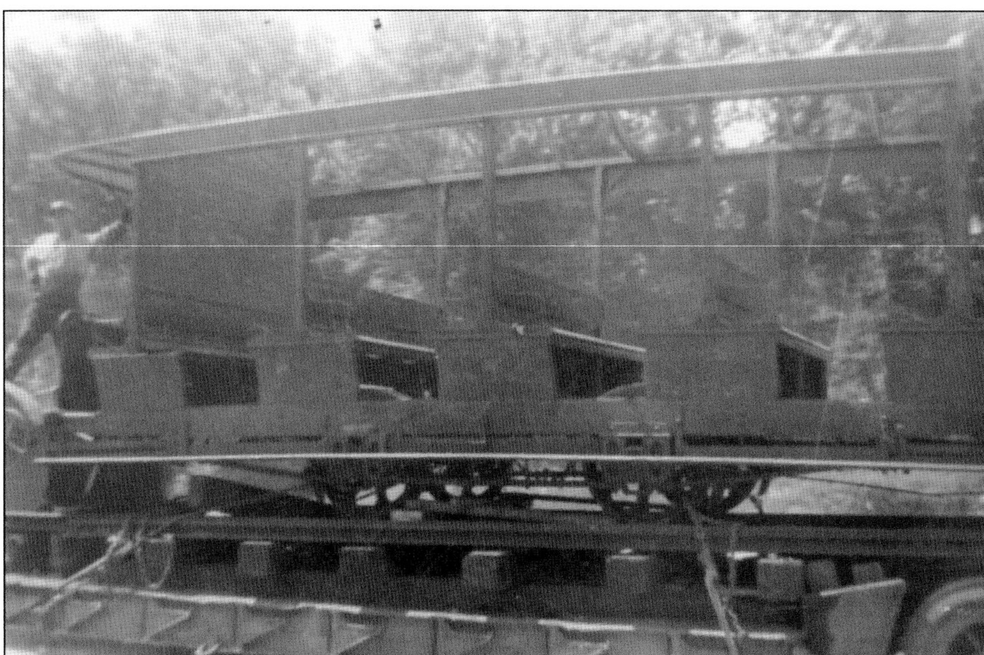

One of the original passenger trolleys also survived for display. This is a picture of it being loaded.

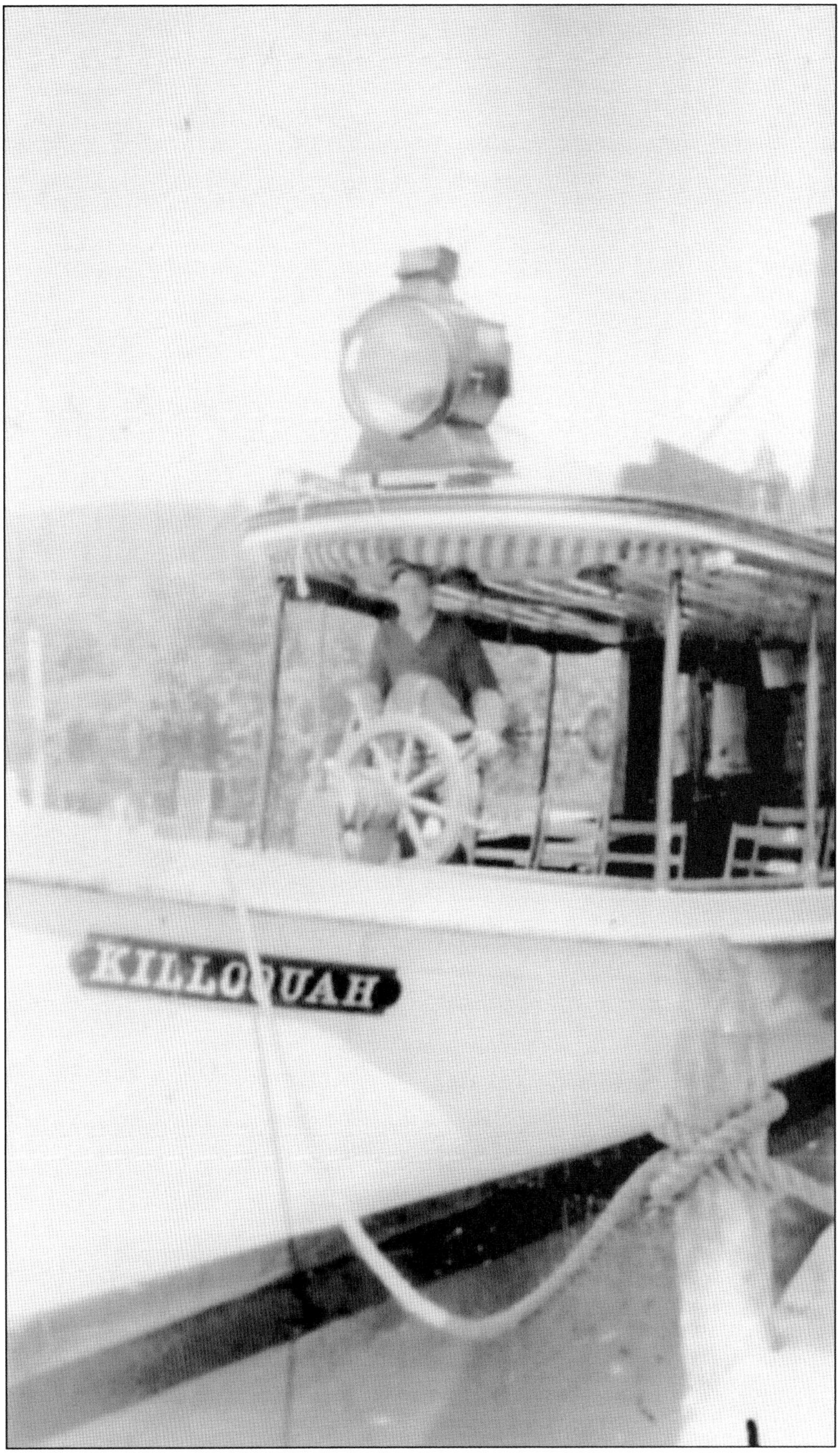

Most of the steamships of the William West Durant era around Raquette Lake have disappeared. The *Killoquah* sat in dry dock in Raquette Lake village for years.

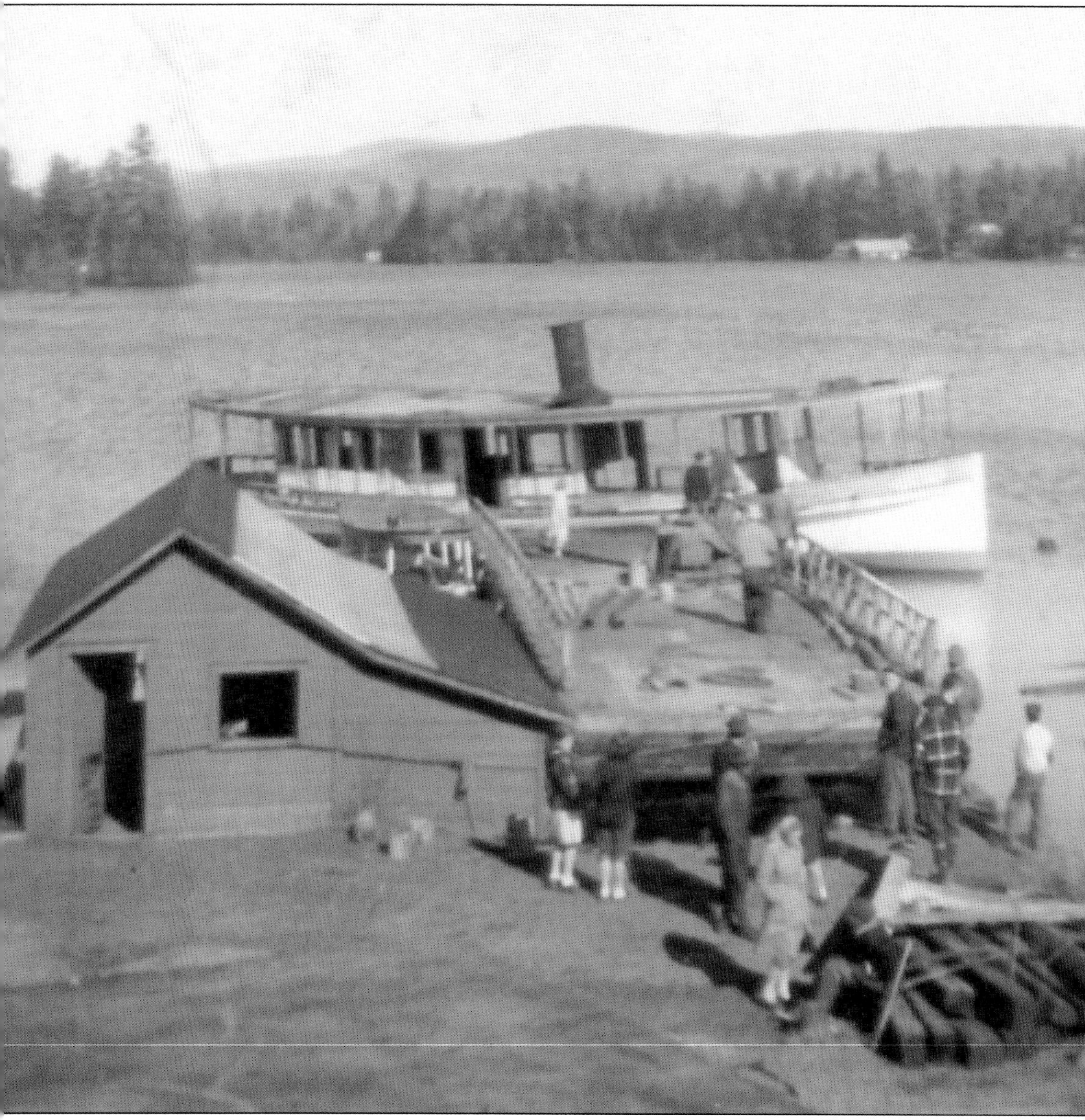

Then, around 1944, the *Killoquah* was floated and sent to the Raquette Lake Girls Camp and used as an art studio along the waterfront.

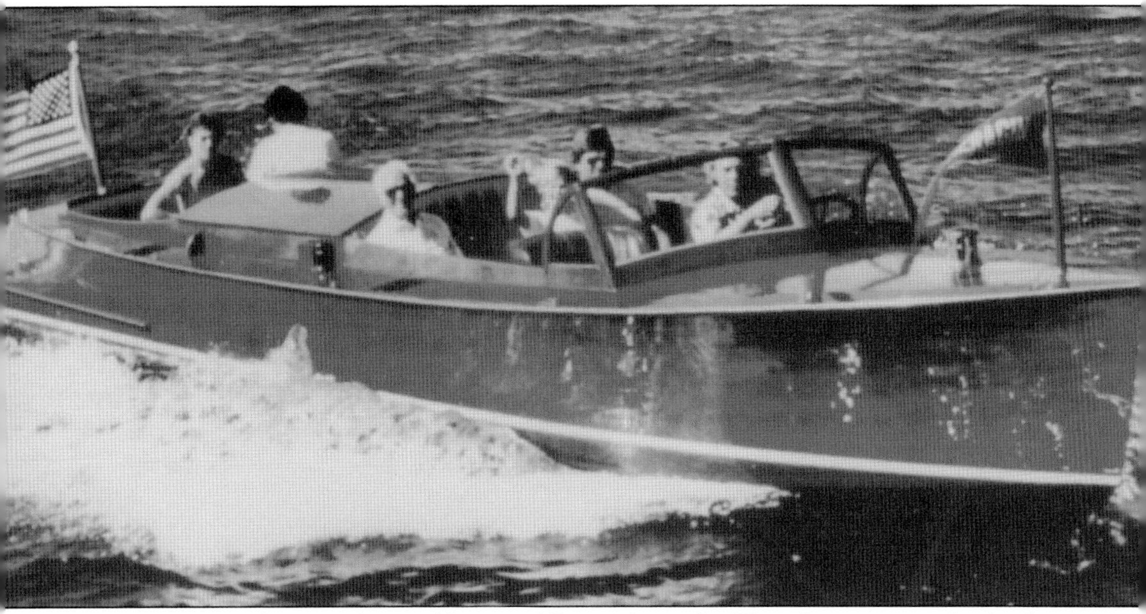

Even after the Antlers Hotel was sold, Samuel Evans's boat, the *Weneederagin*, sat in the Antlers boathouse. When more room was needed there, the boat was floated to Burkes' Marine, where it sat for years on land. Finally it too was rediscovered and was lovingly restored.

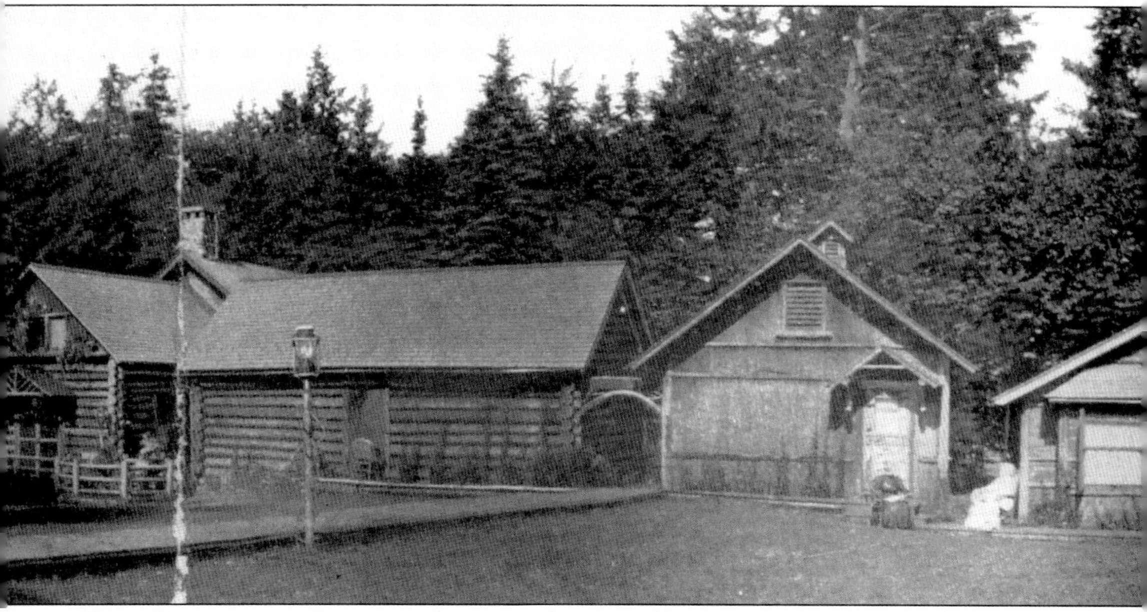

Tioga Point saw much activity for years. Ike Kenwell's Raquette Lake House ran until its destruction by fire. Then the Platt family lived at a compound. Samuel Evans expanded on the properties, prior to New York State running a conservation camp there. During that time, Robert Collier's boat, the *Skeeter*, was stored in a barn there along with the steamer *Osprey* from the Ladew family. Both boats survived and are in the Blue Mountain Lake Museum. Unfortunately the camps at Tioga were all destroyed. Pictured here is the Platt family compound.

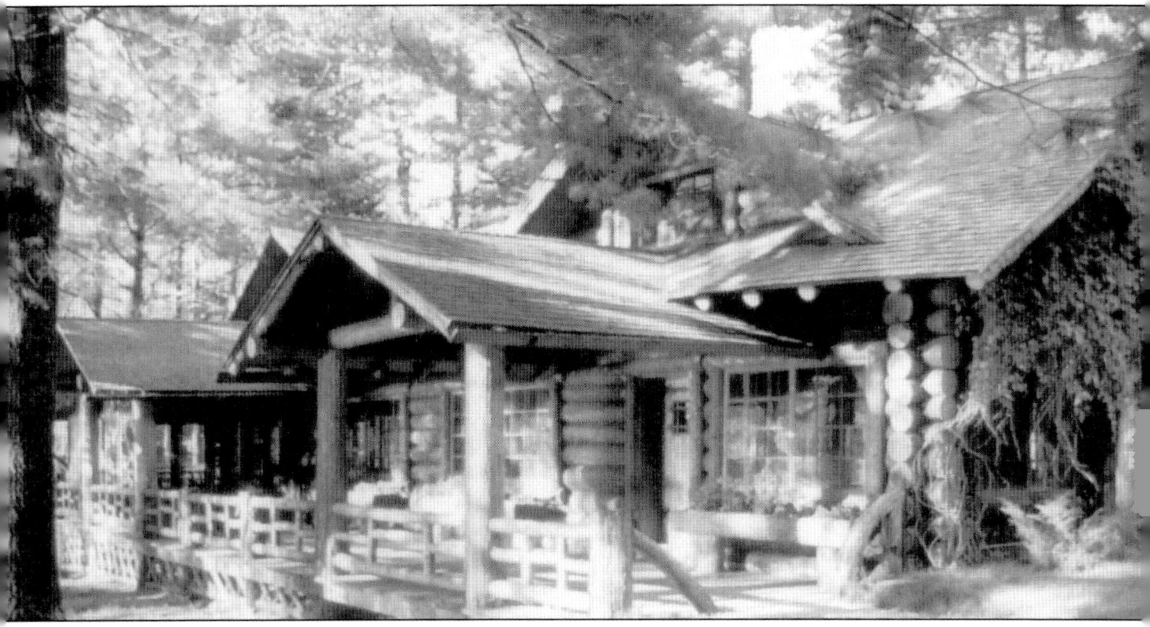

The Great Camps Huntington, Echo, Uncas, Sagamore, and North Point are a reminder that there once was a gilded era. Some are visitor attractions; others are private homes. Here is the surviving main house at Great Camp Kill Kare.

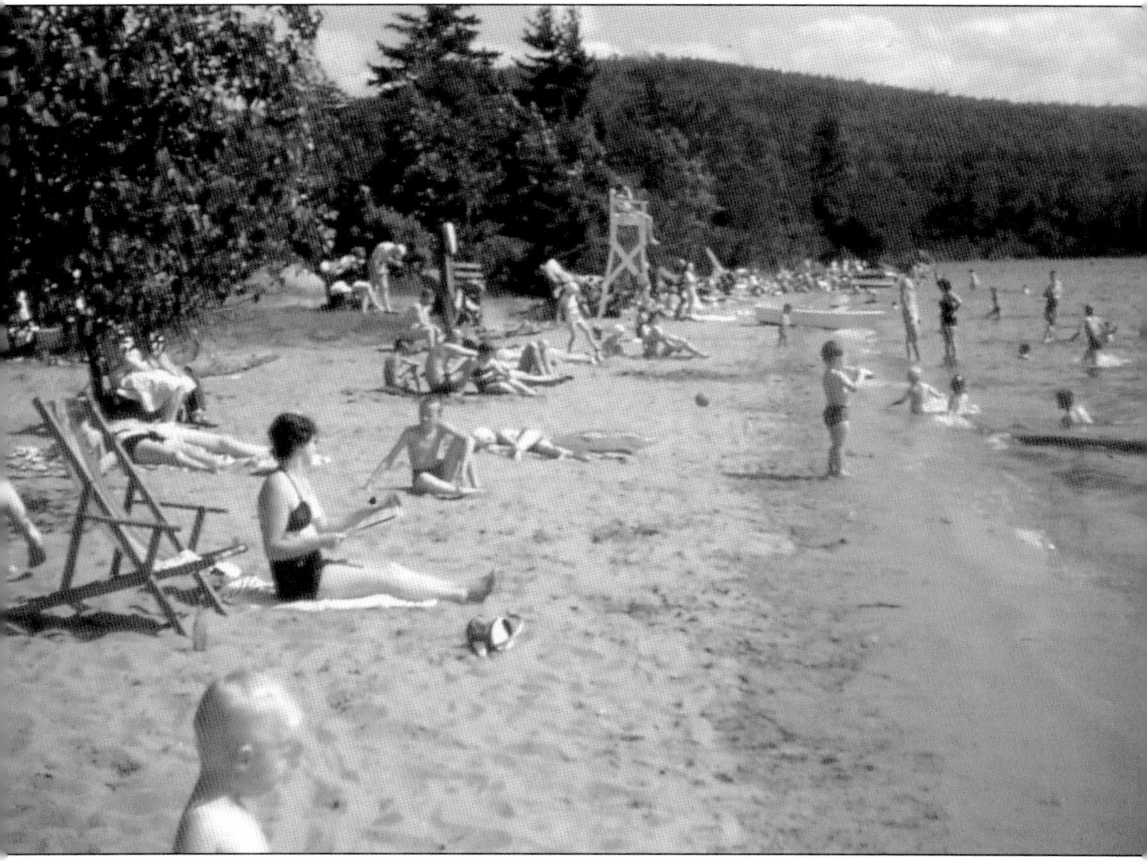

Around the lake, for instance, many views have changed. The Antlers and Hunters Rest Hotels were subdivided and sold. Brightside Camp was split and became a partial company retreat. Sunset Point Camp was split up. Camp Marion is gone. Chauncey Hathorn's is the state campsite at Golden Beach.

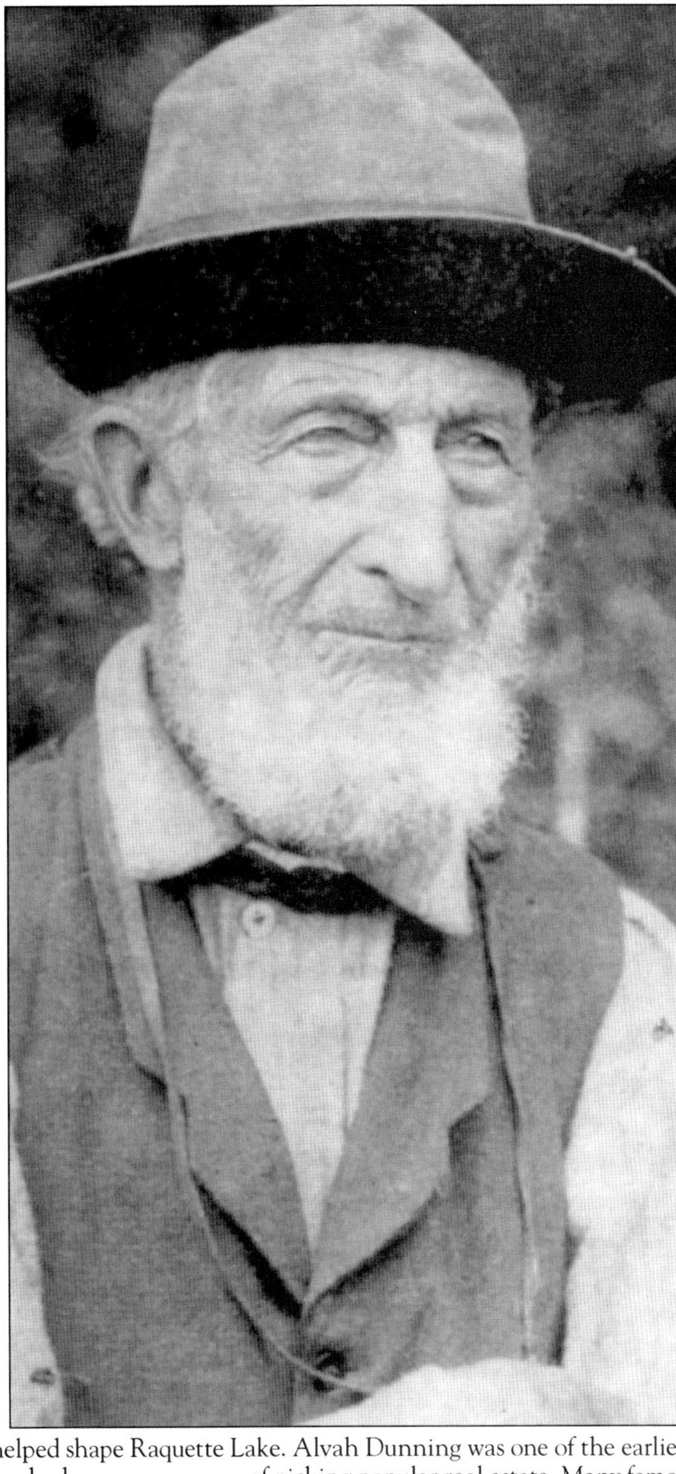

Many people helped shape Raquette Lake. Alvah Dunning was one of the earlier Raquette Lake guides. Dunning had an uncanny way of picking popular real estate. Many famous locals chased him off. When he lived at Brown's Tract Outlet, the Raquette Lake Railroad moved him in order to start building the current village.

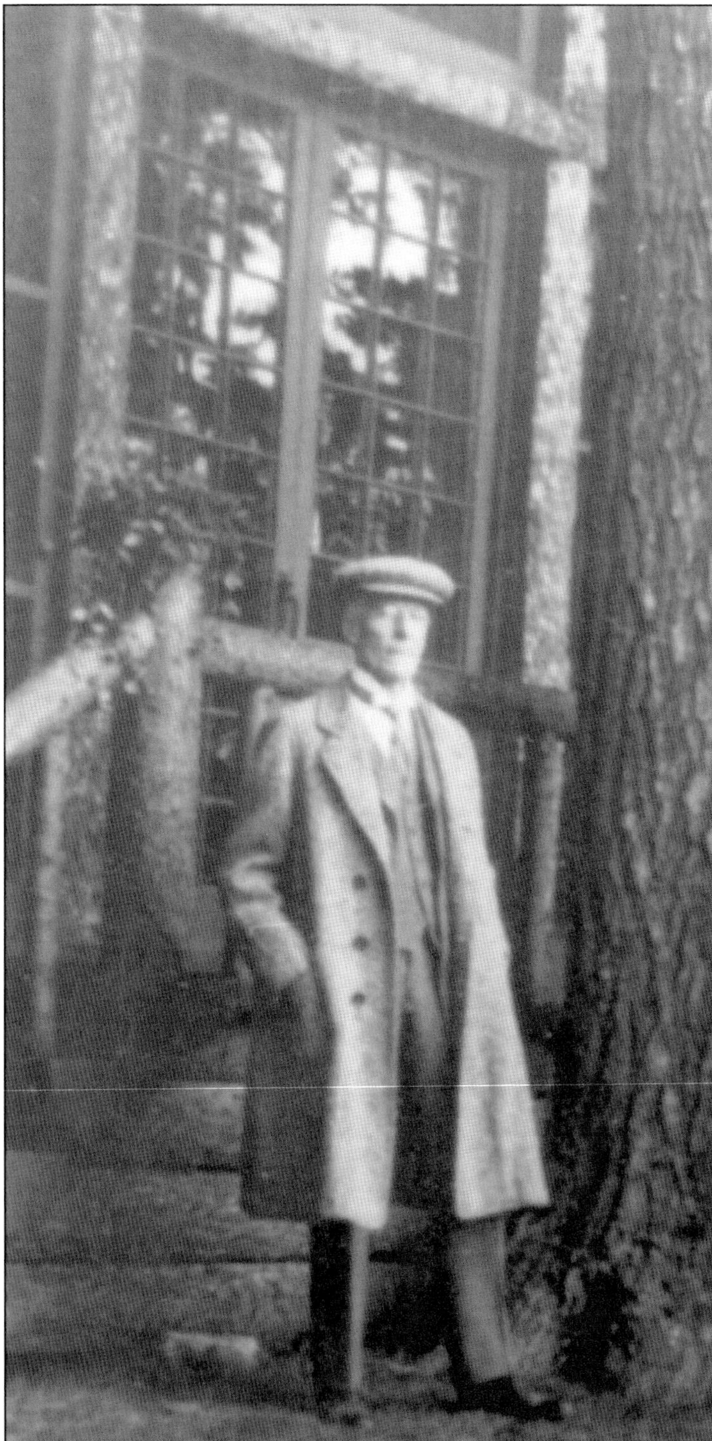

William West Durant was the father of the Adirondack great camps. Around Raquette Lake, he constructed the likes of Camp Pine Knot, Great Camp Uncas, and Great Camp Sagamore. His camps were sold to other notables who brought their people to Raquette Lake.

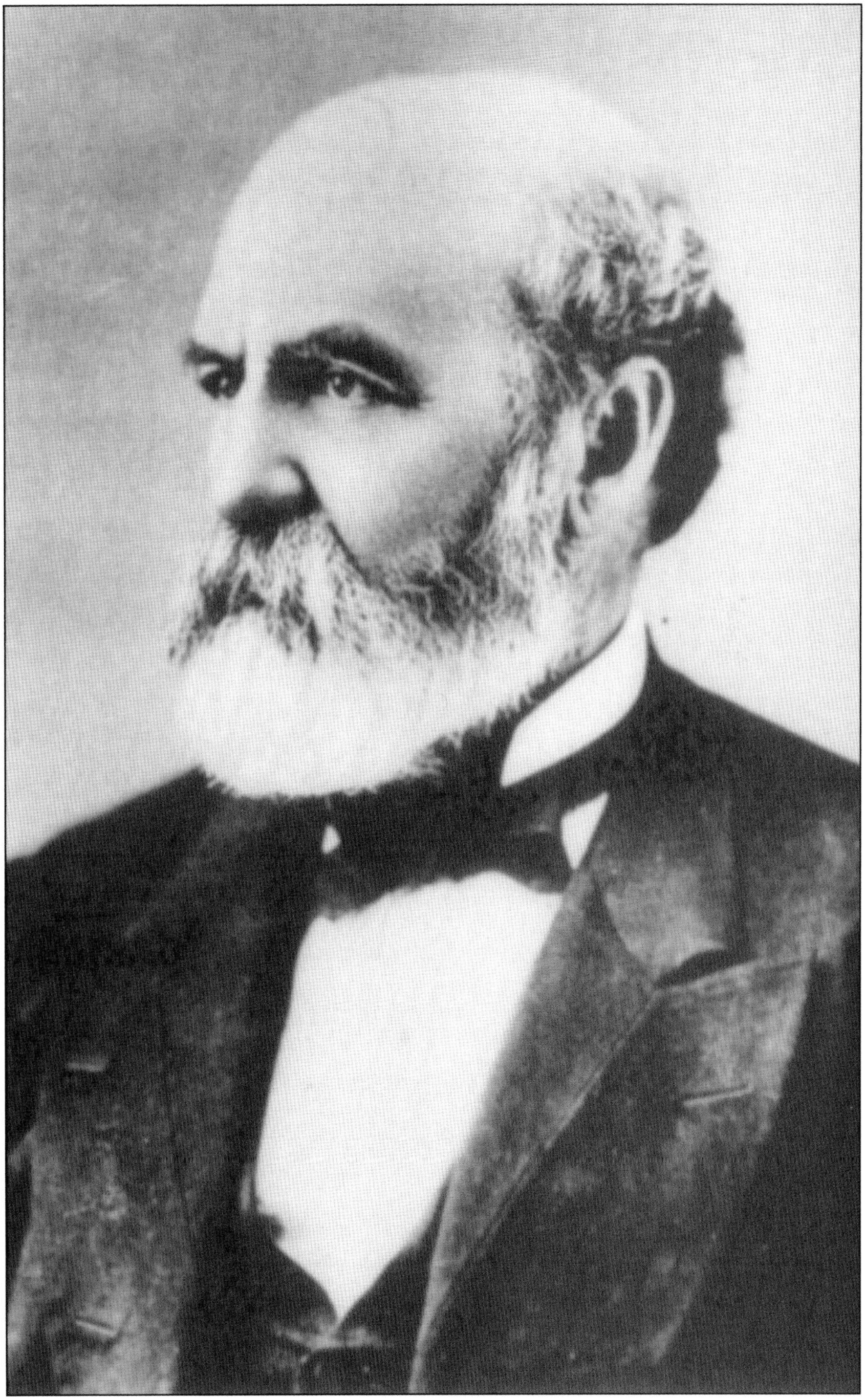

Collis Potter Huntington came to Raquette Lake when he purchased Camp Pine Knot from William West Durant. Huntington arranged financial help for Durant from other powerful men and was also instrumental in starting to form an alliance of businessmen for the Raquette Lake Railroad.

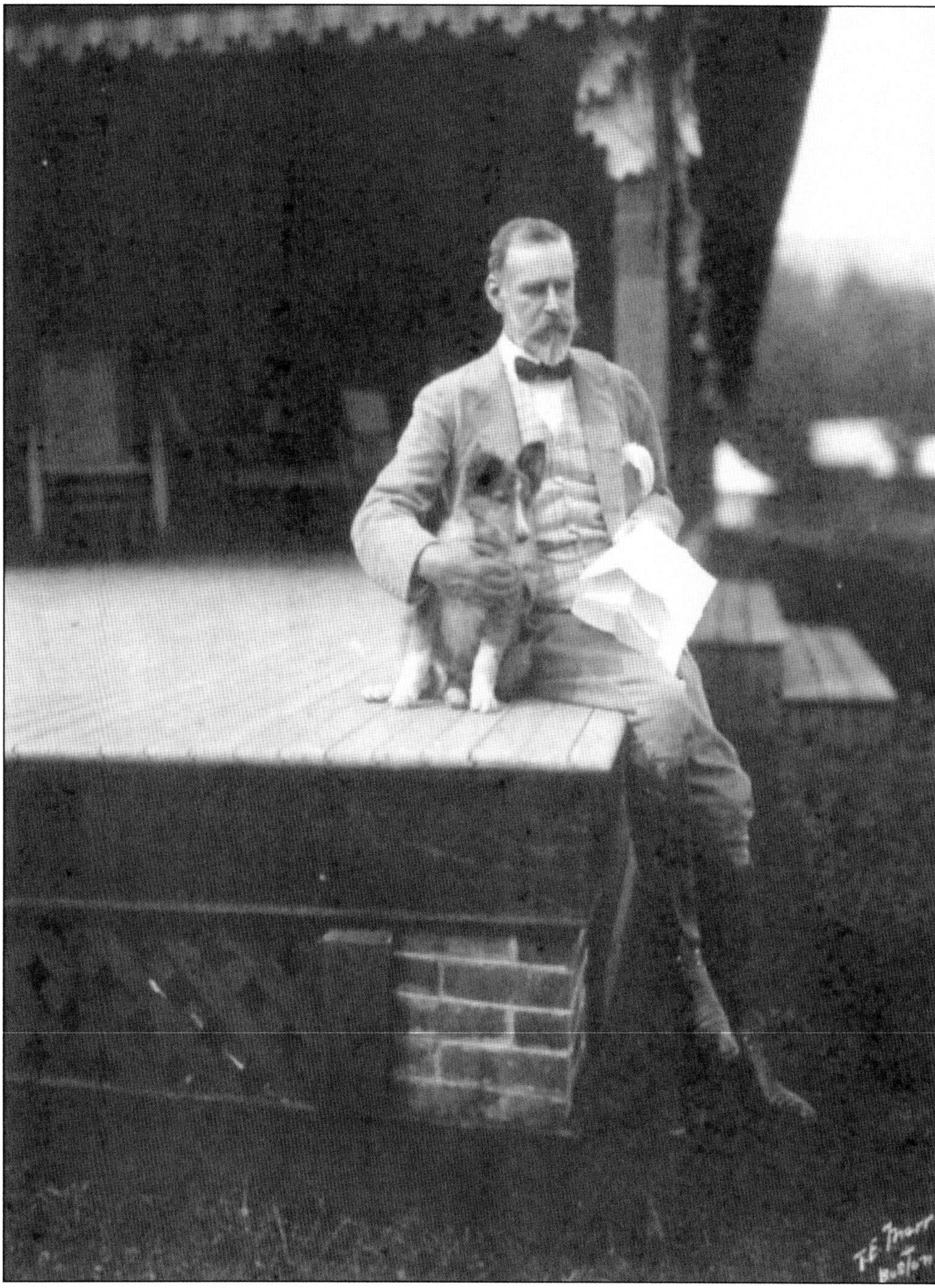

William Seward Webb already had his railway going in the north woods traveling to the northwest of Raquette. The Raquette Lake Railroad spurred off his line at Carter station.

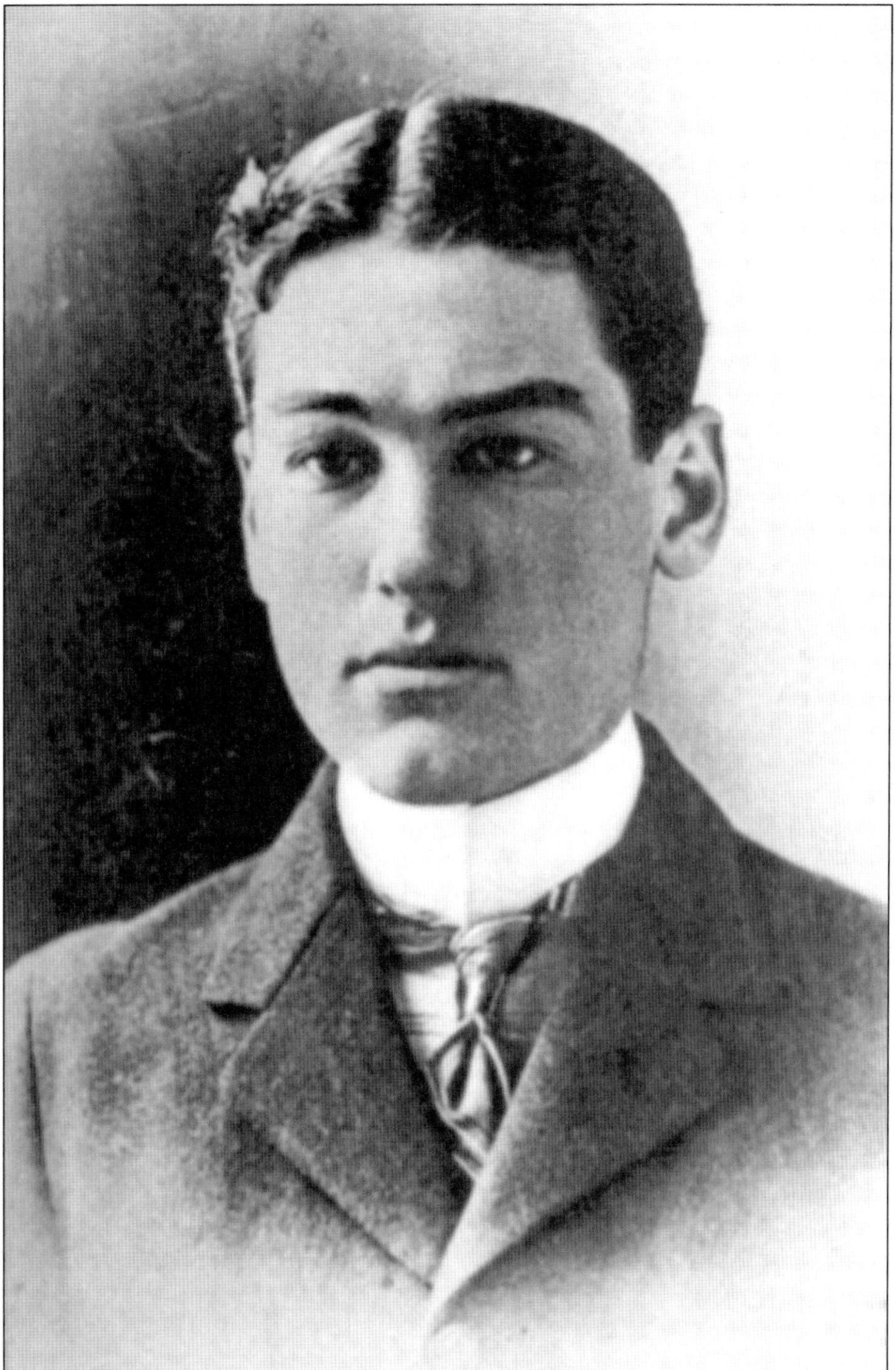

Alfred Vanderbilt and his wife were not just occasional visitors at Raquette. It was not unusual for this family to be in attendance at Great Camp Sagamore even in winter. Vanderbilt died aboard the *Lusitania*, but his widow, Margaret Emerson, brought to Great Camp Sagamore important guests who included diplomat George C. Marshall and Madame Chiang Kai-shek.

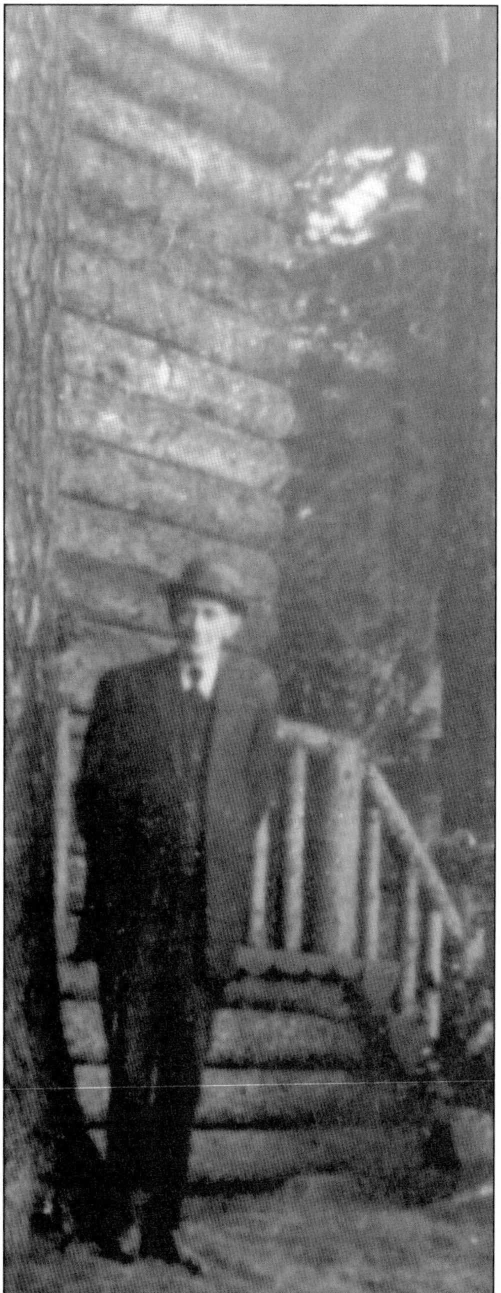

Brothers John (pictured) and Maurice Callahan, along with Dennis Dillion and Patrick Moynehan, bought Raquette Lake Transportation from the Webb conglomeration. John Callahan worked for William West Durant when Great Camp Uncas was under construction and later was caretaker there. Moynehan had contracts with Webb and W. C. Whitney for lumbering on and around Raquette Lake. Moynehan built warehouses and storehouses in the current Raquette Lake village and eventually built the Raquette Lake House. In 1900, when the Raquette Lake store was opened in the current village location, Dennis Dillion was manager. The Callahans and Moynehans, together with Dillion, created the supply company.

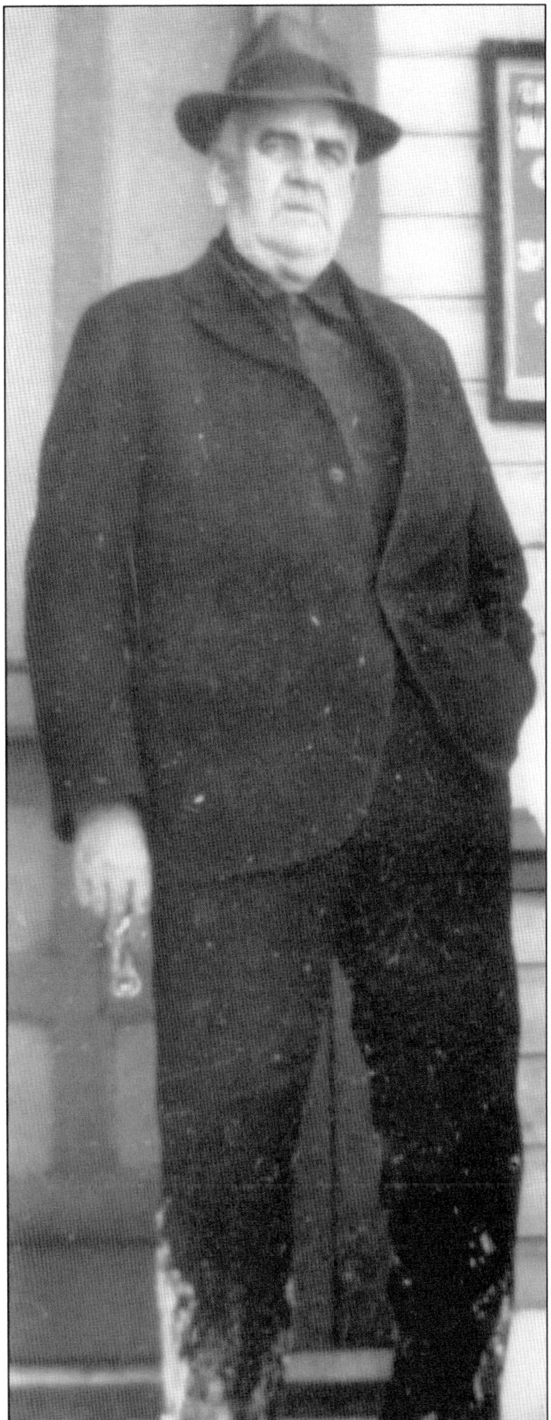

Gov. Al Smith was a friend of Dennis Dillion and visited the village on several occasions. Dillion was also the village judge until his death in 1948. At that time, his son Dennis Dillion Jr. took control of the store and supply.